The Travels 'n Travails of Paddy Egan

Paul W. Mathews

Published by Warrior Publishers, 2024.

While every precaution has been taken in the preparation of this book, the publisher assumes no responsibility for errors or omissions, or for damages resulting from the use of the information contained herein.

THE TRAVELS 'N TRAVAILS OF PADDY EGAN

First edition. July 9, 2024.

Copyright © 2024 Paul W. Mathews.

ISBN: 979-8224248834

Written by Paul W. Mathews.

Table of Contents

The Travels 'n Travails of Paddy Egan
1880 — 1952
Paul W. Mathews

HISTORICAL FICTION

"Do you have a magic spell to return someone to life?" she said.

"No," the witch said, "I'm sorry."

"Oh."

"Why don't you tell me about them?"

"Will that bring them back?"

"For us. For a little while. Stories are a different kind of magic."

Steal not this book my honest friend
For fear the gallows should be your end,
And when you die the Lord will say
And where's the book you stole away?

Acknowledgements

I would like to thank the following for all the effort and help in providing information in my (and my sister's) heritage search.

Linda Emery, Berrima District Historical and Family History Society Inc (Mittagong).

Irene Sheppard, Cemeteries Officer, Wingecarribee Shire Council, particularly for locating our grandfather's final resting place in Bowral.

Sherri Longmore, Executive Assistant, Junee Shire Council, particularly for locating our grandmother's final resting place in Junee.

Michelle Richmond, Local Studies Historian, Northern Beaches Council (Sydney), especially for providing information about Manly and Fairlight.

Helen (Morgan) Honeysett for providing useful ancestry information and documents, and for being a communicative sounding board for some of my "crazy" Sherry-laden ideas.

Michael Bankes, grandson of Roger V. Bankes, Victoria.

Norma Meadley and her assistants, Narromine Local Studies, Local and Family History.

Macquarie Regional Library.

Sharon Bonthuys, Journalist and writer, Narromine.

Elizabeth Egan for her assistance in researching many issues.

The Noel Butlin Archives Centre, Archives Program, Australian National University and Tooth and Company Limited. http://hdl.handle.net/1885/126084 Condon's Railway Hotel/ Junee Hotel.

Dr. Paul W. Mathews.
July 2024

Map of NSW

Gilgandra
Tottenham
Quirindi
Murrurundi
Port Macquarie
Dubbo
Scone
Taree
Narromine
Muswellbrook
Wellington
Mount Hope
Trundle
Forster
Peak Hill
Mudgee
Singleton
Bulahdelah
Condobolin
Raymond Terrace
Carcelligo
Parkes
Molong
Nelson Bay
Forbes
Orange
Hillston
Bathurst
NEWCASTLE
Canowindra
Lithgow
Wyong
West Wyalong
Grenfell
Gosford
Griffith
Cowra
Oberon
Young
Leeton
Boorowa
SYDNEY
Cootamundra
Narrandera
Crookwell
Mittagong
WOLLONGONG
Junee
Kiama
AGGA WAGGA
Yass
Goulburn
Finley
Gundagai
Nowra
Tumut
CANBERRA
LEGEND
kilometres
1 6.5 million
SEALED
Freeway

Names of characters

Main Characters:

Bankes:

Mercedes (Dorrie), (1882-1936)

Madeline/Maddie, (1884-1953)

Elaine, (1889-1958)

Roger, brother to the above (1890-1933)

Egan

*Anthony/Da, Paddy's father (1855-1934)

Bridget Ann (nee: Ryan), Paddy's mother (1864-1914)

***Paddy (Patrick) / George A.,** son of Anthony and Bridget Egan (1880-1952)

Emily Etta Egan (nee: Oakley, Sands), Paddy's 1st wife, and de facto? wife to George Arthur Sands (1888-1925)

Clara Violet Egan, (nee: Lampe, Keough), wife of Robert Lampe, Paddy's 2nd wife, 2nd daughter of Patrick and Rachael Keough (1898-1931)

Rose K. Egan, (nee: Lansdown, Everett), Paddy's 3rd wife. (1878-1941)

Adele Egan, (nee: Moore), 4th wife of Paddy Egan (—1952+)

*Arthur/Arty Egan, son of Antony and Bridget Egan (1890-1933)

Alice Egan (nee: Elliott) (1898-1974), Arthur Egan's wife

Arthur William, Jnr., (1914-), son of Arthur and Alice Egan

Grace, (1918-), daughter of Arthur and Alice Egan

John, (1916-), son of Arthur and Alice Egan

Leslie/Les Robert Elliot, (1920-) son of Arthur and Alice Egan

Gordon W., (1912-), son of Arthur and Alice Egan

*Teresa Agnes Green, (nee: Egan), daughter of Anthony and Bridget Egan, wife of John Green (1885-1953)

*Grace Lillian Herring (nee: Egan), daughter of Antony and Bridget Egan, wife of George Herring (1893-1956)

*William (Bill) Egan, son of Anthony and Bridget Egan, Paddy's youngest brother (1902-1975)

*Mary May Goodwin (nee: Egan), daughter of Anthony and Bridget Egan, wife of Frederick Goodwin (1886-1926)

*Eleanor Egan, daughter of Anthony and Bridget Egan (1884-)

Lillian/Lilly May (nee: Egan), Paddy's eldest daughter (1928-2002)

Elizabeth, Paddy's granddaughter; daughter of Lillian nee: Egan (1949-)

Mark Messenger, Paddy's grandson, son of Lillian nee: Egan (1953-)

Gordon, Paddy's grandson, son of Lillian nee: Egan (1951-)

Marjorie Smart (nee: Egan), Paddy's youngest daughter (1930-1980), wife of Henry Smart

Keough, Patrick (1867-1938)

Keough, Rachael (nee: Jones), wife of Patrick Keough (1873-1950)

Keough, Hannah, youngest daughter of Patrick and Rachael Keough (1901-1967)

Gee, Nellie (nee: Keough), eldest daughter of Patrick and Rachael Keough (1892-1930)

Gee, George, Nellie Gee's husband (1864-1951)

Lampe, Robert, husband of Clara Lampe (nee: Keough, Egan) (1882-1918)

Lampe, Ruth, daughter of Robert and Clara Lampe (1919-

Lampe, Wally (Walter), first/eldest son of Robert and Clara Lampe (1921-)

Lampe, Jack, second/youngest son of Robert and Clara Lampe (1925-)

McKinnon, Mary (1868-1924)

McKinnon, Flora, daughter of Mary McKinnon (1898-1962)

McKinnon, Hugh Alan, son of Mary McKinnon (1904-1928)

McKinnon, Hilda (nee: Kain), wife of Hugh McKinnon (circa 1903-1937)

Tempest-Mogg, Ethyl. Woman who was bequeathed by Flora the boarding house in Manly in 1962.

Bayliss, Walter Mason, (1866-1952)

Minor Characters

May, Lili

Ling (Ling), Anthony Egan's Dubbo housekeeper

Mack, train guard, Cootamundra to Dubbo

Mary, unknown 'aunt' in Gundagai

Merv, railway supervisor, Dubbo

Mr. and Mrs. Woodley, guardians of Emily Oakley, Dubbo

Mr. E. Lamb, Paddy's boss at some time in Bowral-Moss Vale

Barney (Mr. Barnes). Paddy's friend in Cootamundra.

Erica Barnes (wife of Barney)

Joseph Nutter (1914-1989, husband of Lillian Nutter (nee: Egan)

Gilda, Rose Lansdown's aunt

Ned, a horse

Noddy, a horse

Egan, Lampe and Keough Lineages

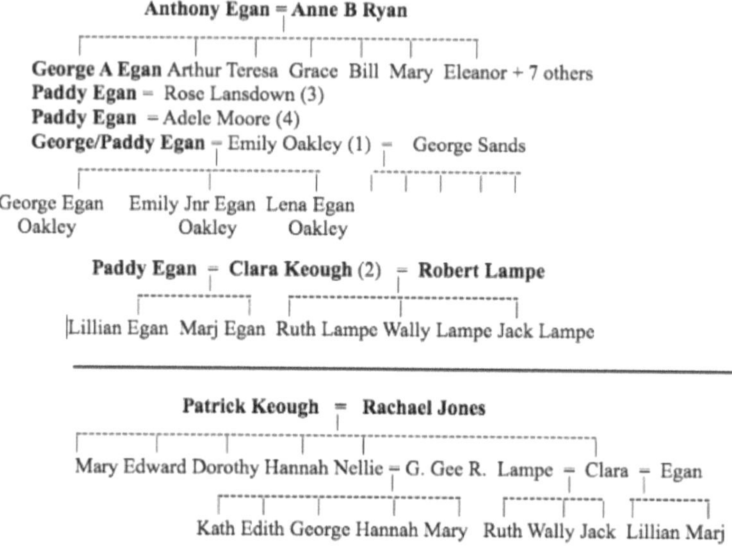

(1-4 First to fourth wives).

One

Gundagai — Cootamundra 1932

"Where we going, dad?" Lillian asked in her four-year-old squeaky voice.

"Narromine."

"Huh? Never mind?"

"Narrow-mine, not never mind," Paddy gruffly corrected.

"Oh... Why?"

"To see your aunts."

"But we see 'em now, here, dad, in Gundee Gay."

"Other aunts... And uncles, and grandpa. Now, up you go," Paddy huffed as he lifted Lillian onto the footrest of the small, four-wheeled buggy that belonged to his 'sister'-of-sorts in Gundagai. "Sit still and hang on," he added as he heaved himself onto the two-seater, "or old Ned here will get spooked."

"Is Marj coming?"

Lillian (4) and Marj (2) Egan, circa 1932.

"No," he snapped, as he waggled the reins to get the lone horse walking.

"Oh... What about Wally and Jack?"

"No."

"Is it far?"

"Aye, a long way. 'bout three days."

"Oh golleee. Where we gonna sleep, dad?"

"On the train, Lilly. On the train."

"What train, dad?"

"We getting train at Cootamundra. You can sleep then," he briefly explained as the horse trudged slowly down the drive from Mary's sheep farm at Gundagai where they had been staying the last few weeks.

Map showing Gundagai, Wagga Wagga, Junee, Coolamon and Cootamundra, up to Cowra and Forbes in the north.

The sun was just beginning to break over the eastern hills of the Southern Tablelands. He wanted to leave before dawn so as to avoid any confrontation with 'Aunt Mary'—some vague relative of Rachael Keough, Paddy's mother-in-law. He had told Mary that he was taking the buggy only to go into town that day, but he had other plans. Lillian interrupted his thoughts again, always asking questions.

"Who our aunty, dad, in Never Mind?"

"Me sisters. Grace, Teresa, Lilli May...."

"Lilly! That's my name, dad."

"Aye, sure is. You were named after her. And your grandpa there, too."

"And grandma?" she asked excitedly, meaning Paddy's mother, Bridget.

"Nah, gran's not there."

"Where she, dad?"

"In Heaven, Lilly."

"Oh. With mum?"

"Yup. With yer mum. But yer mum's sister's there, in Narromine. Yer aunt Nellie," he quickly added to distract her from memories of her mother.

But this wasn't exactly true. Fact was Nellie had also died, in October 1930, just a few months before Clara in January 1931, and it would seem from the same causes. The Keough women seemed to think they were cursed somehow, quite a few of them dying youngish, in their thirties. In the case of Nellie, her parents, Rachael and Patrick Keough, had tried to travel from Junee by car up to Narromine to attend to Nellie's illness but got stuck by major floods before Parkes and so had to turn back. It seemed they cared more about Nellie than Clara, though, so Paddy often thought; they didn't even attend Clara's funeral or contribute to a headstone in Junee cemetery, so she was buried in an unmarked plot. But he knew Nellie, married to George Gee, had had a daughter, so *she* might be a good stand-in for Lillian's aunt, even though technically she was a cousin.

"Wow. I sure have lots of aunts, then, eh dad," Lillian interrupted Paddy's thoughts once again."

"Aye, Lilly. Lots. Fourteen or so in Narromine and Dubbo."

"Where's Dubbo, dad?"

"Not far from Narromine. We be going there too."

"So like a farm? Like aunt Mary?"

"It's a town, Lillian, like our town, Junee, or Coolamon, but bigger. Now settle-in, have the mutton sandwich I made yer. You haven't had no breakfast yet, and it's a long trip."

Paddy reached under the seat and pulled out a worn, sun-bleached canvas bag, all the while keeping the reins wrapped loosely about his arm. He rummaged for a paper bag and a flask of water, and handed them to Lillian.

"Eat a bit o' that, Lillian. We'll stop in about a' hour for tea. You can have a boiled egg then."

Lillian took as big a bite as her small munching chops could manage, right into the middle of two thick slices of white bread covered with country butter, in which was wedged a good slice of thin mutton. Paddy looked at her, thinking that would keep her quiet for awhile. He pulled out a pre-made rollie from the pocket of his flannelette shirt, and in the still, cold air managed to light it up. He was thinking, as he had been for the last year or so, what was he to do with Lilly?

When her mother, Clara, had died about a year earlier, in January 1931, Lillian was not even three years old, and a younger sister, Marj, was only one—very much a babe in arms. Luckily for him and for Marj, Clara's parents, Rachael and Paddy's namesake Patrick Keough in Junee, had more of necessity taken the little one. They had already been straddled with Clara's three other kids: Wally, born in 1921, and Jack in 1925, and their sister, Ruth, born in 1919 just after her father, Robert Lampe, had died of influenza.

It had always been left unsaid who the father was of the two boys, although now as Lillian began to develop her facial characteristics, it was easy to see some resemblance among the kids. And, after all, Paddy *had* been in Junee since 1920, so it wasn't unlikely he had been courting Clara for some time. But she had decided that if Paddy weren't to marry her she couldn't give her two son's his name, whether he was the father or not. And Paddy knew, although he never told anyone, that he *couldn't* marry—not just yet, he kept on saying—because he was already and still married. It was all so complicated.

So, five kids he had had to worry about. He had whittled that down to just one now, Lillian, his shiralee. Jack, Wally and Ruth had been taken by Clara's relatives in Goulburn, while Marj stayed in Junee with the Smart family into which one of Clara's sisters had married. Paddy did have a bother remembering who was who in that Keough clan.

Paddy and Lillian meanwhile idled along on the dirt road to Cootamundra railway station, as Lillian curled up on the hard wooden seat and fell asleep with her head on an old jacket of Paddy's. With the silence, except for the soft clonk-clonk of the horse's hooves on the dry, hardened earth, Paddy had time to think out his plan: Get to Coota, sell the buggy on the cheap, jump a freight train to Dubbo, then on to Narromine a few days later after he had got wind of who was about and who might take Lilly for awhile. He wasn't sure for how long, it would depend if and where he could find work. But he knew he couldn't drag Lilly about the countryside and work at the same time; the country was in the midst of a Depression, it was hard enough as it was finding a bit of scab labour. Turning up at a work yard or farm with a kid might be useful in getting sympathy, but most likely employers would whinge they had to look after the kid, and they had no time for *that*. Besides, if he found a woman he could shag up with, she might say no, thinking if he's got a kid, he's got a wife. No, he had to be free, free to follow the work at a whim, and what he knew best was working on the rails, which might take him anywhere for days at a time. Besides, it was better for the kid to have some place a bit stable.

After another hour or so Lilly woke up, and rubbing her eyes looked around, distracting her dad from his thoughts.

"Where we at, dad?" she grumbled. "We there yet?"

"Nah sweetie, long way to go. Maybe another six hours," he told her flatly, not realizing that clock time meant nothing to a four-year old.

"I have t' pee, dad," she whinged.

"Oh, ok. We'll stop up here a bit. Give the horse a rest and feed, make some tea."

Paddy was never a man of many words. A few minutes later he pulled the horse and cart over to a green patch under a tree, where the horse could find a bit to graze. He lifted Lilly down and told her go behind the tree for a wizz. Meanwhile, he gathered a bit of wood and set to making a small fire and putting an old, blackened billy in its midst to boil the water he had poured from a hessian water bag. Dropping a few spoonfuls of tea in it he then put a feedbag over the horse's muzzle, grabbed a tin bucket from the back of the buggy and headed down to a creek nearby that he had seen.

"I'm hungry," Lilly declared mournfully when he soon returned.

"Well, you didn't finish ya sandwich, did yer."

"I don't like it. 'Snot fresh no more, like aunty's kitchen."

"Then I'll have it. You can have a boiled egg, and a biscuit with tea."

"What kinda boil egg?"

"What you mean? It be a' egg, all eggs t'same."

"Brown or white?" Lillian insisted.

"Why!? It don't matter if brown or white or pink! A' egg a' egg."

" 'Snot. Aunt Mary say brown egg nicer."

"Then it yer lucky day, girl, it be brown," he declared looking in the swag.

"Are ya sure, dad?"

"Sure as I be Paddy Egan."

"You not be lying t' me, dad?"

"I never lie to yer Lillian. *Never.*"

Lillian sat on a rock and ate the hard-boiled—*brown*—egg that Paddy had de-shelled, along with a small slice of buttered bread which, he hoped, would be fresh enough for her fussy appetite. Then he gulped down the rest of her unfinished sandwich, dunking it a few times in the boiling tea. Sitting next to her he poured the brew into a big tin cup, added a spoon of sugar, and helped her sip, telling her over and over to be careful, it was hot.

Breakfast done, he stood up, lit a smoke and moseyed about a little, with Lillian following him.

"We going now, dad?"

"Oh aye."

"My bum hurts, dad. On the wood seat," she again complained.

"Orright. Wait a minute."

Paddy put out the fire, threw the horse's nose bag and water bucket in behind the seat, and tucked the other stuff under it. He secured the leftover tea in the billy, thinking it be quicker next time to just heat up the brew. Then he lifted Lillian up and put an old shirt on the seat for her skinny, boney butt. Climbing up he pulled on the reins to get the horse back on the road and yelled, "Walk on!"

For awhile they travelled on in silence, Lilly content for now to look about and sing some ditties she had learned from her kinfolk in Gundagai. When she got bored after thirty or so minutes she asked Paddy if he had brought her book with him.

"Aye, I did a'that. Under the seat. You scamper down there and git it," he told, while hanging on to her shirt with one hand so she wouldn't fall off the buggy.

Clambering back up she was content once again to flip through her favourite book, one that aunt Mary had given her to teach her to read. It was all about birds—magpies, kookaburras, galas, colorful Rosellas, the big white cockatoos, and her favourite, the cute wagtail. There were colour pictures and a short story about each one. She read as much as she could on each worn page, but had to ask her dad when she got stuck on a word or two... Then she would break into an imitation of each bird's song, smiling at Paddy at the end of each rendition, seeking his approval. He pulled her into him so she could lay her head on his free arm. On and on they trudged as Lilly sang and hummed, until she grew weary and dropped off to sleep, leaving Paddy with a largely blank mind, other than drumming in his determination to move on, to get away from the Smarts and the Keoughs, who didn't much like him, he knew.

After leaving Junee he and Lilly had stayed in Goulburn, hoping to catch some work with his sister-in-law's extended family, but they lived in houses, not on farms, so it soon became evident to them that he was more of a lay-about—not for wanting to work, but because of a lack of work to do. He tried to make himself useful to the Keoughs and Smarts, cutting wood, hauling water, a few home repairs, and so forth, but which hardly compensated for the food he and Lilly ate. He often felt to be the butt of unspoken wrath.

Some of his kin-in-law commonly made him to feel that he had already burdened them with Clara's kids, whether it be 3 or 5, that he should have been more responsible when living with her. Maybe if he had taken more care she'd still be alive, as some relatives no doubt thought, even though he reckoned he had done the best he could, and if Clara's kin could have been more inclusive. But what none of them had twigged to was that many of the Keough women were cursed with a biological short fuse.

Indeed, back in Junee one of the Smarts, the older lady of the clan, the matriarch so Paddy thought, gave him short shrift often, one time telling him in no uncertain terms that she wished he had stayed in South Africa, that everyone would have been better off. This comment came on the back of him telling his mother-in-law, Rachael Keough, that he had spent a few years back in 1901 at the Boer War, and had even been wounded, that he was a patriot and hero, and therefore should be respected if not wholly compensated.

But the Smarts overall weren't necessarily all that smart; they had little inkling of the rest of the world, and even less of the Boer War. For them, after WW1, any war simply meant deprivation and loss, and a growing dissociation from not just Europe but indeed the whole world. It may have been the war to end all wars, as the cliché they had heard a thousand times claimed, but in the 1930s it had not ended their poverty and the irresponsibility of men who returned and bred kids like rabbits. "Nuffin to do wif t'war," he muttered to himself. His own mother had 14 kids in the 1880s, and that was well before 1914.

These reminiscences and thoughts twirled about in his head for another hour before Lilly once again awoke, sat up, rubbed her eyes, and looked about.

"Where are we dad?" she murmured.

"Oh 'bout half way I 'spect," he lied to fortify her. "You want some water?"

"Yes please." Lillian was almost always polite.

He pulled the water bag in from where it hung on the outside, and keeping the reins in one hand helped Lilly gulp down a bit of cool water.

"I need pee, dad," she sheepishly told him

"Again! Must be the tea. Orright, let me find a shady spot."

A few minutes later he again pulled the horse and buggy off the road. Jumping down he went around and fetched Lilly, who went behind a nearby bush. Then he gave the horse a bucket of water. After that he also went behind a bush to wee.

When he came back he said, "Let's walk a little while, do us good to stretch the legs."

Putting the water bucket back in the tray he held Lilly's hand and with the other led the horse out onto the road, once again heading northwest to Cootamundra. He had no idea what the time was, but reckoned by the warming sun and the fact they had left Mary's farm about five o'clock, it was near 9am. He knew it was 33 miles between the towns and that horses could do about four miles an hour. Taking into account the stops they had made, Ned and the pair of disheveled humans should be about a third of the way to Coota. It was becoming dreary, and Lilly would soon be growing bored and impatient. He thought he might be able to pick up the pace a little before it got too hot and the horse would need a good rest. Walking awhile beside the animal might motivate it, and after lunch get it to a canter that would cover about ten miles. Whatever he was to do, he couldn't foresee getting into 'Mundra before four o'clock.

They set off once again, initially at a rapid walk, Paddy having to almost drag Lilly as she stumbled, then eased back to a stroll. At one point he carried her on his back, then put her in the buggy alone, as he led the horse.

After an hour he joined his kid in the buggy and took up the reins once again. It was slow going, whatever he did to pass the distance. If he had been on his own he would be content to lean back on the wooden seat, smoke, think, hum.... But he had a 4 year old kid who needed constant attending to.

After another twenty minutes, with Lilly having returned to her book, he looked up at the sun, now high in the sky, thinking it might be later than nine. Looking ahead he saw another carriage coming their way, so he jumped down and ran to hold the horse's head. He thought to ask the travellers what time it might be, and how far to Cootamundra.

The oncoming buggy came to a halt as Paddy put up his arm to wave them down. The travellers were an older man and, he assumed, his wife. Exchanging greetings they told him they were on their way to visit a neighbour's farm for a reading of the Gospel, and it was in fact past eleven o'clock, the man said, looking at his fob watch.

"How far to Cootamundra, then?" Paddy enquired.

"Oh, it's twenty miles from our place, we know that for sure. Our gate is just up the road. You better go in and get some hay for that horse and give him a rest. My boys will fix ya. Then set out at two, you'll catch a cooler breeze by three. Tell the boys we met on the road, Sam's me name."

"Aye, thank you, sir. Ma'am. We'll do just that. It's tiresome journey orright, and the kid's a bit bored."

With nods and gestures Paddy jumped back on the buggy and got the horse moving, following the given directions.

Fifteen minutes later Paddy and Lilly on the horse and buggy pulled up at a neat farmhouse, quite big, so it seemed. Two lads in their late teens or thereabout came out to see who was visiting.

Paddy explained he had met their father, he guessed, Sam, on the road, and asked if he could put the horse in the stable with some hay. Having unhitched old Ned and put him to feed and rest he found Lilly at the farm house chattering away with the two boys, who invited the visitors in, out of the growing heat, and said they had some cold chicken, cooked by their mum that morning, with fresh bread and tomatoes.

The boys were friendly, talkative and hospitable, so after lunch Paddy had a lay down in the verandah's shade, while Lilly went off with one of the lads to see the chickens, the large vege patch, and to feed a baby goat. She felt for a time as if she was back at her aunt's farm in Gundagai, and the time moved quickly for her.

At two o'clock Paddy hitched up the horse again to the buggy and lifted Lillian onto the hard seat. The boys donated the left over chicken and bread, with some goat cheese, all wrapped in brown paper, and with many thanks Paddy and kid set off once again for Cootamundra.

As they hit the road Paddy said, "It be only two more hours, Lilly. I get old Ned do a bit of a trot on the flats. It be night time when we get there."

"Can we stay at that farm, dad? It was nice. And the boys are like Wally and Jack."

"Ah, we cannae stay, 'fraid not Lil'. We got a train to catch if we ever gonna get to Dubbo."

"But dad," she whined, "I'm tired of travel'n, I wanna stay at the farm."

"Maybe when we come back. There be other farms at Dubbo. Yer aunts got farms up there. You'll see. Have a sleep, then we be in Coota before yer know it."

Lillian once again curled up on the wooden seat, padded only by Paddy's worn shirt, and resting her head against him once again began reading her book. Fortunately she fell asleep soon, probably tired from running about Sam's farm and the good tucker she had put away. Old Ned trudged on until they reached a smooth flat part of the road where Paddy could get Ned to do a trot for twenty minutes.

And so on they went, on and on.... Twenty miles seemed interminable. Paddy couldn't wait to get to Cootamundra and have a beer with a mate he knew, Barney, then catch a train in a day or so, and be able to just sit back and let the steel wheels do the work. He was hoping Barney could put them up for a night, maybe get a good feed, borrow a few bob, and help in selling the horse and buggy for a pittance, he imagined. He figured his sister-of-sorts had plenty of money, and if she wanted the transport back she'd soon find out where it was at and pay out the little Paddy was expecting to get for it.

It was a little after 5pm when Paddy caught sight of Cootamundra as they came over the last hill. It was getting dark, but a few lights of the town twinkled in the distance. He woke up Lillian, who yawned, rubbed her eyes and sat up, scratching the nits in her unruly long blonde hair.

"We almost there, Lilly," he said to cut off her inevitable questions about where they were or how much longer.

Lillian craned her neck forward to see, and stared into the twilight. "I'm hungry dad," she said after a few moments. "And need pee."

"Ok, we can stop for wee, but you have-ta wait till we get to Barney's for eating."

He stopped old Ned, gave him his bucket of water, and then lifted Lilly down, who ran behind a bush to do her business. Meanwhile he rolled a smoke and lit up, while he had the chance.

Back on the buckboard he told Ned to walk on.

"Who's Barney, dad?" Lilly piped.

"Friend o' mine. Mr. Barnes. We just call him Barney. He works the rail line."

"Does he drive the train, dad?"

"Nah. He does odd jobs, you know, clean up, digging, paintin', repairs..."

"Oh." Lillian fell to silence, to take in some of what Paddy had told her, a little disappointed that Barney wasn't a train driver; she had hoped he might let her into the driving cab. But after a while she again started asking questions:

"How long we staying here, dad?"

"Just a day or so. Then we catch t' train."

"Is Ned coming with us?"

"Haha. Don't be daft, girl. Cannae take a horse on the t' train. Barney'll look after him... Till we get back," he added, to allay any concerns Lillian may have had about not returning to Gundagai or Junee. Truth was, he didn't know what would happen, although he did hope one of his relatives in Dubbo might take her for awhile.

By 6pm it was getting cold. Lillian wrapped her father's shirt about herself, covering almost all of her small body, as they descended the last small hill down into town. It wasn't a big place, so it didn't take long to drive Ned through a few streets to stop at a rather ramshackle house behind the rail station.

Paddy tied up the horse and gave him some water, then lifted Lilly down. Taking her hand he stepped up to the front door and banged a few times. A moment later the door swung in to reveal a plumpish older woman, perhaps in her late forties, with frizzy curly black hair, dark eyes, wearing a cotton dress covered with a dirty white apron. She looked at Paddy and the girl, immediately thinking they might be looking for a handout.

"Evening, ma'am," Paddy greeted in his best manner. "Patrick, ma'am, Egan, from Junee. Is Barney home?"

"Oh! Egan, eh. Ain't seen yer fer...how long...?"

"Been a few years, missus. Barney about?"

"You know where he be at this time o' night. Down the pub," she answered in a surly tone.

"Oh right. Yeah, of course. I'll go down, then, bring 'im home."

"Oh yeah. Good luck with that. You can't take the girl there but. She yours?"

"Oh aye, Lillian. My oldest. Just four."

"Ya better leave 'er 'ere, tell Barney 'is dinner's almost done. Don't be long!"

"Thanks ma'am."

Turning to Lillian he told her go with the nice lady, who might give her a bite to eat.

"No, dad, I wanna go wif you."

"Ya can't, Lil, I'm going t'pub a little bit. Kids not allowed."

"Maybe you not come back...?" she protested.

"I'm coming back, Lilly. Promise. I gotta come back for Ned and the buggy, haven't I? Just going down the road, t'pub."

"Come on in, Lillian," the woman, presumably Barney's wife, assured the child. "Your Da's coming back for dinner, and get the horse. C'mon, let's get something to eat."

Reluctantly Lillian followed the woman into the house with a looksee over her tiny shoulder, wondering if her dad was coming back, as Paddy without a backward glance strolled off to the *Station Hotel*, barely 500 yards away.

Barging through the tall doors of glazed-glass set in solid wood frames, Paddy readily espied Barney leaning on the bar, nursing a schooner of *KB* beer. He had put on weight, Paddy could see. His 5' 8" was now a bit plump and his head balding, with only a sunburnt flabby neck and round face protruding from navy blue overalls and flannelette shirt.

The bar was almost empty, it being near 7 o'clock closing time, so it wasn't hard for Barney to recognize the newcomer who sauntered over to him.

"Barney, mate!" Paddy cheered. "What's that ya drinkin'?" He turned to the bartender, a big surly fella with colonial grey lamb-chops sprouting from his fat ruddy face: "Two more of the same," he ordered, pointing to Barney's schooner.

"Almost closing time, ya know," the bartender told him, which carried the suggestion that Paddy should buy-up or miss out.

"Then you better make it three," he smiled. "And two long-necks when ya ready."

"Well, blow me! If it ain't damn Egan from Junee!" Barney declared. "What, you flush with cash these days?"

"Nah. Wouldn't say flush. Got a few bob though."

"Oh aye. How'd ya get here? Walk?"

"Not quite. 'Orse 'n buggy. Old Ned did the walking," he chuckled. "Had ta, got me a kid, four year ol', her ma died a year back."

"Oh, shit. That's bad luck, mate. So what brings you up this way? There no work here-abouts."

"Ya, I know. On me way to Dubbo…" Paddy gulped down half of his first schooner in one shot. "Geez, I needed that!" he declared wiping his lips on his shirt.

"So where's the kid? And the buggy?"

"Your place. Ya missus said 'urry up, ya dinner's ready."

"Oh yeah, yeah. We finish these off first. We can open them bottles at home, after."

This line of conversation was good to hear, as Paddy surmised now that he had a place to bunk for the night.

He went on to tell Barney what he'd been doing the last few years, everything leading to his marriage with Clara in 1926, the two girls he'd fathered, the youngest barely a year before Clara had taken ill and died, and the juggling of scrap work he could come by since and looking after Lillian. And now how he was heading to Dubbo hoping to find greener pastures.

"Ya not thinking of going by buggy, ar's ya? It's near over two-hundred mile!"

"Nah. Train."

"So what ya gonna do with the buggy and 'orse?"

"Well, was hoping someone would wanna buy 'em. Going cheap." He gave a wink at Barney.

"Not me, mate. I no need for a buggy. I don't goes nowheres. Can ask 'round tomorrow, though, I guess."

On that note both Paddy and Barney began on their second beers, just as the barman called "Time, gentlemen, time!" This meant they had ten minutes to finish off their drinks—an easy task for the two men.

Not having much to eat all day Paddy was a bit unsteady on his feet as the two mates rambled back to Barney's house. Lillian came rushing to her dad when she heard them and grabbed his leg, babbling about what she had been doing: helping Mrs. Barney, as she called her, in the kitchen, playing with 7 year old Barney Junior in the back yard, having some tucker—Irish stew—and playing Snap at the kitchen table.

Barney took a seat at the table and pointed to Paddy to do the same, as Barney's wife, Erica, dished out some stew and plain bread. It didn't take them long to gulp that down, then move to the back verandah. Sitting on some stools with their backs against the wall Barney opened the two long-necks. For an hour they smoked, drank and chatted about the past, about the people they knew in common, the state of unemployment, and Paddy's plans, which he kept as vague as possible.

By nine the two fellas had finished off the beer, so Barney pulled out a sizeable flask of rum and poured each of them a large unmeasured draft with a dash of water. Barney was glad to share an evening of relaxation with an old mate, and Paddy likewise, something with which he was all too familiar given the lack of employment he had experienced over the last few years.

Even though he had gotten the dole tickets when he was out of work, they were barely enough to buy food to put flesh to bone. Often he would skimp on meals himself, and exchange a ticket for grog, or cash-in to buy grog. It was a dismal situation, and nought he might do to fix it, he thought, so he might as well get what little pleasure he could.

A few years past Clara had worked, doing a bit of laundering, cooking or cleaning in a local Junee hotel, and kept control of the little money they ever had, and Ruth, Wally and Jack minded Lilly and Marj. All was good, even if only basic. He loved Clara, and not unreasonably thought Clara would look after him as he got older. But when Clara suddenly took sick and eventually passed away in early 1931, the two boys and their older sister, Ruth, were shunted off to make themselves useful to their Keough grandparents, who had a fruit shop in Junee. A short time later Rachel and her husband Patrick Keough sold the shop and took the 3 kids to Goulburn, where they would in the end mostly grow up. The Keough grandparents became their legal guardians, but never actually adopted them.

Marj and Lillian, on the other hand, were taken in by 'Great aunt' Lillian 'Mary' Smart in Gundagai. She was a formidable matriarch, treating the two girls as though they were her own, which left Paddy to fend for himself there, for a little while at least.

He had a hard time figuring out how it had all happened, how he had got to this situation. It wasn't that he didn't care about Lillian, but what did he know about being responsible for a four year-old, and a girl at that? It was all a wife's business. Lillian needed a home, educating, stability, playmates, and *he* needed money to achieve even a skerick of that. Now, it seemed his life had come full circle, and that everything was in conflict with one thing or another. He was getting too old for this sort of shite anyway, nearing 52. Sure enough he was strong and fit still, but just mentally he didn't want to take on any responsibilities.

At 11 o'clock the two men staggered indoors, with Paddy readily falling on to a sofa that Erica had made up as a bed of sorts. Barney joined his wife in bed, smelling of rum, while Lillian lay in an old cot at the foot of the bed. She was tired from the day's travelling, exhausted by the seemingly endless bumps and rocking of the buggy. Erica had already put old Ned out in a back paddock with a few other horses for company.

Erica was up by 7am, preparing a breakfast of eggs, toast and dripping, and a sausage apiece. Tea was brewing on the wood stove. Erica checked on Ned and gave him some welcome oats.

It seemed the Barney family was doing alright in this economically depressive time; he was employed by the NSW Railway Department, needed as a general hand to help shunt, operate boom gates, maintain the station and nearby goods depot, and any other required jobs. Cootamundra was a significant rail junction or hub for mostly freight trains to the north and south, that carried grains and other agricultural produce. The passenger trains all went via Goulburn into Sydney, where passengers would change over to the north-west line that would take them to Parkes, Dubbo, then Narromine and beyond as the line was extended westward.

Paddy and Barney got up at eight, had a wash, and tea. Erica kept the food warm on the ever-heated stove until they were sufficiently recovered from the previous night to eat. Barney suggested they go into town with the buggy and pass the word around that it was for sale. Paddy was hoping to get ten pounds for it, but there wasn't a great deal of demand in this hick-town, and the Great Depression had curtailed money even amongst the well-off. He might have to settle for seven or even five pounds. If worst came, he might convince Barney to take it for five, and then *he* could sell it at his leisure for seven or ten. It would probably be better that way, because Lillian would then think they were coming back for Ned.

The two men went to the three hotels in Coota and chatted with each of the barmen, who allowed a small handwritten notice about the sale to be put up amongst many others on makeshift noticeboards. Then they returned to the Station.

"No trains today, mate," Barney informed Paddy after looking up a schedule sheet. "When were you thinking of leaving?"

"Anytime. The sooner the better. Need to get this kid settled."

At this moment Lillian came around the corner of the Station. "Are we going today, dad?"

"No pet. No train today. Tomorrow, Barney?"

"Sure is. Passing through here at ten. I'll signal 'em slow right down so you can get on at the brake-van."

"Thanks mate."

"What the brake van, dad?"

"The last carriage, Lil'."

"What we doing then? Can we go t' town?" she pleaded.

"Sure. Why not. C'mon, then, we walk in. Have a look about."

They left Barney to go about his Station work, what little there was of it, and strolled into town, consisting primarily of a quiet main street of various small shops, a hardware store, some minor factories and foundries, a dispensing pharmacy, and at right angles a few side streets of little remark. The occasional horse-drawn carriage trundled by, and even fewer motor cars were parked here and there. They found a green park with nothing but a swing, so Lillian was content to play on that while Paddy rolled a smoke and idled his time in the sun.

At noon he bought two more bottles of beer and the two Egans headed back to the Station, Paddy thinking his amber donation would compensate for a lunch-time feed. He wasn't wrong in this regard, with Barney ushering them in to share in some cheese, freshly baked bread, and thick ham slices. After lunch he and Barney sat on the back verandah to imbibe of the two bottles.

The afternoon wore on slowly, and it was hot. Paddy had a lay down on the sofa, with doors and windows open to let *some* air circulate. Barney Jnr. took Lillian out to the paddocks to look after the horses, and down to a stream nearby. Erica had a cuppa tea then called on a neighbour, while Barney went to the Station, which, with its thick brickwork, was considerably cooler than anywhere else. *This* was Cootamundra, like a hundred other small rural towns of New South Wales.

As the heat dissipated and the sun sank in the west, Barney and Paddy headed for the pub. It was six o'clock. Erica admonished the two men to be back by seven, she had cooked a beef pie with mash, and wasn't going to have it spoil.

The two men again sat at the bar of the *Station Hotel* and yakked, with Paddy having to fork out more shillings in reciprocation for the Barnes' hospitality. No one had contacted them about the buggy and horse, leaving Paddy to have to ask Barney for a 'lend' of five quid the next day. At 7 o'clock they returned to the house and mostly repeated the previous night's routine.

By ten the next morning Paddy, Lillian and Barney were tired of waiting for the scheduled train. But, although a little late, it could eventually be seen puffing up from the south, hauling open wagons of grain covered with tarps. Barney walked up the track to signal it to slow down, and as it reached him he jumped onto the driver's cab. It slowed even further, to a snail pace, as Paddy and Lillian walked to the rear end of the platform. As the brake van came level he hoisted Lillian onto the van's small verandah and then quickly followed suit, gripping on to the old water-bag and a knapsack containing minimal clothes and a bit of food. They waved a cheerio to Barney, as the train again began to pick up a little speed.

"That's it, Lilly. That was Cootamundra... Let's go inside, see what's what."

"We going t' Never Mind now, dad?" she asked with a happy smile.

"Aye."

"And we come back for Ned?"

"Aye."

Two

Perth 2021

Mark knocked on the front door of his sister's house, an old 1980s bungalow with cement roof tiles, sagging gutters, a chimney that had been blocked up years ago, but red double-brick that kept it relatively cool in the summer heat of Perth. It was a bit narrow inside, and cluttered, with several pieces of past-used-date furniture that might collect a few dollars in an antique shop.

Finally, Elizabeth hobbled to the door; her arthritic right knee had been playing up again. And the wrist brace on her left hand didn't help with her doing much housework, or anything else for that matter. Both ailments were burdensome in looking after their mother, Lillian—or Mary or Dara or Susie—depending on who was addressing her. Dad always called her Susie; no one knew why. But her real name was Lillian May Egan, born in Junee just before the Great Depression, in 1928.

"Hi," he greeted his sister who, a few years older than himself and indeed the oldest child in the family, was touching 74. "Mum up?"

"Yeah. She's still in bed, though, having a cuppa."

"Well, that's fair enough. It's only nine o'clock. She *is* retired, you know." He winked.

"Ha! She's been retired thirty years!"

"I'll go see her," he told her. "You make the tea. Strong. A little milk, two sugars, and hot!"

Elizabeth went off to the kitchen to make the tea as directed. Mark could hear her banging, as usual. In fact one of her childhood nicknames was 'the Banger'. Mark slipped into Lillian's bedroom after a light tap on the half-closed door.

"Hi ma. I see you're awake."

"Of course I'm awake. Been up since seven. You know as a country-bred girl we get up with the chickens. I been going through some pictures and letters." She waved a free hand at the scattered documents on the bed.

"Good. Memories…?" he queried with a raised brow.

"Lots. Too many. But sometimes I get a bit mixed up, when and where, you know…"

"Yeah. That's ok. That's why we'll record everything and try to get you to focus on one thing at a time. So, are you up to continuing from yesterday?"

Mark was referring to the project his sister and he had seemingly undertaken, beginning a few weeks previously, of documenting their mother's life and travels, building a family tree that went as far back as the 1700s, according to what they had discovered so far. Elizabeth had found in some way or another they were related to the Bugdens, one or more of whom came out from England, Donhead Saint Mary or thereabouts more precisely, and worked for the famous Macarthers around Camden, near Sydney. Poignantly, one of the earliest ancestors had married in 1626—exactly 300 years before Paddy was to marry Clara…

"Sure. Nothing else I have to do," Lillian answered. "But I have a doctor's appointment at two, you know."

"Yup. We can take you. So, where do you want to do it? Here or in the office?"

"You go and have your tea. I'll get up. Give me the dressing gown."

Mark handed Lillian her dressing-gown, and left her to get herself ready. He headed out to the kitchen to have his tea. He said to his sister:

"Have you cranked up the computer?"

"Yeah. First thing I do. It takes so long to get going."

"Good. You know how to light the kerosene lamp under it then?" he chuckled. "Ma'll be out in a minute. What are we doing today?"

"I don't know. Best to get her to start at the beginning, again, if we can. Yesterday did a lot of sorting... Photos, letters, notes. We can read some of the letters and stories she's written and try to expand on them, jog her memory..."

"Ok. You're the typist. I'll handle the tape recorder. You jot down notes on the PC, like we did before."

For the last few weeks Mark and Elizabeth had worked together to get Lillian to reminisce about her life, hopefully beginning when she was a child, and identifying some of her ancient relatives from the 1920s to the early 1950s. This was combined with some vignettes of sorts that she herself had written long ago about her past travels, living arrangements, people she knew... But these had to be expanded and clarified. In addition there were letters by her, or to her from her own siblings from many years ago, mostly in the 1960s. Photographs had to be organized and the people and places in them identified and dated.

Looking about Elizabeth's office—and now also his mother's since she had moved in several years ago—while sipping his tea, he considered how this 'mess', as he thought of it, had even happened. Their brother, Gordon, long ago had started collecting bits and pieces about their father, now deceased some 30 years. He collected dad's medals and his military history of being a POW on the Burma railway in the 1940s, and had typed up dad's 3 diary books. Not much one for writing and collating and organizing, and getting a bit old himself, Gordon gave it all to Elizabeth in the hope *she* could and would put it all together in a book. With editing and research assistance from Mark, the diary was published as a 100 page précis of his life with a focus on his war years.

But dad's lineage was so totally different from ma's. *He* had been born in Yorkshire, enlisted in the Army Medical Corp at the drop of a hat in May 1936, just before his 22nd birthday, ended up in India, and then as bad luck, perhaps, would have it, he was in Singapore when it fell to the Japanese in 1942. Surviving that, he immediately migrated to Australia, and by 1949 had married their mother. The rest was history. He never returned to Britain.

So, having completed his story Elizabeth thought to balance it with a narrative of their mother's life, using *Ancestry.com* as a starting point, along with any other documents she could find. Having their mother alive still, now aged 92, and the Covid Pandemic still in full swing that kept half the population confined to their homes, Elizabeth and Mark could tap into her living memories.

They had begun by organizing documents and photos, scanning and digitizing things, tracing relatives past and making connections. This was not only so as to organize the material but also to enthuse their mother in the project and jog her memories. Often, of course, her tattling would be all over the shop, so Mark made it a point of having a tape recording running at all times. It's not that Lillian's memory was bad, or even forgetful, just muddled, and while she could recall events and saw the connections in her own mind, articulating them in a coherent way required patience, checking and back-stepping.

Lillian came into the office, now using a walker-frame to steady herself. She always had bad feet, rather than arthritis. Chilblains, she said. Probably a result of wearing high heels all day for about 30 years at work, first in a hospital as a secretary of sorts, and later standing all day as a Chemist's assistant. And in between times on her feet taking care of four kids and a household.

She took a seat in a high-winged comfy chair. Mark seated himself in a swivel chair and started the tape recorder, while Elizabeth sat at the PC awaiting instructions.

"So, mum," Mark began, "we found this old black and white photo of a young girl and an older man, looks like he could be a relative. Do you know who he is?"

Possibly an Egan relative with a child, both unknown. (Date unknown).

She took the picture and instantly recognized it, so it seemed. "That's me!" she smiled. "Oh... Wait. I *think*. Maybe. Maybe Marj, or even *her* daughter, Violet. I don't know...." Mum looked a bit sheepish. "And I don't know who *he* is. Not *my* dad. Maybe an uncle, or grandfather Keough, Patrick Keough. Or could be old man Egan, my dad's father."

"Do you know where and when it was taken? Or who took the picture?"

"No. None of it. Not a clue. But the girl looks about four, you can tell," she observed to try to be helpful. "But honestly, can't say who they are, at all."

"Here's another one, of your mother," Mark gently said, hoping it would not upset his own mum. "Clara, yes?"

"Yes," she sighed. "I didn't know her much, she died when I was about three and a half or four."

"Nineteen-thirty-one," Mark confirmed. "Just after Marj was born."

"Yes. Poor mum," Lillian commiserated, turning the photo over and over in her frail hands.

"So what happened after, ma? After Clara died? There's a note that you and Paddy, your dad, went travelling…?"

"Oh yes, we travelled. Walked mostly, or sometimes by train. Sometime later…, I was well over four when we started. I was born in June, you know. June 'twenty-eight. So musta been nineteen-thirty-two or 'thirty-three. We went to Gundagai. Dad said he had a sister there with a farm. Aunt Mary."

"So, do you recall who was there, at Gundagai?"

"Oh, so long ago. All I remember is that it was a big farm, with sheep and cows and goats and horses."

"And the people there? Who were they?"

"My relatives, of course. The Keoughs, on my mother's side. My mum was born in Gundagai, you know."

"Anyone specifically you can recall?" Mark asked, not wanting to lead her with names.

"Aunt Mary! I remember her. She ran the place with an iron rod."

"And cousins?"

"Oh yes. Lots of kids. But I don't remember their names."

"But mum, we can't find any aunt Mary in Gundagai. Paddy's sister *maybe*, a Mary in Dubbo, yes, but she died in 1926, so you would never have met her. In fact, we can't find any *real* sister of Paddy, *or* a brother. Did he have any at all?"

"Yes, of course. Especially aunt Mary. In Gundagai. But she was a Keough, I think, not an Egan. And some up north 'round Dubbo, I think. Not sure, now. And there were my mum's sisters and brothers... And her mum, my grandma, Rachael Keough."

"The Keoughs?"

"Yes. But my dad didn't get on so well with them."

"So no brothers or sisters of your *father's?*"

"No. But he did have a sister somewhere, Mary something, I think."

"Seems everyone was called Mary... So, ma, let me get this straight: the only relatives you knew, aunts and uncles, were the Keoughs?"

"That's right. Dad didn't have any relatives in Junee, but, I *think* he had two brothers in Bowral. Marj told me much later in the 'sixties. But I never met 'em."

"Ok, we know about them. But for the moment, you mentioned maybe some sisters in Dubbo? And 'old man Egan'?"

"He was dad's father, my grandfather, I *think*."

"So, you're saying Paddy had relo's in Dubbo?"

"I expect so. That's why we went there. But I don't know really who they were. Just, I met an old man there, and dad said he's my grandfather. But I don't know if it's true."

"Ok, we'll get to that soon. Meanwhile, so you went to Gundagai? How did you get there?" Mark persisted, now changing tack.

"Oh... I don't know. Walked I guess..."

Lillian seemed a bit concerned she couldn't recall, and therefore couldn't answer the questions as well as she might like.

"I think we walked from Junee, then got a train...*maybe.* I remember going on a train, sometime..." Lillian shrugged her shoulders and looked a little uncomfortable.

It was about 25 km from Junee to Wagga and maybe 50 km then to Gundagai by train, or even 50+ km in total by a more direct route, walking, but no train. The train lines at the time went from Wagga Wagga through Junee then to Cootamundra and up to Parkes and Dubbo, and beyond, but they were solely freight trains. The passenger trains went from Wagga through Gundagai, Goulburn and on to Sydney.

"So what did you do in Gundagai, mum?"

"Played, of course! I had cousins and it was a farm. I was too little to do much, but we fed the chickens, helped bring in wood for the house, feed the horses and pigs...and goats, too. But you didn't get on the wrong side of the fence with *them!*"

"So it was a farm, and you had a good time?"

"Oh yes. It was fun. I had cousins there, and my aunt Mary—maybe her, I'm not sure... Maybe aunt Rachel. Anyway, *one* of them, she ruled the roost with an iron rod. Every Sunday we'd go to Church into Gundagai, riding on a wagon."

"How long were you there, ma?"

"No idea," she shrugged. "Time didn't mean anything then, especially to us kids. But I know it was cold when we got there, so musta been winter, or coming-on."

"Ok, so what happened? Why did you leave and where did you go? You wrote a kinda diary entry here, says your father stole Mary's buggy and horse, and you went somewhere."

Mark showed his mum a note she had written some years before when she was trying to record her history. She already had some poems and stories written, and indeed published, in some writer's club magazine, and people generally thought they were good. So this scrap of a narrative that Mark showed her was just one part of that project, but she had not got far with it.

"Well, I do remember *that*. We went all the way to Narromine!"

"Narromine? Near Dubbo? Why on earth…? By buggy?"

"Oh no. We got the train at Cootamundra. I remember, because it was fun, in a way, but also very long. And, I think we didn't have much food."

"Ah, ok. But can you start at the beginning. In Gundagai. Grandpa Paddy stole the buggy? From your aunt Mary?"

"I think so. All I know is it belonged to her. She had a buggy *and* wagon, and about three horses. We took old Ned. I remember his name. Ned. I miss him. He was my favourite. Old, and gentle. Like my dad," she added with a smile.

Mark silently thought this could be a long story, and it was nowhere near yet at hinting at how Lillian ended up in Parramatta, and then Manly, by the seaside. And because she *had*, she met his own dad, Joseph, and subsequently Mark and his siblings were born and grew up in an idyllic part of Sydney. But all that was to be in the future, about 20 years into the future. Little did Lillian know, or would understand if she did know, that in the 1930s and '40s her future husband would be grueling his way through a Japanese POW camp in Singapore while she was in Manly enjoying life as much as she could in ten years' time, at age 14.

But that was to come. For now they had to figure out the narrative of movements and relations, beginning in Gundagai in about 1932.

After about thirty minutes Lillian said she needed to get up and move about, to keep her joints working, she explained with a smile. As she shuffled out with her walker she half turned and said: "You know you have to ask Roger."

"Roger? Who's Roger?" Mark exclaimed.

"Roger Bankes, of course. I told you. He was the brother of the three Bankes sisters. Ask Roger!"

She went out to the back porch and sat in the sun, with her eyes closed. Mark could keep an eye on her through the back door.

He turned to Elizabeth:

"Well, we got something. I don't know who this aunt Mary at Gundagai is; we haven't been able to find any mention or documentation of her. We know some Keoughs lived there, but no trace of a Mary. And it can't be Mary Egan from up north, in Dubbo, the one who married Goodwin, because she died in 1926."

"And Roger Bankes died in 1933, so a bit hard to ask him!" Elizabeth confirmed by looking up the family notes.

"I know. Bit hard to dig up skeletons and ask *them!*"

"So what now?" asked Elizabeth. "Doesn't seem to be any of Paddy *Egan's* relatives. It's odd that everyone else we came across having lots of siblings but he has none."

"Oh he had some, in fact, many," Mark insisted. "Why? Because he is not Paddy Egan, he is *George* Egan. That's my theory. Mum pretty well as much said so, when she referred to 'old man Egan.'"

The problem had evolved of Paddy—or *George* Patrick Egan—not having any record of his birth date or location, other than what *he* stated in 1926 on his marriage registration to Clara Keough. It was so odd: it seemed like Paddy didn't exist prior to 1926. He had said then that he was born 'on a ship' off the coast of Western Australia, *and* in 1888, and that his parents were Anthony Egan and Bridget Egan nee: Ryan. Elizabeth and Mark had found extensive records of these two and their 14 children, including a Mary, many of them born and raised in the Bathurst region then living much of their time in Dubbo or thereabouts. And one of the sons, the first born, was George A. Egan, born in 1880 in Cudal, not so far from Bathurst from whence his parents had come. On Paddy's death certificate he was listed as 73 years old, which meant he was born also in 1880, not '88. And then it gets interesting: Mark told Elizabeth that as more documents and records were discovered, George A. Egan of Dubbo totally disappears from the planet in 1917, in Sydney, and lo and behold Paddy Egan—George Patrick Egan—turns up out of thin air, in Junee, and just a few years later, with no known sibs, just when every other man and his dog were having 10, 12 or even 14 kids! Now their mum, Lillian, is telling Elizabeth and Mark that she and her father, Paddy, had gone to Dubbo and Narromine, Anthony and Bridget Egan's stomping ground....

"Yeah yeah. I'm still not convinced," Elizabeth declared.

"What would you like?" Mark retorted. "A pound of flesh? Photographic evidence? DNA?"

"All. But DNA would be best, I think."

"Then why is mum telling us she and her father went to Dubbo, and Narromine of all god-forsaken towns? And just when Roger Bankes was there!?"

"Ask Roger...," she flipped.

"Funny. You don't go trooping half-way across the State on a whim in the middle of the Great Depression for no reason. And I tell yer, it's because he *did* have relos there!"

"It's because Roger *was* there."

"But Paddy didn't *know* that. There's no connection between Paddy and Roger before they met, that we know of. There's no connection between them before nineteen-thirty-two. In fact, we can't even be sure they *did* meet, other than mum telling us to ask Roger. She could have met Roger at Parramatta for all we know."

"But..." Elizabeth gave up, exasperated. "Anyway, what's next?"

"You keep tracking relatives, and taking notes on anything she says."

"She keeps rambling, jumping from one thing to another," she informed him.

"That's why you have to write notes on what she says, we can use them to fill in details later."

"And she's been typing stuff, but I haven't had time to look at it."

"Ok. I will tweak her story of the trip by horse and buggy from Gundagai to Cootamundra...," Mark affirmed. "It starts with what she has told us and the little story she wrote about it."

"Then we can read it to her, so she might be able to fill in some gaps and tell us what happened after."

With that settled he went out quietly to say goodbye to his mum, but she was asleep. Without disturbing ma he told Elizabeth to keep an eye on her, to wake her in fifteen or so minutes, and look after her, and reminded Elizabeth that mum had an appointment at 2pm with the doctor. Meanwhile, Elizabeth could keep doing what they had all been doing for the last several weeks about mum's history and narrative.

He would call again tomorrow.

Mark returned to Elizabeth's house at 1pm the next day, hoping by this time mum would have had lunch, a nap, and be more energetic. She was as usual fine, except in terms of memory and story-telling that was not much better than previous days. Again they sat in the office, and Mark began to lead her. He thought that perhaps by telling her story, part one, as he understood it, she could nod assent or correct as necessary. A linear narrative might also help her organize the past.

He began to read and embellish what he had written about her trip from Gundagai to Cootamundra, adding bits and pieces as she was prompted, and correcting errors. The narrative to date had got Lillian and her dad, Paddy Egan, to Dubbo, first by horse and buggy, then by freight train from Cootamundra.

Tomorrow Mark and Elizabeth would try to get more details than hints about their stay in Dubbo and Narromine, and whence they went afterwards. They were keen to know how their mum ended up in Parramatta and then Manly.

After an exhausting ninety minutes Mark got up to leave. His mother again suggested he should ask Roger, that he was in Narromine. Somehow for Lillian the past and the present were fused into one.

Three

Dubbo 1932

Despite the train wheels doing the 'walking', it was a long boring journey from Cootamundra to Dubbo. It was meant to be 8 hours, but with all the stops and the adding of wagons, and the naturally slow speed of a steam freight train, it became twelve hours. This meant they got into Dubbo at about 11 o'clock that night, when there was not a peep to be heard in the growing but nevertheless sleepy town, one that Paddy had left behind some 14 or 15 years previously.

There was no chance of getting a bite to eat, or a place to sleep. The brake-man, a kindly elderly gent close to retirement, so he said often enough, told them they could sleep in the van, which would at least give them some safety and comfort and, with a small potbelly stove, warmth against the chilly country nights.

At first the train ride was all excitement for Lillian. She could look out the grimy side and rear windows and wonder at the countryside rolling by, the plains of grass or grains, the scrub to the left and to the right, the occasional tree; and she could wander about the small confine and ask a thousand questions which the old man, Mack, was only too glad to answer and embellish with a yarn. He had done this trip the proverbially hundred times, and was thankful to have company. As far as Lillian knew this was the reality of train travel; she didn't know there could be plush carriages with seats, corridors, a canteen, a lot of people, and a WC.

And it was the latter that began to pose problems after two hours on the rails.

"I need pee," Lillian whispered to her dad.

For men it was too easy: just open the back door and stand on the shelf-like back board. But for women, for a girl, it wasn't going to be so easy; the train couldn't just stop for a pee. Much to Lillian's embarrassment Paddy had to inform Mack of his daughter's need.

"Oh aye. Not to worry. It's all fitted out, here, you see," he told them as he opened a small hatch in the floor. "You sit on this box 'ere, that got a hole cut through it, and it sits over the hole in the deck. Mind for splinters, and don't fall down," he chuckled kindly.

Lillian gave a gasp and a look of terror.

"It's orright, Lilly, I'll hold ya. Go on, git on the box, like Mack says."

"But... I'm shy, dad."

"Don't be daft, girl. How many times I bath you, eh? Go on, we look the other way."

"But dad...." she whispered even more softly. "I gotta do number two."

"Then do it, Lilly. No one's awatching. Mack's standing out on the front porch. I'll get the water bag, so ya can clean."

Lillian finally had to succumb to her natural needs, so she sat on the box holding her dad tight and lifted her short cotton skirt up to her thighs... She didn't have any underwear, so Paddy now realized. Undergarments were something he neither took notice of nor could afford.

Recovering from her ordeal and discomfort Lillian was now as frisky as a playful cat. But she soon calmed down as hunger begun to bite. Paddy rummaged amongst their belongings and pulled out some boiled eggs that Erica had given them, with bread wrapped in brown paper, and slices of cheese. Mack didn't have much he could share, other than an apple which he cut into slices, as he secured the billy on the pot belly stove.

After that meagre meal the men smoked and chatted idly, until Lillian pestered them to play Snap. Another hour went by, and

Paddy encouraged Lillian to have a nap by laying himself down on an old rug. Thankfully, he thought, she was still young enough to want an afternoon sleep. But this was not to last long, perhaps two hours, and by four or five she would be hungry again.

It seemed like his whole life now was measured by each and every hour and each morsel he had to procure. He could begin to empathize with a magpie mother with its squawking chick. He couldn't carry a lot of food, even if he could afford it, because much of it would go off. He was confined to bread, barely fresh, and cheese, boiled eggs, biscuits or plain cake, and if lucky some ham which had to be eaten quickly before it spoiled. Salted corned beef was the better option, but even that was expensive. At least if he had rum he could go into a stupor and forget his hunger.

By five o'clock both Paddy and Lillian were awake, and again she needed to pee. After that she grew listless, and again hungry. No wonder, since she ate like a sparrow.

"What do you do, Mack, for dinner?" Paddy was forced to ask.

"We'll be in Forbes soon. Half way. Pretty big town. There's a canteen near the railhead, and we stop to change drivers. You got a few bob? I can get ya some cold chicken and salad, or veg. That do?"

"That'd be good, thanks Mack."

Paddy rifled through his money bag tucked in his pants, and found a few hardly-spare shillings, which he gave to Mack to do his best for some tucker.

At 6 o'clock Mack had returned and the train again began its slow haul for the next 4 or maybe 5 hours toward Dubbo. Paddy encouraged Lillian to eat up, telling her there be nowt else till morning. He prolonged the meal as long as he could, as a way of occupying Lilly's inevitable boredom. She hadn't had much running around in the day, it might be difficult to get her to sleep; he just hoped she would run out of steam before too long. Having to amuse his kid every hour wasn't what he had counted on when they had set out from Gundagai.

Fortunately she did settle down on the rug at about 8pm, which meant she might now sleep the whole night through. And that was, luckily, the case. The train finally rolled into Dubbo goods depot at eleven, and being so late there was no disturbance in unhitching trucks or shunting. Mack secured the brake and left for a boarding house, saying he would be back about eight in the morning.

Paddy would have given a jumbuck for a drink, but it was already the wee hours as he lay down to sleep, and nothing at all was open.

Mack returned as scheduled, his appearance waking the Egans. He put the billy on the stove and fired it up. If there were nowt to eat then they could at least have tea.

"How'd you sleep?" Mack asked, to make conversation, although not disingenuously.

"As good as it gets," Paddy rattled with a dry throat. "Thanks."

"So where you off t'day?"

"Go see me ol' man first up. Got his address," he indicated by patting his shirt pocket.

"Still kicking, then?" Mack asked, thinking that if Paddy was fifty-something his father must be over seventy.

"Was a few years ago, I know. We'll see. Got a few other relo's about, too."

"Ok. Good. Have some tea, then, before you go."

Gathering up their stuff after the cuppa, Paddy and Lillian bade farewell to Mack, and headed into town.

"Where we go, dad?" Lillian asked as they trudged across tracks and down streets.

"See your grandpa."

"Oh. Grandad Paddy? In Junee?"

"No, Lil', your *other* grandpa, *my* dad. We in Dubbo now."

"Golly gee! How many granpa's I got, dad?"

"Just two, Lilly." He avoided trying to explain the relatives on her mother's side and father's side, it could bring up her own mother's death.

"And how many uncles, dad?"

"Lots. And lots of aunts."

"Wow. I lucky, eh dad. I got many many," she said with glee and gave a little twirl in the street. "When we go t' Narrow Mind?"

"Tomorrow, maybe."

After about 30 minutes they arrived at Bligh Street, in a more seedy part of town, not far from the local goal, and by the river. It wasn't that the street was so far from the Station, about three blocks, but that Lillian was a dawdler, and whinging at times about being tired, and hungry, so Paddy had to carry her from time to time.

In Bligh Street they found a rather run down white weatherboard cottage with a red tin roof, an untidy front yard, and rickety fence. Paddy led the way to a sunburnt brown front door and rapped. They had to wait quite a few moments before the door was opened slowly, and an old man leaning on a wooden walking stick peered out.

"Hi dad. Long time no see..." Not getting a positive response after a moment, Paddy added: "George, dad. It's George."

"George? Egan?"

"Aye dad. Come up from Junee."

"Thought you married," the old man spluttered. "Nellie said you married. Where's ya missus?"

"I'll explain later," he replied giving Lillian a quick glance. "This is Lilly, my kid. The oldest."

"Oh aye. Ya better come in then. I get Ling make the tea."

"Ling?"

Anthony Egan, not looking all too well, not surprisingly at age 70-plus, turned and led the way into the dimness of the house. Before turning into the front room, the lounge, he yelled down the short hall, "Ling! Ling!"

A chunky, short Chinese woman, perhaps in her fifties, although Paddy found it hard to tell, came shuffling in from the kitchen. She stopped short on seeing the visitors.

"Make some tea, Ling. *English* tea."

Anthony hobbled into the lounge and took his seat in a high-winged soft chair.

"Whose that, dad?" Paddy asked again, moving into the dank interior that smelled of incense mixed with some kind of cabbage smell.

"Oh, that. Ling," he dismissed the query. "Housekeeper."

Lillian clung close to Paddy as they took a seat on a dilapidated sofa.

"Is that gran'pa, dad?" she whispered.

"Sure is. Your grandpa Anthony."

"He old, dad," she very quietly whispered in his ear, that Anthony couldn't possibly hear even had he tried.

"So you living here, Da, on your own?" Paddy enquired to get a sense of the situation he was currently facing, and assessing his father now that his eyes were adjusting to the inside dimness.

Anthony was still a tall man, with broad shoulders, although somewhat bent now. Even though he probably wasn't going anywhere, he was dressed in a baggy dark-grey suit, with a flannel vest, and white shirt that was buttoned to the neck. He still sported a bushy moustache, silver-white, that extended down his jowls at either end, matched by equally bushy eyebrows over deep, angled eyes. His straight large nose looked even bigger today against a more ashen face that was blotched with varicose veins, and he continued to wear his old round hat of felt that had no style, which obscured his unkempt curling dark hair.

Anthony Egan (Date unknown).

Paddy could well imagine why Lillian might think of him as a bit scary and old.

"Ling," Anthony finally answered. "She stays here. Gave 'er a room for keeping 'ouse. Works down the vege market part time, brings 'ome some fresh vege. Can't go pass that!"

"Is that her first name, or last?"

Anthony looked at Paddy with a perplexed frown. "Bugger'd if I know. I just call her Ling Ling 'n she comes a-running."

"Where did ya find her, then?"

"Narromine. Ran a vege patch with her hubby. He died, so she came with me down 'ere." Anthony didn't think it needn't have more explanation that that.

"Ah. I see... And the others...? My sis, Grace? Teresa? The boys...?"

"Gone. All gone," he dismissed with a brief wave of his large hand. "Off here and there, the big smoke, married.... Lot of catching up *there*, boy. You been gone a long time."

"Yeah, about fourteen, fifteen year. Got two kids. Marj, she be about two now, and Lillian, 'ere, going on five. Their ma, well, you know..." he indicated without saying by a flick of the eyes and his brow.

"Nellie too, ya know? Her sister, 'bout two year back."

"Aye, I heard. So whose left in Narromine?"

"Not a one. Few new folk: Bankes, McKinnon.... What brings you up this way?"

Just then Ling brought in a large Chinaware teapot which she placed on a small sideboard. Then hurried out with barely a glance at the visitors. She returned in a moment with three large tin mugs and proceeded to fill them from the teapot.

"Sugar, Ling. 'Fraid its black," Anthony told them. "Ling never seen milk tea. It's early. You eaten yet? I don't eat till late. Maybe it's time. Ling!" he bellowed, as though perceived stupidity could be compensated for by volume. "You cook, eggs, eh. Cook. And bacon or ham. Cook." To ensure she at least remotely understood he pointed to his mouth, as if wanting it stuffed.

Ling nodded obediently then left for the kitchen.

Paddy got up to pass the tea mugs around, giving Lilly the smallest and telling her to be careful, it's hot.

"I'm hungry, dad," she quietly whimpered.

"I know, Lil'. Ling's cooking some eggs. Wait awhile."

"How long you stayin'?" Anthony asked after taking a sip of his tea.

"Don't know. Depends. Gotta find some work, but need someone look after Lillian 'ere."

"Not me, lad. Too old for that shite. Had my fair share already. Fourteen of yer kids we raised. Done *me* duty."

"Mmm. So no one 'bout?"

Anthony shook his head and took another sip of tea. "You can try Nellie's kid, she be 'bout twelve by now, just her and her pa, up in Warren."

"What 'bout me other one, Emily junior?" Paddy asked in a vague way so as not to indicate to Lillian that she had a half-sister, who would be aged about 23 by now.

"Oakley? They gone. Big smoke. Newcastle I been told."

The name Oakley irked Paddy. His first love, three kids, two dead, she left him for dead for another man, all gone sour, very sour.

"Any work 'bouts here, Da?" he asked to change tact.

"Have to ask about. We do that after brekky. Come on, bring yer tea."

Like his son, Anthony was a man of few words. He pushed himself up from his sunken chair, grabbed his stick, and led the way to the kitchen.

Paddy had to hand it to the Chinese, they could whip up a voluminous storm in the kitchen at the drop of Anthony's round felt hat. Ling served up a Chinese omelet as big as a frying pan, fish cakes lightly battered, and steamed rice laced with cabbage. What Lillian couldn't finish of her share, Paddy polished off, with gulps of black, sweetened tea to follow.

Anthony hobbled out to the back verandah and lit up a pipe, while Paddy followed and rolled a cigarette, leaving Lily to poke around. The view was of lush green rolling banks down to the river. Father and son sat on wicker chairs in the morning sun.

"We finish these, hobble into town. I don't get around so fine no more. See who's at the pub, ask about for a job. How you stacked for money?"

"I got a few bob. Not much. Lillian stay here, alright? With Ling?" Paddy checked.

"Sure. Will be a great conversation," Anthony chuckled.

"So how do you get on Da? I mean, you got a pension or something?"

"Sure 'ave, for what it's worth. A pittance. Had a few plots, sold 'em off. Some savings. Was working 'til about five year ago."

"And the house? Yours?"

"Sure is. Lot, stock and barrel. What 'bout you? What you planning?"

"Gotta find some work, dad. But hard, and can't drag the kid 'round. Need to shunt her off, at least for awhile."

"Can't help you there, boy. I too old for that, told yer. I like me quiet. And no room 'ere. Go up Narromine. See Nellie's clan. McKinnon. Hilda McKinnon, too. She got a boarding 'ouse. And Roger Bankes. Newspaper fella, he's a nice chap. Smart too, might have some ideas."

"Ok. Tomorrow. For now, let's go to the pub, ask about some jobs..."

It being almost noon, now, Paddy and Anthony headed off to the *Milestone* pub within shambling distance for Anthony. They had to assure Lillian they were coming back, and give promises of going swimming in the river. In any case, they both needed a bath. Ling also cooed Lillian with suggestions of helping her make spring rolls. Finally, although reluctantly, Lillian acceded on the payment of thruppence from Anthony.

They walked in silence mostly, Paddy noting that not much had changed in his absence. He was startled that his dad, always a robust hard working man, a labourer in anything that was going—mining, shearing, rail work, roads, horses, a jack o' all trades—had come to this: infirm and barely able to look after himself. Just like his old man, Paddy had been a roustabout and jack of trades, and wondered if this would also be his own fate. At 52 now, he would barely be able to look after his growing daughter even in ten years time.

They arrived at the pub after ten or so minutes, even though it was only two blocks from the house. Anthony bought the first round of schooners, and Paddy a second one for himself; his father said he didn't drink much these days on account of his age and rheumatoid. Customers were pretty sparse, and none of the few nor the barman could direct Paddy to any employment. After an hour or so Paddy decided to head up to the train yard and ask about any work, leaving Anthony to shuffle home on his own.

Paddy wandered about the train yards and asked whoever looked officious about possible work, stating he had experience over the last 20-odd years on the southern line down to Bowral and later to Junee, and earlier on the Dubbo-Narromine line and out to Nyngan, that he could turn his hand to anything. None of the bosses had anything that day, but told him come by early, 7am, tomorrow and the next on speck. This was about the best news he had had for a long time.

He returned to Anthony's dwelling to relay the good news, then took Lillian down to the river for a 'swim' and a bath, and to wash their clothes. Anthony was agreeable that Lillian could hang about the house for a day or two while Paddy earned a quid, and to which Lillian, now familiar with the old man and Ling, agreed. As evening came on Paddy went down to the *Milestone* and bought only two long-necks of *KB*; his money was fast running out. But he thought it better to invest in a little reciprocation with his father in the hope he and Lillian could stay on at the house for a few days.

After another early dinner of rabbit, potato, cabbage again, and rice, Paddy invited his father out to the back verandah for a smoke and the beers, that had remained cool enough in a bucket of water.

"Only a glass for me, son. 'Nuff t'put me t'sleep."

"Sure, Da," Paddy affirmed, glad he would have almost two bottles to himself. "I'll go early in the morning, see of I can get a day's pay at the depot."

"Tell 'em you know me," his father encouraged. "Everyone knows me. I been 'ere near-on almost twenty year, now, ever since yer ma passed."

"I know, Da. You moved back from Narromine a year after, 'bout 'fourteen, 'fifteen, wasn't it?"

"Aye. More work down 'ere. Nuffin to keep me in Narromine."

"Where all the others, then, Da? I only know 'bout Arthur and Bill in Bowral."

"They still there. Teresa, Grace an' Mary moved to Sydney. You know Mary married that fella, Goodwin...?"

Paddy nodded. "Aye."

"Well, she died in 'twenty-six."

"Aye. I heard, from Grace. The year I married Clara."

"Aye. Well you know Lily Grace married in 'twelve, to that fella, Herring. Then moved down to Sydney, near Parramatta if I recalls right."

Grace Lillian Herring nee: Egan. (Date unknown).
"And the other Lily? Lily May?"

"Still in Orange, so I do believe. Don't get much writin' from any of 'em."

"And Lena? And Mag?"

"Ha! Lena, not a word. Margaret somewheres in Sydney."

"How you know that Roger fella, in Narromine?" Paddy asked, redirecting the talk.

"Oh him. Through McKinnons. Whole bunch of 'em up there. Hugh McKinnon, ran a bakery up there. Not sure him, or a nephew maybe, died young, in 'twenty-eight, just twenty-four year old, mind.

Sad case, 'cause his ma died just a few years before. Their folks from Junee. You might know 'em?"

"There's a few McKinnons down that way, Da. Some of 'em got a few quid, too."

"That be right. Hugh left a wife, Hilda. Set her up in a boarding 'ouse in Narromine. We all went to Hugh's, thingy..."

"Funeral," Paddy filled in for his Da.

"Na. Funeral in Sydney. That where he deaded and buried. His mem'r'al service. In the church. Roger was there reporting it. We got talking. Go see him, George. He knows what's going on."

"I will."

"And Hugh's ma had a boardin' 'ouse too, in Sydney, near the beach I 'ear. Gave it to her daughter, Flora if I recall. She came up for the service. Big turn out, got yakking to 'em all, I did. Some kerfuffle about Hilda owing money t' Flora. I reckon she came up to see what else she get 'er claws inta."

"When was that, Da?"

"Oh...," Anthony scratched his chin, trying to think; he knew himself that he had a hard time remembering when things happened. "Not long 'go... Maybe two, three year. She come up 'ere thirty...nineteen-thirty, if I recollect correctly."

"And you went up there? To Narromine, for a Service?"

"Aye. Just look about, you know, old times... See what's new."

"I see. Ok, then, I'll head up that way for a few days, when I get a bob or two. Go see Nellie's man and kid, as well, I guess."

"George Gee. They in Warren."

"Not far. I'll hitch a ride maybe."

"Well, I'm goin' t' hit the sack. Seven a-clock. Ling wake yer at six."

George-Paddy said goodnight to Anthony. Lillian came out to replace him, clutching her dad's knee. She babbled about what she had been doing, mostly rolling and folding dough for Ling, baking bread, prepping veges for chop-suey, and learning a bit of Chinese which she repeated with distorted expressions. She seemed cheerful and occupied for the first time in about a week, as well as well-fed and clean. She was now happy enough to stay at the house while Paddy went off to work, or at least look for work, and also pleased to have a grandpa she could take a short walk with.

They stayed on the verandah awhile. Paddy didn't know what to say, how to talk to a four-year old. He just let her babble, nodded, answered her questions with mono-syllables, and drank the warming beer. In between Lillian's tattle he wondered about his brothers and sisters, all thirteen of them.

Oh he knew several had died at birth or soon thereafter; his parents seemed to pop out a sibling almost every year, sometimes twins. In fact, as far as he could figure, at least 5 of them had died, and the only remaining ones with whom he occasionally had some contact were Grace and Teresa. Arthur and Billy in Bowral he had good direct contact with when he was in that area, before he had moved on to Junee in about 1919, or was in '20? But he found it a bit awkward even then. Arthur had his own young family, and everyone had their own jobs and lives, yet he was the eldest in the family and should be showing leadership, stability and responsibility. But at that stage he had nothing: no job, no money, no wife or family to speak of... Now, in 1932, back in Dubbo, his growing-up place, he had come full circle, and the only thing he had was a kid in tow. His shiralee.

But he was still fit and strong, at six foot with broad shoulders and big arms, so he could work. And he was a likeable guy, so the women said, with dark sandy hair, green eyes, a long nose, and firm chin. Although he didn't say much, he got on ok with most folks—except the Keoughs and their extended kin, the Smarts, of course.

Four

Narromine — Warren 1932

Paddy Egan was up early the next morning, having remained largely sober the night before. He had drank only the two bottles of beer. He couldn't afford any more, and his old man was no longer a big drinker and so not a good drinking companion.

Ling—or was it Ling Ling?—was also up and rekindling the stove, hoping to brew some tea quickly. The water was boiling in five minutes and she had some fried eggs on the hob, also. Language was a problem, though; she seemed to understand more than she could speak, so pointed at the eggs, at Paddy, then the plate on the table, mumbling something incomprehensible, but Paddy got the drift. He took a seat as Ling served some tea, then the eggs, and even 'toast-bread', she was able to say, and a fat sausage.

'Wow. This woman is good,' he thought. 'Da seems to have hit potluck with this one.' He gulped down his fill and finished off the tea, then thanked Ling. Then she wrapped a warm sausage, cheese and bread in butcher's paper and put it in a hessian satchel. These she thrust at Paddy as he was putting on his coat, again mumbling something, and pointing to her mouth, as if to say 'food'. He assumed it was for his lunch. All he could do was smile and say thank you a dozen times. It crossed his mind that Lillian would be safe with Ling, for a few days at least. And he thought it might be good if she could stay with Ling and his father for a good while longer, but his father had said no. And what would happen if his dad died—it could be months before he knew of it and came to collect Lilly.

He left the house soon, and quietly; he didn't want a crying scene with Lillian. His dad would distract her and assure her that Paddy was coming back, and he'd left all of his meagre belongings as if to prove it, just as he had left Ned with Barney on the pretence of returning to Coota.

He headed for the rail yards, about a 15 minute brisk walk from the house. Even though it was early summer the country air was crisp at a little after six. Taking long strides he arrived in good time to find three other blokes huddled about an open pit fire, who, like him, were waiting for a chance to earn a quid. He silently wished some of them would leave, or were no hopers, thinking there may not be enough jobs for four men. But playing it friendly he introduced himself and soon found one of the men, Stuart he said, was just a free-loader willing to do a scrap of work for a free train ride to Narromine. That left just him and two others. He prayed the boss would be out soon before any more workers came scrounging; he knew he was experienced and good, but he was also older, and had no friendly contacts here to push him along.

Merv, the boss, came out of a warehouse a few minutes later. He was a big but overweight fella, about Paddy's age, which might endear him a bit toward Paddy; he could only hope.

"Ok fellers," he boomed, "let's get moving. Need load those sleepers there," he pointed down the track, "on t' flat car, and the tools in the wagon. Gotta replace some today before we get a derailment. Up in Narromine." The four men nodded acknowledgment. "Any of you's got experience with re-railing?" Merv looked around.

"Aye, sir. I've done my fair share of track laying, even up on t' Narromine-Nyngan line, a few years back," Paddy proudly declared.

"Good. Then ya know what ya doing, I s'pose. It's ten bob a day. Finish it off and there might be another ten bob tomorrow."

"Right fellas," Paddy directed, taking a bit of a lead. "Let's get them sleepy logs on board. Train ain't gonna wait for ever," he chuckled.

With that they all headed down the track and, working in pairs, began stacking 30 sleepers on the flat wagon, then threw whatever tools were at hand into the brake van. Merv climbed up and took the one and only seat, followed by the workers who sat on the floor boards. He told one of the guys to go tell the driver they were ready, and a few minutes later they felt the jerking forward motion.

Merv pulled out a notebook from his top pocket and listed the men's names as he asked each one.

Paddy turned to Stuart, who was about thirty years old, and asked him in a friendly way if he lived in Narromine.

"Sure do, mate. Family's there. Heading home."

"Ah. That's good. You don't happ'n t'know a Roger Bankes up that way?"

"Ha! Everyone knows Roger! Small place. He's the newspaper guy."

"You know where I find him, then?"

"Sure, he's got an office in town. You can't miss it? What fer?"

"Oh nuffin special. Me dad told me to look 'im up, that be all."

Their chat was interrupted by Merv yelling over the noise of the wheels and rattles and the wind rushing in and around the van as the train reached some speed.

"Listen up you fellers. We'll see how it goes t'day. If need be might have t'stay overnight. No point having this train go up and down the line empty. There's a cheap boardin' 'ouse in Narromine, two bob a night. Not to worry, though, New South Wales Rail will pay up."

Everyone was silent for a while in light of this news. Merv briefly returned to his notebook, then soon took up a newspaper. Paddy was a bit worried about Lillian if he didn't return that night; he hoped his dad would be able to sooth her. He sat back and held his silence, thinking all things, knowing it was only 25 miles so they'd be at

Narromine in about an hour, maybe about 8.30am. So he wasn't so far from Lillian, he thought. But she wouldn't know that...

Meantime, back at the house Lillian had woken up and ambled out to the kitchen. Ling babbled incomprehensively to her, as she had done with Paddy, about the tea, eggs and toast-bread.

Lillian looked around and began to wonder.

"Where my dad?" she ineffectually asked.

Ling just babbled again, Lillian able to catch only one English word, 'work'.

"My dad. Daddy? Where daddy?" she persisted.

Ling pointed toward the front of the house and again said the monosyllable word 'work'.

"Work? What work?" she quizzed with a discernible frown.

Ling shrugged. "Work." Then she made motions as though she were a train, a steam train with all the sounds of 'choo-choo' and 'toot-toot'. Lillian was a bit confused, and worried. 'Work?' 'Or gone, on a train?' her little mind turned over. She went to the parlour, with Ling on her heals. Ling pointed to his belongings of a water bottle, billy, knapsack, large knife, and other blankets. Seeing these Lillian knew her dad would never leave without them, especially his knife, so he must have got a job and would be back. But Ling couldn't tell her when.

"Gran'pa? Where gran'pa?" she persisted.

Ling pointed to the bedroom where Anthony was still asleep. It was only just past seven, so Ling pantomimed sleeping. Lillian seemed to understand and returned to the kitchen to have her breakfast.

Afterward she helped Ling tidy up the kitchen, and watched as she cooked some more eggs and a sausage, while waiting for grandpa Anthony to wake up. So she wandered out back to explore. A few wallabies and a rabbit were out grazing by the river; she couldn't swim, in fact she was a bit timid near water, so didn't approach them.

She quickly became bored. She had no one to play with, no toys, no work to do, and only one book that she had read a hundred times. So she wandered about aimlessly, singing ditties to herself for a while until grandpa came out with a cup of tea. She ran up to him.

"Where my dad?" she demanded.

"He's got a job, Lillian. On the rail. Back tonight," he answered nonplussed, staring out to the fields.

She huffed. "He didn't tell me."

"He wasn't sure. He's gotta work, ya know, get some money."

"He coming back?" she insisted, still with some disbelief.

"Sure is. All his swaggy stuff is here, ain't it?"

Again she huffed. "I got nuffin to do."

"Well, then, let's see. Ling's going down the market. You go help her. See if she buy you some candy."

With that he went inside and spoke to Ling, managing somehow to explain that Ling should take Lillian to the market before it got too hot.

Shortly afterwards Ling took Lillian by the hand, and carrying a large shopping bag of hessian in the other, set out for the market. Even though they couldn't talk much, Lillian was happy to skip along on a new adventure.

Paddy and his team arrived in due time, a few miles past Narromine. They clambered out of the brake van and onto the flat tray, rolling off the sleepers at spots designated by Merv as the train slowly puffed along. After a mile or so the train halted; the workers gathered the tools out of the van, while Merv put together a fire and started a large billy boiling. Everything now gotten off the train, it backed up the track a mile, while two of the men walked up-track to place red warning flags.

Merv found a seat on a large rock, and invited his men to get a cuppa and have a smoke. He told them there were three sections to do, so they might be on the job tomorrow as well. All organized, they set to work in pairs: unhooking the rails from rotten sleepers, pulling them out, digging new channels and slipping a new sleeper into each one and tightening the track to it, before moving on to the next.

At noon they stopped for lunch. Finding a shady spot they all sat about as though it were a picnic. Paddy was glad Ling had made something for him, simple as it was. They got another cup of tea and smoked, Merv telling them it was too hot to work, to take a snooze until two o'clock, but they'd have to work early the next day to make up for it.

Merv roused them at two, and they again set to work, finishing at about five o'clock. Throwing the tools back into the brake van that the train again brought up, they climbed in and the train reversed back to Narromine.

"Now gents," Merv solemnly told them as they came into the town, "we'll go to this boarding 'ouse I was tellin' yer 'bout, run by a widow by the name Hilda. There's a pub down the road a bit, but there be no getting drunk, orright! You do that on yer own time back in Dubbo or wherever. Two bottles each, yer 'ear. Dinner at seven, sharp. I'll give yer each half-pay fer t'day, so yer can buy some baccy or what not. The rest when we back at Dubbo... Except Stuart 'ere."

Everyone nodded or murmured assent then followed Merv to the pub he mentioned. Paddy was as keen as the others to down a schooner, and quickly order another. Each of the men, other than Stuart who left for home, bought two long-necks and again followed Merv up the dusty road a hundred yards to *'Narromine Nights'* boarding house *'for refined gentlemen'*, the old painted sign said. Beneath it in small letters was *'Hilda McKinnon, Proprietress.'* They took a spot on the front verandah for a while.

It was close enough to seven o'clock when Hilda came out and called them to table. There were no other guests, so Merv introduced his team of three. Hilda served up rabbit stew with mixed vege and fresh bread, saying a friend of her owns a bakery down the street, that used to belong to her husband's kin, so she thought, but Hugh had been deceased now about four years.

They all chatted without much purpose. Amidst a lull Paddy asked Hilda where she was from, noting he knew a few McKinnons in the Junee area.

"Oh yeah, that'd be me husband's side, and sister-in-law, Flora. Them and me are really from Sydney, but have relo's in Junee. You know 'em?"

"Nah. Not really. Know *of* 'em but. Auctioneer and horses, i'nit?"

"Yup. Cousins and uncles."

"I see. So what brings you up here, to Narromine?" he probed.

"My husband... Ex-husband. Hugh. He passed away four years ago, now, in 'twenty-eight. Very young. Only twenty-four. We only married one year, can ya believe *that!?* His father, or grandfather, maybe an uncle, I can't remember who, or some other distant relo I don't know who, had a bakery here. We only 'ere a short time. But then Hugh's mum had died a few years before, so we went back to Manly."

"Manly?"

"Yeah, Sydney, on the harbour, the beaches... My mother-in-law had a boardin' 'ouse, so it passed to Hugh, my husband, and his sister, then he died in 'twenty-eight and it passed to his sis', Flora McKinnon. I don't now what she done with it now. That was about two year ago, nineteen-thirty."

"So you came back here?"

"Sure. We already set up this boardin' 'ouse, and had connections with the bakery, so a chance to make a quid, and I had a bit o' experience with Hugh running the 'ouse in Manly. But his sister didn't like me all too much, so I headed back here. In fact, she and me had a bit of a run-in over some money Hugh had borrowed, back in nineteen-thirty."

"Aye. Ok. Nice," Paddy nodded with acknowledgement, not sure he followed Hilda's time-line. He then got up and grabbed one of his beers from the ice chest and sauntered outside to the front verandah, taking a few hefty swigs as he sat on the steps. 'Not a bad sort,' he thought to himself. 'And young, couldn't be much older than twenty-six or twenty-eight. Doesn't seem to have kids... I wonder...?'

Indeed, Hilda was not a bad sort. She was in her mid to late twenties, as Paddy surmised, slim and tall, with sharp features topped by long auburn hair tied up in a classical bun to keep it out of the work she had to do. Her fair skin would suggest that she seldom ventured into the western NSW sun. She commonly wore a straight, plain black dress, not for reasons of mourning, but more as to present an authoritarian appearance in her business, where she had to deal with all kinds of often uncouth men.

A little while later, after Hilda had finished cleaning up the dining area, she joined Paddy out front, taking a wicker chair to one side.

"You ever been to Manly, Paddy?"

"Nah. Not me. Sydney, oh aye, but just the city. Long time ago."

"Oh. Well, if you get down that way again catch the ferry across. You can stay at Flora's boardin' 'ouse," she laughed. "I can give you the address if ya like...?"

"Sure. Why not. Never know."

"Yup. You and yer missus, eh, a day at the seaside."

"Not married, ma'am. Got a kid, but, in tow. Four year old."

"I see. So where's yer missus?"

"Dead. 'Bout a year or so ago. In Junee."

"And left yer with a child?"

"Aye. Daughter. It hard to find work trooping 'round with her in tow. You got kids?" he added in order to pursue his own agenda.

"No. We never had. No time. Hugh died young, told yer that. And was sickly before he went."

"You want kids but?"

"Ha! Maybe. If I meet the right feller. For now, I'm too busy with this place," she nodded behind her.

"Mmm. I'm looking to board her for awhile. Hard times, y'know. Gotta earn a quid y'know. An' wha'd I know 'bout raising a girl, eh?"

"You got no relatives who can take her?"

"I'm looking. My Da's in Dubbo, but he's too old. Had a sister-in-law in Warren but she died two year ago. Don't suppose her widower would take Lillian, my kid. He not blood."

"No brothers, sisters?"

"Oh sure, them about, but got their own families." He took another large swig from the bottle to fortify himself, or perhaps drown his miserable thoughts. "And we didn't always get on. Haven't seen 'em for yonks. I left Dubbo 'bout nineteen-eighteen."

"Wow. That's 'bout fourteen years."

"Aye. So you wouldn't be wanting to take on a lil' helper here, in ya 'ouse?" he boldly suggested.

"Ha no. Too young, Paddy. Maybe if she was a bit older.... Go see Roger Bankes, he might know something or someone."

"Oh aye. Me Da likewise said that."

"So you going back to Dubbo tomorrow?"

"Guess so. Lucky enough to get two days work. But we'll hitch a ride up here again to see some relo's and this Bankes fella. Be orright if we stayed here a bit?"

"By all means. You can always earn yer keep for a few days, if that suits ya?"

"It sure does, miss. Just a few days 'til I know where we goin' next."

"Ok, then. See you in a few days. I'm off. Early to bed for me. Lock the door when you come in, and turn off the lights. Oh, by the way, your room's number three."

"Aye. Thanks. I won't be long."

Hilda went inside. After a few minutes Paddy followed in, retrieving his second and last bottle of beer. He returned to the front verandah and swigged on the long-neck amidst a few rollies. At ten he also retired for the night.

The next morning at 6am Merv woke up his team of three, hustled them down to the kitchen where they were pressured to gulp down some scrambled eggs, toast and tea, with Merv saying they started at seven. Hilda was busy shoving freshly cooked meat patties and cold chicken into a cardboard box with bread and cheese for their lunches. Merv handed over a few bob for the accommodation, and a tenner for the food. Then they all set off for the rail line, where the train was already waiting.

Much of the day was a repeat of the previous day's work, until all the new sleepers were securely placed and Merv checked the track was straight and level. At four they headed back to Dubbo, sitting in the brake van again, as Merv tallied wages and expenses, eventually handing over to each of the men another ten shillings. He told them to check with him each day for any future work, he being happy with their past efforts.

They arrived back at five o'clock, and after unloading and storing the tools each went their separate ways. Paddy walked back to his Da's house in great expectation of a bath in the river and a good feed from Ling, and the joy that Lillian would have on seeing him. But first he stopped at the *Miletsone* for a lager. He had only one, then bought two long necks and headed 'home', thinking everyone would be wondering about him.

Lillian was the first to come running to the door when she heard Paddy knock on the unlocked front door then opened it wide. She came running from the kitchen where she had been 'helping' Ling, and grabbed his leg, crying and babbling all sorts of lamentations and regrets and endearments, demanding to know where he had been and why he had not told her or why he had not written. He picked her up and soothed her as much as he could, saying it was fine now, he was 'home', and trying to distract her by asking what she had been doing. She then turned to babbling about going to the markets, baking bread, making 'sping wols' as Ling showed her, having a 'swim', and going for a walk with grandpa.

By this time Anthony had heard the commotion and came out of his bedroom. He nodded to Paddy and said, "How'd ya go?"

"Good. Two days work, a quid. Tide me over but."

"Sure will. Any outlook?"

"Merv said check in each day, see what happens. But I got a plan to go up 'n see that Bankes fella. Met that lady, Hilda McKinnon..."

"Ah aye. I know'd her. C'mon, let's eat. Ya canna tell me 'bout it after."

Lillian was all talkative and helpful in serving the dinner of some Chinese concoction of which Paddy had no idea, but it was food, and tasted good. He took a good share of the spring rolls that Lillian persisted in giving him with a smile anticipating his approval.

Straight afterwards Paddy took Lillian down to the creek, even though it was now dark, but still warm. Paddy surely needed a clean up, and Lilly was not much better. Clean and dried they sat on the back verandah, Lillian holding her dad's leg so he couldn't run off again, she thought, as he opened a bottle of beer. Anthony came out to join them.

"Only one for me, son. Now, what's this 'bout Hilda?"

"How d'ya know her, Da?"

"Oh everyone in these parts knows the McKinnons. She married a fella called Hugh, and one o' his relo's had a bakery in Narromine. Young fella, Hugh, nice chap, but he upped and died 'bout four year ago. Before he did but, his ma died and left him some property down Sydney way. So off he went, never came back... Dead there."

"And his missus? Hilda?"

"She came back. Nuffin in Sydney fer 'er. Hugh's sister, seems, got the property. So come back to that boardin' 'ouse, been runnin' it ever since."

"Aye. I see. We stay there last night. No kids, she tells me," giving a nod in Lillian's direction.

"And not int'rested, I take it," he affirmed with a glance at Lillian.

"Nah. But we go up there in a day or two, see if she might'n change 'er mind. Or go see Nellie's old man."

"Gee?"

"Aye."

"You see Bankes?" Anthony asked.

"Nope. No time. Hilda told me 'bout him, so I'll look 'im up fer sure."

"Aye. Then rest up tomorrow. I hittin' the sack," he indicated as he finished off his glass of beer. "Night."

"You alright Da? Bit early for bed idn'it?"

"Not the best, boy," Anthony explained as he lifted his big frame from a chair. "Just getting old, feelin' tired, that's all."

"Aye. Ok, night Da."

Paddy and Lillian stayed out on the verandah awhile longer, until Lilly fell asleep on his chest. He carried her inside to Ling's room, then returned to the verandah to finish off his second bottle, and to think.

He wondered how old his Da was, figuring he must be 75, and what might happen when Anthony died. He had no property to pass on, as far as Paddy knew, other than the worn-out house, and in any case his sisters would probably swoop on anything that did remain. In the meantime he had to deal with his immediate problem of earning a regular wage, having a place to live, and finding someone who could take better care of Lilly than he could. He would have a rest the next day, then the following would ask down at the rail yard. If there was nothing going then he'd get Lilly and jump a train to Narromine, hoping Hilda would let him stay there a few days in exchange for a bit of work.

The next day he followed this plan, this time making the effort to explain to Lillian he was going to look for work or he'd come back straight away and they'd go to Narromine to see her cousins.

Almost invariably he returned to the house at 7.30, having lost out at the rail yard: there was no work at all that day. Merv told him there was a train coming through at nine, so he could jump on that for a shilling, and the kid could go free.

"C'mon little'n," he told Lillian, when he got back. "Let's get our stuff, there's a train soon to Narromine."

"Are we coming back?" Lillian whined, although also excited they were going somewhere.

"Aye. Sure we are. Be just a few days. I'll leave a note for yer grandpa."

Scrounging about for a piece of paper and pencil he scribbled a note to his father then hurried outdoors with Lillian dawdling behind. Fortunately she had managed to tell Ling through pantomime that they were going. Ling quickly followed Lillian, babbling loudly and carrying a hessian bag. Lilly opened it and saw some food, the likes of 'sping wols', chicken, rice, bread and cheese, so she thought. She gave Ling a hug to say thank you, and Paddy equally dipped his hat.

They made it to the station just as the train arrived, and grabbed a few empty seats in a rather empty carriage; seemed not too many were traveling these days, and especially to Narromine. Likely most would have got off in Parkes or Dubbo. Lillian was delighted with the space and luxury of the carriage, clambering over one seat or another and wandering up and down. At this moment she loved her dad more than ever for such luxury and excitement.

About forty minutes later the train pulled into Narromine station, with which Paddy was all too familiar, although it was about

14 years since he had been there—apart from the brief visit the day before. No conductor had come along, so he was a shilling ahead. They walked up to Hilda's boarding house, where he rang the door bell.

"Well, if it ain't Paddy!" Hilda declared. "And this must be...?"

"Lillian. Or Lilly if you like."

"Well hello, Lillian. I'm Hilda. Welcome."

Lilly hid a little behind her father's leg, a bit shy at first.

"Come in, then. Let's have some tea. Everyone's out by this time. You here for work or just visiting?"

Hilda led the way to the kitchen where she put together the makings of tea, and offered Lilly a biscuit. Settling down at the table, waiting for the tea to draw, she asked: "So, what is it? I guess if you've got yer kid then yer visiting?"

"Aye. Come up to see 'er cousins. Gee, in Warren. And that fella, Bankes."

"I expect you be wanting a place to stay then...?"

"Aye. Was hoping, missus. Maybe I can do some work for a room, and Lilly can help a bit in the kitchen."

"Sounds good to me," she smiled. "You can have a room, so long as you change your own sheets and tidy. There's a load of washing to be done, and wood to chop. You up to it?"

"Aye. Nuffin too hard for Paddy Egan," he chuckled.

"Good. Then finish yer tea. When yer going to Warren? And *how?*"

"Thought we'd look about town first, today. I haven't been 'ere for quite awhiles. Maybe look for that Bankes fella. Then can do some laundry fer yer. How's that sound?"

"Fine by me. You might have t' ask about town if anyone's going out Warren way, get a lift. I ain't got no horse. I'll ask around a bit, though."

"Thanks ma'am. Ok, then, we can put our stuff in a room and head on out."

"Dad, we got this food Ling give us, for lunch," Lillian whispered.

"Oh aye. Mind if we put some o' this in yer icebox, ma'am?"

Hilda took the bag and placed the contents in the icebox, then showed them a room with two single beds. They left their gear there and headed out to the street.

"Where we go dad?"

"Just a wander, Lil."

The two strolled hand in hand down the main street, which was just about all there was in Narromine. Past a hardware store, a blacksmith and saddler, the pub—which was closed until noon—a grain merchant, the front end of a cattle sales yard, a small church and attached school, empty, and vacant blocks of land, weatherboard homes sparingly placed, a doctor's and dispensary combined, a general grocery store, and further on a small office at the front of a larger house with a sign that read 'Narromine News'.

"C'mon, we go in here," he told Lillian, who frowned with a puzzled look. But then she just shrugged and followed him.

Opening the door he encountered a youngish woman, he supposed, sitting behind a desk covered with all kinds of papers, and not much less than the several tables around the office stacked with newspapers and files.

"Morning," she pleasantly said. "What can I do for you?"

"Aye. I was hopin' t'catch Roger Bankes...?"

"Not in, I'm afraid. You can try after one, or I may be able to help you?"

"Nah, thanks. I think I needs speak with Mr. Bankes 'imself."

"Well, as I say, after one, but can never be sure. Or you might find him about five at the pub. Usually goes there," she smiled.

"Ok. Thanks." He turned to go, then turned back again. "Do you know how I can get out t'Warren?"

"Train I guess, if you don't have a horse. The line's still open. But you have to get off at Nevertire. It doesn't go into Warren itself too often, nowadays. That's about five miles, so you can use the public handcar at the station to get into Warren."

"Aye. Yes, of course. Thanks for that."

"Getting back is another thing, though. You need check the timetable, as unreliable as it is," the woman added.

"Thanks again." Paddy tipped his hat in appreciation and opened the door, ushering Lillian out.

"Who that man, dad? Roger? A bank robber?"

"No sweet. That's his name, Roger Bankes. He be a newspaper man I wanna speak with, that's all."

Lillian shrugged, oblivious to her father's mission, and turned back the way they had come. "C'mon dad, it lunch time. Ling give us that food."

They strolled a little quicker than before, with Lilly skipping along. There wasn't much else to see or do than they had already. And it was near-on noon.

Arriving back, Paddy told Hilda of their walk, and of what the newspaper lady had told him, saying he would go down to the station later and find out when the next train was due.

"Ok. Why don't you go wash up. Lunch is soon. I'll heat up yer chicken and things fer you." Turning to Lillian, she said with a smile, "Why don't you help me set the table, Lilly."

"Yes, ma'am," she smiled back with heartfelt thanks that she could *do* something.

So Lilly set about helping to arrange the table under Hilda's direction and supervision.

"Just one dish at a time, we don't want be breaking any, do we?" she kindly remonstrated. "Then knives, forks and spoons. The knife goes on the right side, the fork on the left..."

"Which one is right?" she questioned.

Hilda raised Lilly's right arm. "This is your right arm," then lifted her left one. "And this is your left. Do you think you will remember that?"

Lillian shrugged.

"Then how about we tie a ribbon on your right wrist..."

"Where do spoons go?"

"At the top," Hilda smiled as she tied a neat pink ribbon onto Lilly's right arm.

Carefully Lillian laid out six white porcelain dinner plates, then the cutlery as directed. Then put some chipped cups next to each place and added two sets of salt and pepper shakers.

"Are you gonna marry me dad?" she blurted unashamedly, out of the blue.

Unfazed, Hilda simply said, "No."

"Why not?"

Rather than say she didn't want to marry *Paddy*, she replied, "Because I don't want to marry. That's all."

"Why?"

"Because I don't want to get married and have a bunch of imps, like some women who have ten or twelve kids. Besides, I was married once, and in a way I am still married to him."

Hilda was of the view that she *had* been married, had survived through the War, then the good carefree times of the 'twenties, and now it was hard in the Depression. *Now* was not the time to be burdened with more mouths to feed. Besides, in a way her heart was still with Hugh, it was too soon to abandon him.

Lilly couldn't quite comprehend this notion so had to ask: "Huh? So where is he?"

Recalling that Paddy had said Lillian's mother had died recently she thought better to answer more obliquely. "He's off somewhere. In the army. Not sure when he'll be back."

Paddy returned a little while later, looking a bit refreshed, and took a seat with Lillian and Hilda. She had heated the spring rolls and chicken a little in a fry pan, toasted the bread, and laid out the cheese and some butter.

"You expecting more guests?" he asked, glancing at the other three plate settings.

"Maybe. You never know when they might get back."

"Aye. So what you want me doing this arvo?"

"Washing. I just haven't had a chance. There's a tub out back, it's pretty straightforward. Then just hang 'em up to dry. When you come back from the station maybe you can chop some wood."

"Aye. No problem. You can't get enough wood piled for winter."

The remainder of the lunch break was largely silent, with Hilda darting in and out to do one thing or another, finally settling down for another cup of tea with Paddy, Lillian having gone out front to find something playful.

After the tea he and Hilda went out back; she showed him the laundry set up. The sheets had been soaking in a large copper overnight, so all Paddy had to do was transfer a few each time to a washing tub filled with fresh water and turn a handle a dozen times. It wasn't connected to the electricity, and the old gasoline engine that used to drive the washer had long since given up the ghost. After washing he had to put each item through a wringer then hang them up to dry.

"Aye. I'll get the knack o' it, but. My first missus always wanted one of these contraptions, but we never had but."

"First wife? I thought the one in Junee that died was your wife, Paddy?"

"Aye, she be that, but not the first," he revealed as he hauled two sheets from the copper to the washer tub and begun to turn the handle. "Was married before, in Dubbo, lived in Warren for a time in fact. She was only seventeen, but me also a wisp, twenty-one or twenty-two. I just come back from Africa, the Boar War ya know."

"When was that?"

"Aww, 'bout nineteen-o-three if I recall. Emily 'er name, Oakley. You know her?"

Hilda shook her head. "So what happen to her?"

"Oh, we had three kids, two died but. I was away working a lot, on the railways. When I come back one day found her shacking up with some other fella, George Sands, give her more than I could, she said. That was about nineteen-fifteen thereabouts. Went on awhile, then in 'seventeen I enlisted in t' World War."

"So you went off to fight in Europe?"

"Nah. Home duties. They said I getting a bit long in d'tooth, and been suffering malaria I picked up in Africa, and buggered hand—been shot, ya know. So we parted company."

"And Emily...?"

"She musta thought I be dead. She buggered off to Newcastle with that other fella, had a few kids with 'im, I 'eard. Me.... I went to Bowral, had a brother there, then Junee. Then I 'eard she dead in 'twenty-five. Got married to Clara the next year, my second missus."

"So you didn't divorce?"

"Couldn't. Catholics ya know. Besides, cannae afford to."

"And the girl in Warren...?"

"Nellie. She Clara's sister. But she dead about a year before my missus. Nineteen-thirty I think. Left a few cousins for Lillian, that she never seen. So hoping, blood ties, you know..."

"Yeah, Worth a try I 'spose. Well, I'll leave it to yer."

With that Hilda wandered inside the house to do more chores, thinking now that, although Paddy was handy and not bad looking although getting on in years, he had too many wives and kids for her liking; he was a good 25 years or thereabouts older than her, and came with baggage.

An hour later Paddy went in search of Hilda, and told her he was walking into town, to the station, to check the train times, and asking her to keep on eye on Lillian.

"Okee. I might give her a writing lesson, basic, you know. She was asking me before."

Paddy's eyes lit up, above a wide smile. He had long wanted Lilly to learn to read 'n write properly, to go to school even, but he and she were always on the move, or he fumbling about to earn a crust, and he knew next to nothing himself about how to teach even the basic three-Rs.

"Goodo! That'd be great. See you soon. Then I'll get stuck into tha' wood."

Another hour went by during which Hilda begun teaching Lilly the alphabet and how to write letters and simple words. Paddy came back, with news that there'd be a train about ten tomorrow. Then he went out back to chop wood until almost five o'clock.

At that time he came in and had a wash, planning to go to the pub, not only for a drink or two but also hoping to meet up with Roger Bankes. To placate Lillian he promised her that he'd be back about six for dinner, and the next day she'd be meeting some cousins.

He quickly strode down to the *Narromine Pub* and ordered a schooner. The place was mostly empty, and the two men who had taken up seats in a corner didn't look like newspaper men. He asked the bartender, who said he'd give Paddy a nod when Roger came in.

He didn't have to wait long. Paddy had just about finished his drink when Roger Bankes sauntered in, dressed in light beige trousers, a white shirt and grey jacket. He was younger than Paddy had expected, perhaps about forty, with a good crop of black hair, some chin stubble, and soft features.

The barman called Paddy over from his window seat he had taken, and said to Roger that this feller, the stranger, had been waiting for him.

"Afternoon, Mr. Bankes," he greeted. "Paddy Egan, from Junee. Can I get yer a beer?"

Paddy thought he should begin by being a little generous first time around, since he didn't know what to expect from the newspaper-fella, but was hoping to extract some information.

"Sure."

Paddy ordered two schooners.

"From Junee? You're not related to the Egans around here, then?"

"I am, as a matter o' fact. Anthony Egan me dad. Got kin all 'round the place."

"Ah, yes. I know Anthony, and some of his kin. But haven't seen you about. What brings you up from Junee?"

"Aww, visiting me Da and folks, looking fer work. Me wife's sister, Nellie Keough, or you might know her as Nellie Gee, out at Warren. Well, not her exactly, 'coz I know she passed two year ago. But hoping to catch up with nieces and nephews."

"You're with your wife?"

"Nope. Sadly she also passed away 'bout a year or so ago, not long after Nellie. But I got a kid, Lillian May, she not ever seen her cousins, you know what I mean?"

"Sorry to hear. I heard of the Keoughs down Wagga way, and met Nellie when I came here in 'twenty-eight. Odd, my wife's name's also Nellie, Nellie Duncan from Melbourne," he chuckled. "Here, I have a picture of her. I always carry it with me."

Roger Bankes' and Nellie Dunstan's wedding, St. Johns, Clifton Hill (Melbourne),
with Bob Dunstan and Charlot Ward in the background. 1926.

"Nice. Very pretty," Paddy respectfully approved. "When that be?"

"Nineteen-twenty-six."

"That be so!? Same year I married Clara."

"Indeed! Well, the Lord *does* work in mysterious ways... And here's one of me, nineteen-twenty-eight, outside my office, when I came up here."

Roger Bankes outside his office of the Narromine News, circa 1927-28.

"Of course I reported Nell's passing," Roger continued after showing Paddy the two rather ragged black-and-white photographs. "Yeah, and so I met George Gee. Nice chap."

"Hope so. I never met him, meself. Was hoping he could look after me kid awhile."

"How old is she?"

" 'Bout four, going on five."

"Ha! I don't like your chances there, mate. George's got six or seven of his own. Mighta been different if Nellie was still alive."

"Ah, I see. Anyways, I going out to Warren tomorrow, look around. Used to live there, yer know."

"Oh. When was that?"

"Ah, 'bout nineteen-o-two, o-three. Got married to a girl, Oakley, out there, till she passed on."

"Geez, mate, you don't have much luck. I don't know any Oakleys, though. Where you staying?"

"Here? McKinnon's."

"Ah, Hilda's. Nice lady that. But sad story. She tell you?"

"Yeah, about her hubby dying and the boarding house down in Sydney."

"So what's your plan? Finding work I guess, but difficult if you've got a five-year old toting along?"

"That's about it." Paddy finished off his beer, as Roger was going slow. He ordered a middy now, to give Roger a chance to catch up.

"Hilda won't look after the little one, then?"

"Nah. She said she too busy, and Lillian too young."

"So what work do you do, Paddy?"

"I can turn me hand to anything. Labourer, used to work on the railways, farm work..."

"Well... I don't know anything going 'round here. It's hard times, could get harder. I was gonna suggest Sydney, but I hear they just lining up at places looking for a day's work."

"Yeah, I heard. Was thinking going to Bowral. Got a brother there, Arthur, might be able to find me some work. Me Da said he's got a long-time job building some kinda dam or some such."

"But the kid holding you back?"

"Don't get me wrong, but yeah, who gonna look after 'er while I at work?"

"Let me think on it. Might be able to help yer there a bit. I got three sisters in Parramatta. Spinsters. Older than me. Might be willing to take on a helper awhile."

"Parramatta eh? That'd be good. She'd like that, all the people and shops and things. And I could get up from Bowral to visit."

Roger looked at his watch. "Getting on to six, I better get home. I usually just drop in here now and again to catch up on any news. But as you can see, as quiet as a church today. Let me give my sisters a call, see what they think."

"Fine. Anything would be good."

"Meet me here, then, tomorrow, if you're back from Warren. I'm usually here about five. Or the next day..."

"Aye. Thank you. I sure will catch up."

Roger finished off his single beer and said good night to all four people in the pub before heading home. Paddy lingered a little, to give Roger some space, then finished off his second beer. He bought two long-necks, and headed back to McKinnon's.

He found Lillian setting the table again, and Hilda stirring another rabbit stew. He put his two beers in the icebox and took a seat. Two other men had since arrived in the dining area; they looked like travelling salesmen or real estate procurers. He introduced himself and engaged in small talk until Hilda dished out a stew with home-made bread.

Finishing the meal the two men retired to their rooms, Paddy thinking they weren't too sociable, or perhaps just not with the likes of him dressed in an open-neck grey shirt, a shabby brown coat and faded dark blue pants. He retrieved a bottle of beer and headed out to the front verandah, leaving Hilda to clean up with some help from Lillian.

Twenty minutes later Hilda joined him on the verandah, as she had done previously.

"You find Roger?"

"Aye. Sure did. Had a chat. Says he has a sister or two down Parramatta, might be able to look after Lillian awhile, and I can look fer work or go down Bowral. I got a brother there, he might get me a job."

"So you'd leave her with strangers?"

"Aye, what else canna do? Anyways, they aren't 'zactly strangers, if Roger says they ok, then fine. He seems like a decent fella, educated, well dressed, friendly... And they be women."

The point was not lost on Hilda, but she held her tongue. There was no point trying to explain to Paddy that women can be the worst, especially in the domestic sphere.

"Why don't ya take Lilly to Bowral?" Hilda queried.

"Nah, too hard. You don't know me family. They got their own mouths t'feed, and we didn't 'zactly get on, ya know what I mean? Easier fer me to get a job and shack up somewhere, alone."

"But yer gonna go back for her, right?"

"Sure I will. When things get sorted. An' I can visit. There be a train through to Sydney. It ain't far."

"She'll miss you."

"She get over it. It only for a short time, and maybe she canna go t'school, and there be plenty things to do in Sydney, not like out here in the sticks."

"Oh well, your kid. Up to you. But if it goes bad, maybe ya can bring her back here, if she a bit older..."

"I keep that in mind. Problem but, no work 'round 'ere."

"Yeah. And no one knows how long this shite gonna last." Hilda gave a sigh and shrug.

"Yer right there. Makes me wonder then how Roger is doing so well. Can't be too many folks 'fford a newspaper each day."

"There still some can, it be only 'alf a penny. And not every day. Besides, not the sales that brings in the quids, it be the advertising. A few bob for a small ad."

"Aye. But who 'fford even that? Businesses going t'wall every day."

"Ahh. But you don't see, eh? They *gotta* advertise in hard times to get people in the door, drum up business, or they *will* go bust," Hilda explained.

"I see. Makes sense."

"And… The paper goes far and wide. Where else folks gonna get their news? Most don't have radio, or sold *them* long ago. When a fella's done with reading it, he passes it on."

"Well, I ne'er thought 'bout it, fer sure. So, yer not just a pretty face then, eh. You knows stuff, too."

"That's me! Smart and beautiful."

"Aye, you are at that. And I guess Roger owns property 'bouts here?"

"Nah. Don't think so. Just his house, back o' his office. So no rent t'pay. And his Da owns a few plots in Parramatta."

"So not short of a quid?"

"That be right. Why? You planning on robbing the Bankes?" Hilda gave a long loud laugh at her witty joke.

When she had recovered her composure Paddy replied. "Nope, not me. I ain't no bank robber. Hard working, honest fella, that's me. Just wondering, that' all."

"Yup. And money and knowing folks and stories give 'im a lot of influence. Yer don't wanna cross swords with no newspaper man."

"Not me. I gets on with anyone."

"Well, I better get some things done, and turn in. Night."

"Night."

The next morning Paddy and Lillian came down and had some breakfast with Hilda. The other two guests had gone out already. Paddy was pleased to see Lilly again help as much as she could in the kitchen, thinking that Hilda might take a shine to her and find her useful. Meanwhile, he went out back for an hour to split wood for kindling. At nine they got ready, and leaving most of their swag in the bedroom, headed down to Narromine Station to await the train to Warren. Lillian was again excited to be going somewhere again, and not least in the comfort of a real carriage.

Late as usual, the train steamed in at quarter-past ten; it stopped only briefly, letting off a straggle of passengers, and allowing Paddy and Lillian to board.

It was less than an hour to Nevertire. Disembarking, and the train pulling out in less than a minute, Paddy espied a handcar on the spur line going to Warren. No one was around, since small stations with platforms of barely 100 feet didn't have station masters, but he knew the routine. Crossing the tracks, carrying Lilly so she wouldn't tumble on the ballast or, for her, the big rails, he got to where the handcar sat idle next to an old signal box. Opening that he chalked on the clean blackboard inside his name and Gee's name as the person he was visiting, then in the column marked "To Warren" he put in the time, 11am he figured, and then the next column marked 'N'tire' he put 5pm for his expected time of return. It wasn't the best system, but seemed to work alright. Anyone wanting the handcar meanwhile would know when it would be back in Nevertire, and where it and its user were in the meantime.

Paddy lifted Lillian on to the front seat and told her to hang on tight. He gave the car a push then jumped on and began the push-pull motion on the vertical handle, and away they went. Once it got its momentum it was easy. Lillian was exhilarated by the contraption, the ostensible speed, and the wind blowing in her face. At a casual speed they covered the five miles into Warren in 30 minutes.

Paddy let the handcar slow as they approached a bumper, then applied the brake.

"C'mon Lilly, off we get," he told as he lifted her down.

"Wheee, dad! That was fun," she smiled, flushed in the face from the wind. "Can we do it agin?"

"On the way back. Meantime, let's walk, not far."

"Where we go dad?"

"See your cuz. The Gees. In Chester Street, just up here a wee bit."

It was only a five minute walk; Warren was hardly a big town, and having lived there back in the early 1900s Paddy knew the way. Not much had changed. Turning into Chester Street they walked past several rather dilapidated weatherboard houses with front yards of mostly dry, long, dead grass and scrub, until they reached number ten. It was as quiet as a Churchyard, and as equally nondescript as all the other houses in the street, the only difference being, it seemed, was an old goods-wagon standing down the side of the house of peeling white paint.

There was no gate, indeed no fence, so Paddy led the way up a well-worn rut to the door and banged loudly, but politely he hoped. The door was opened soon enough by a young lass, maybe 14 or 15 years old, in bare feet and wearing a plain cotton pinafore that extended barely half way down her shins. She looked bedazzled by the sight of strangers.

"Morning miss," Paddy politely said, with a tip of his hat. "I'm Paddy Egan, from Junee."

'Egan'. The name seemed to cause a vague recollection for the girl, and Junee was where her ma had come from. She knew that much.

"And this 'ere's Lillian, your cousin, I believe."

"Cousin?"

"Aye. Your ma Nellie, she be Clara's sister, my wife."

The girl still seemed a bit confused, not quite able to take in the kinship relationships, and not knowing she had cousins in Junee. Ma Nellie's sister? She looked past Patrick to see where the sister might be, perhaps hoping to catch sight of a woman who gave a recollection of her own lost mother, especially since Nellie and Clara were look-a-likes.

Finally she blabbered, "I don't know...."

Seeing her bewilderment, thinking now this girl was not quite the full quid, Paddy continued. "Your Da is George Gee, right?" She nodded. "Well, your ma's sister, Clara Keough, was me wife."

"Where is she?" The girl looked around. "My ma's dead."

"Aye. I know. So Clara is. We came 'ere to see your Da, and Lillian 'ere her cousins. That's you, miss. You got a name?"

All this seemed to confuse her even more, so she simply answered, "Esther."

"Aye. Ya father home?"

Esther nodded. "Out back. I get 'im."

The lass closed the door rather than invite the strangers in and went out back to tell her father about them: "He say he knows ma, dad. He from a place called Junee, and got a kid wif 'im."

George looked at her with confusion; he'd left from down Junee way, Narrandera to be precise, way back in 1909, not long after he married Nellie. He scratched his balding head. That was near-on 20 years ago, he figured. Then he realized he'd have to deal with the visitors. He went to the front door and opened it, with Esther standing back in his shadow.

"Yes?" he asked.

"George Gee?"

"Aye. Who you?"

"Paddy Egan. I was married to your wife's sister. Clara Keough."

"Ah! Yes, I know, Nellie spoke about you from time to time. You didn't come to our wedding, then?"

"Nah. I not a great fan of the Keoughs."

"Aye, I see. So, where is she? Clara I mean."

"No longer with us," he told George, and made a sign of the Cross, to indicate as obliquely as possible in front of Lillian that she was dead.

"I see. Nell's gone also. Two year ago."

"I 'eard."

"So what brings you to these parts?"

"My daughter, 'ere, Lillian. Your niece. She wanted see 'er cousins," he lied.

"They out back. Some of 'em at least. The eldest, Cath, out working, in Dubbo."

"That's good. Mind if we meet 'em? We come all the way from Junee."

"Oh. Yes, of course. Come through then." George then turned to his daughter: "Esther, you think ya can put the kettle on for tea?"

Esther immediately turned and disappeared into the kitchen, then George led the way down a short passageway to the backyard. Paddy and Lillian, she clutching his hand, trailed behind, paused a moment to glance at an old black-and-white photograph of George, the single item on a small hallway telephone-table, divested of its phone. Then, stepping out the back, Paddy and Lillian took a rickety bench seat on an equally rickety verandah.

George called to three kids playing down the paddock. They looked up and could see the strangers, so came running.

"My kids," George unnecessarily stated. "Some o' them, anyways... George Junior, Charles, Bede. And Esther you met. And Sylvia, nineteen she be, out gallivanting I 'spect. The oldest one, Catherine, she be about twenty-somefing I figure, out working. Had seven, but one didn't make it."

"Sorry to hear that. This is Lillian, Clara's oldest, just four year old. Lilly, these your cousins."

"What's cuzzin, dad?"

"They be like brothers and sisters, Lilly. Your auntie Nellie's kids."

Lilly gave him an enquiring frown, wondering who Nellie was.

"I'll explain later, ok. They like your cousins in Gundagai."

Lilly just shrugged.

"Go play with 'em, Lil', I'll chat with your Uncle George, ok."

"C'mon Lilly, we catchin' tadpoles down the stream," Bede, the youngest one at age 13, directed. She grabbed Lily's hand, and all four ran off down the slope to the stream.

"I'll get the tea," George proffered, and went inside. He returned a few minutes later carrying two stained tin mugs, as Paddy was lighting up a smoke.

"Hope you likes it black. No sugar either. Can't afford."

It was the first chance Paddy had of getting a round look at George Bromley Gee.

George Gee (circa 1909).

He was much older than Paddy had anticipated, about 65 so Paddy thought, thin with narrow shoulders, short-ish, and a bit paunchy with age, but having a rather long narrow face and head topped with short, rich-black hair that was now receding from the temple. He had a ruddy complexion with evident spider lines through his hollow cheeks and over his long nose, beneath which the remnants of a moustache hung. Dressed in faded dungarees and a blue shirt beneath, Paddy wondered what Nellie may have seen in him if she was anything as beautiful as Clara, her slender, tall sister. But George Gee was quite a good-looking fella in his day, he reckoned from the photo in the hallway.

But that was in 1909, and George may have been a strapping young fella at one time—although in reality he married Nellie at age 45 when she was just 17. *That*, Paddy thought, was a bit beyond the pale, even though he himself was 46 when he married Clara in 1926, but she at least was 28. But the fact was, there was a lack of young, able men available in the 'twenties because of the Great War, and it was still expected women marry and populate the country, and indeed *needed* to be married for protection. Protection against what, however, was never clear to Paddy; he had only to think of Hilda who seemed to be able to hold her own in every way.

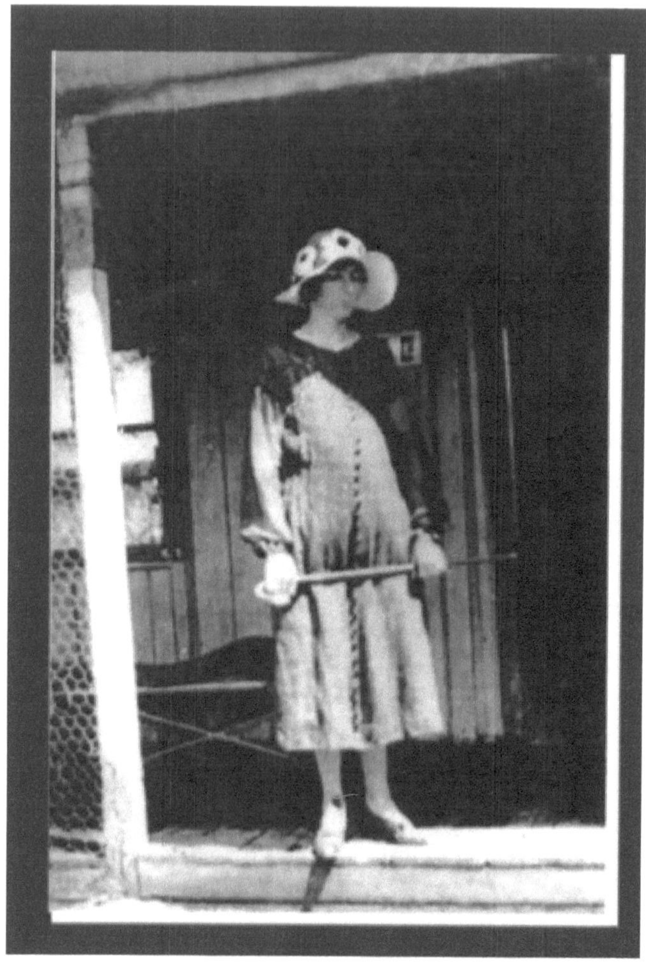

Nellie Gee, nee: Keough. (Date unknown).

"So what brings you to Warren?" George asked again, as if he had forgotten that he had asked not ten minutes before. His voice interrupted Paddy's meandering thoughts.

"Just passing through....Dubbo, Narromine, Warren. Let Lillie meet her cousins... Look for a bit of work, if I can."

"Well, yer won't find no work in this hick place. Barely keep flesh to bone meself."

"You don't have work here, but?"

"Not regular. I still do a bit of carting, when needed. Mostly people selling up and moving to bigger towns, or Sydney even. That my wagon out front."

"You used to do carting before but?"

"Aye. In Narrandera. Me and me brother. But we got into a bit o' bovver, oh.., many years back, eighteen-ninety-four to be 'zact," he told, scratching a bit of hair as if to stimulate some memories. "Went bust. When I met up with Nell, we came up here t'try our luck."

"Aye. I'm looking for work around 'ere, but with Lilly in tow, even harder."

Paddy sensed that George was not going to be very forthcoming with anything—hospitality, lunch, work, and especially taking Lilly off his hands; so he thought he may as well come right out with what he was looking for.

"Yer couldn't take 'er off me hands for a while, then, while I scab some employ? She'd fit in good with your kids," meaning she would have cousins to play with.

"Blimey, nah, mate, can't even 'fford to feed this lot. Rely on the eldest, Cath, to earn us a crust, just get by."

Warren seemed to have lost its soul. Even the school must have shut for the kids to be home all day, every day, and there was no obvious agriculture they could lend a hand to.

"You see them houses," he continued, "coming in the street. All gone. They packed up long ago. An' this drought don't help. The train don't even come in anymore."

"Aye. I got the rail to Nevertire, then the handcar. Used to live up 'ere, was very different."

"Oh aye? When that be?"

"Oh, 'bout nineteen-o-three, thereabouts. Married a local girl, but didn't work out."

"Who that be?"

"Oakley. Emily Oakley."

"Oh aye. I knew of her. She shifted out, aw, fifteen years ago, maybe. Went to Newcastle."

George didn't comment that he knew the story of Oakley taking up with some feller called Sands; let sleeping dogs lie...

"Aye. I know. I got word she died, nineteen-twenty-five it was, fell down some steps."

"Oh aye. So 'ow ya getting back...? To Narromine is it?"

George Gee seemed a bit keen to be rid of the visitors, even if they were relatives, whom he couldn't accommodate in any way.

"Same way as I come. Handcar then jump a train, hoping."

"Good luck with that. The handcar probably gone by now, and trains don't stop at Never' without 'ppointment."

"Oh shite!"

"But might be yer lucky day. I got a load t'take into Narromine. Canna yer drive a wagon?"

"Sure as me name's Paddy."

George Gee went on to explain that he had to pick up some furniture from a house nearby, the folks there were moving out selling what megre belongings they still had. If Paddy could lend a hand then George would let Paddy drive the loaded wagon to Narromine, with his son who was going-on twenty; the boy could bring it back the next day. But George couldn't pay anything for the help, just a free ride; he was hardly making a quid as it was.

That arranged George hitched up the horse to the wagon and with the boy, George Junior, they trundled about a mile, picked up some odds and ends of furniture that would be lucky to fetch ten bob at a store, and drove back to Chester Street. There Lilly was hoisted onto the front seat between her dad and Junior, and it being near 2pm set off at a plod.

George wasn't able to offer any lunch, saying all they had was eggs and toast-bread with dripping, but if Paddy had a bob or two he could stop at Nevertire Station and get a damper with treacle from an old lady's shop there.

It had taken an hour on the wagon to get to Nevertire, where they did stop and Paddy bought two dampers with tea to share. He figured it would take about ten more hours to get to Narromine, maybe longer if the horse had to rest and feed. Paddy settled in the back of the wagon, letting the boy drive for a while, with Lilly happy to babble and sing to G. Junior.

It was a long slow trip. After an hour or so Lilly was sleepy and crawled in to the back next to her father on a bed of hay. He covered her with his coat and old blankets kept in the tray. When he knew she was asleep he clambered over to the front seat where Junior was patiently and rather mindlessly driving the horse. He lit up a rollie and told G. Junior to get some sleep.

He began to wonder what the feck he was doing. This was no place for a four year old, especially a girl. He'd dragged her up to Warren for nowt, and had left all his swaggy gear at Hilda's. He had not foreseen the scarcity of trains, or lack of hospitality at Gee's house, or even the fact that when they did get back to Narromine Hilda's house would be all shut up. Lucky she had told him where a spare key was kept for the back door, but still, he had no beer, and they had no real dinner.

He was also to hope now that Roger could help him out. The middle of a great economic depression, no work, no money, and no one wanted to take his kid even for a while. He wondered of Lillian's grandmother, Rachael Keough, had considered what kind of trajectory she had set him *and* Lillian on by spurning *her* relationship and responsibilities.

Sure, Rachael had taken the little one, Marj Egan, because obviously Paddy couldn't deal with a one year old, and the other three, Ruth, Wally, Jack, carried the Lampe name and the maternal bloodline, and so they had a direct maternal link to the Keoughs. But so, too, did Lillian, who came from the same mother. That's what Paddy couldn't figure. Even so, none of the Keoughs or Lampes came to Clara's funeral or offered to lay a headstone. Now she lay in an unmarked grave, all but forgotten.

The horse plodded on, unmindful of time, other than its own need for food and rest. Twice Paddy had to stop and give it water and put the nose bag on, give it a talking to, a pat and some comfort. He was himself beginning to feel a bit like a horse, just plodding on aimlessly, mindlessly, going where told, seeking out nourishment, and dependent on others for it.

It was near midnight by the time they arrived in Narromine. Paddy parked the wagon out back, woke G. Jnr., unhitched the horse and covered him with a blanket, then put him to pasture. He found the hidden key and fetched the two kids, carrying Lillian up to their room, putting her in the bed with himself, and G. Jnr. in the other. Hilda had left a soft lamp on in the hall, so Paddy quietly stumbled downstairs, hoping he could find a draft of whisky or rum. Instead he found a bottle of beer in the icebox, with a note that read: "In case you need it, H."

He took a few deep swigs of that, thinking, 'Gawd, I could marry this girl', then downed the rest as quick as he could before returning to his bed, with Lillian still sound asleep.

At 6 the next morning Lillian awoke. Rubbing her eyes she sleepily looked around, trying to make sense of where she was, and who was sleeping in *her* bed. After a moment she recalled some of the last 24 hours, and looking at her dad understood where she was and that he shouldn't be disturbed. She slid out of bed, ran down the hall to the inside loo, then slowly trod downstairs to the kitchen to be greeted by Hilda, as cheerful as ever.

"Hello Lillian. I see you and yer dad got back alright. Who owns the horse an' wagon?"

"Uncle Gee-gee, I think," she murmured.

"Gee-gee? That's a funny name for a horse owner," Hilda smiled with a quizzical look. "You hungry?"

"Oh yes please. We had no lunch, or *tea!*"

"Oh my Lord! Then I get ya some eggs and a sausage. Your father should feed yer better. I'll have a word with him."

"Not his fault, aunt Hilda. T'was Uncle Gee-gee, he stingy. Not even a cuppa tea with sugar!"

"Oh, really? Well... Anyways, here's a cuppa for yer, with sugar *and milk.*" She poured out a big mug of hot tea for Lillian, who helped herself with the additives. "The food be ready in a minute."

"Thank you."

"Did you meet your cousins?"

"Yes, thank you," Lillian replied politely after a few gulps of the much needed tea. "Four off 'em, I fink. Esther, she stay in the 'ouse. Then Bede, Charlie, and George. He upstairs sleeping."

"Oh? Really?" Hilda was a bit surprised at this, thinking that Paddy now had an extra charge, and Hilda maybe an extra mouth to feed.

After a few minutes Hilda laid out a plate of fried eggs and a fat sausage for Lilly, then sat down with her own cuppa to watch the ravenous girl devour the food, and to think.

Five minutes went by in silence, Hilda letting the wisp of a girl satisfy herself. When she had finished it all she pushed the plate away a little and sat back in the chair.

"Excuse me, aunty, I need go t'loo."

"Ok. You know where's it at. But mind you wash yer hands after. And wash your privates, too. There's a tub of water and a scoop. You know how to do that?"

Lillian shook her head, which raised some concern with Hilda, she thinking that Lilly's parent, or parents, had sadly neglected her.

"Ok, you go up, I'll come in a few minutes and show you. It's important you wash so you don't get sick, especially with polio."

"What polo?" the child innocently asked.

"It's bad germs, *very bad*." She stopped there, realizing this might frighten the girl, and in any case she couldn't adequately explain that dreadful disease she had heard so much about. All she knew was that the new medical thinking said it was very important to wash after toileting. But clearly it was too much to expect that a man, and perhaps most especially Paddy, she silently scoffed, could supervise this activity. It confirmed her belief that child-raising was a big responsibility and arduous, and therefore reason not to have children underfoot until they had been house-trained.

Emerging from his own sleep, George Junior heard the ruckus from the bathroom, slipped on his shoes and found his way downstairs and to the kitchen, where Hilda and Lillian, adequately clean now, once again sat at the table.

"Good morning young man," Hilda greeted him. "I guess you're George?"

"Yes ma'am."

"Then take a seat, I'll get you a cuppa tea."

"Thank you ma'am," he replied demurely, sitting next to Lillian like a big brother.

"I 'spect you're hungry, too?" she observed handing him a mug of hot tea and adding a dash of milk and spoon of sugar.

"Yes ma'am."

"Then I'll get yer an egg and sausage. How's that sound?"

"Yes ma'am."

Poor uncultured G. Jnr didn't know what to make of this whole situation; he hadn't been forewarned about anything, so could only be on what he thought to be his best behaviour.

It may have been *his* best, but Hilda noted his lack of conscious table etiquette. He ate the fried eggs with just a fork, then using the same instrument stabbed the long piece of meat and ate that from one end then the other.

Hilda wanted to ask about the horse and wagon, but thought she'd wait till Paddy came down; she might only get 'Yes ma'am' from G. Jnr. In the end, after the two kids had finished she told them to go out back and check on the horse. They ran off, gladly, Hilda thought. It was just as difficult for them to deal with an adult as it was for her to be looking after uncouth kids.

She went about her housekeeping affairs for an hour, until Paddy arrived, somewhat disheveled. Hilda knew better not to ask of anything until a man has had a cuppa and a fag. He took his mug out to the front verandah and lit up a rollie. After ten minutes she joined him.

"Afternoon," Hilda teased.

He looked up, rather surly. "Aye."

"What's happen'n with the horse and cart?"

"Gotta drop it off somewheres, from me brudder-in-law, lazy sod."

"Oh. So you two are not the best of mates, then?"

"Aye, could say that."

"So tell me, from the start…" she prodded.

Paddy went over the events of yesterday, about no way to get back, how George Gee was as skint as a dead dog, wouldn't even *think* about taking Lillian, and basically conned Paddy into driving his wagon to Narromine.

"And now I guess I gotta pay for his boy's lodging. I'm getting skint meself, and stuck here, no way to get back to Dubbo."

"You better see Roger, then."

"Cannae. I not even got a bob to buy 'im a beer to get in 'is good books."

"Then you better come get something to eat."

Paddy followed Hilda into the kitchen; she served up the same breakfast of eggs and sausage, and another tea. He gulped it down pretty quick, now beginning to wonder where his next meal and bed was going to be.

"Can't you hitch a ride on the train back to Dubbo, like you did coming up here?" she asked him when he had finished eating.

"Maybe. Depend if the conductor get on, if he does I'll be buggered."

"Then you better get that furniture delivered. I guess the boy's driving back home?"

"Aye. And not a bite to eat to take wif 'im."

"Don't worry about that. I'll make him a cheese sandwich. Meantime, dump the stuff, set 'im on his way before it's late, then go do some chores. I'll lend ya a dina for the pub."

"Aye, yer too kind, missus. Wish we could stay 'ere but."

Hilda ignored the suggestive request and went off to do her own work. She currently had four guests, so needed to tidy up their rooms and get things sorted. Paddy went out back and with George Jnr. hitched the horse. Then he hoisted Lillian on to the buckboard, and all three trundled down the main street about half a mile to a furniture store. Paddy helped George Jnr. haggle with the owner about the price for the shabby bits and pieces they had delivered, in the end managing to get twelve shillings.

"C'mon then, boy. Back to the boardin' 'ouse, then yer can be on yer way. Should be a bit quicker now, without that load."

"Thanks uncle," George answered, but didn't offer any payment for Paddy's efforts, no doubt having been told by his father to not pay him off.

Hilda made some lunch to take with him, then filled a water bag for him and the horse.

"Thank you, ma'am," he said. "I be seeing you then," he directed to everyone.

"Sure. If you get down to Dubbo, or maybe Sydney, look us up," Paddy affirmed. "Got ya 'dress, so maybe we write yer soon."

Lillian gave George a big hug, not knowing she would never see her cousins again, then the boy and horse and wagon set off, back to Warren. They watched the sorry lot trundle down the highway for a minute, before Paddy told Lillian to go inside and help Hilda, while he went out back to do whatever was needed.

At 4pm Paddy came in and had a wash, changed clothes, and checked on Lilly; she had been helping Hilda as much as was able, babbling along, doing some more reading and writing lessons, and generally keeping Hilda company—who actually enjoyed the companionship.

"You missed lunch, Paddy," Hilda remonstrated.

"Aye, cannae take advantage of yer hospitality all the day."

"Nonsense. Here, you eat something before you go drinking. I kept some cold chicken and cheese with bread." She set out a plate for him. "Be back by seven for dinner. Here's a dina, enough to keep you sober," she joked.

Paddy strolled down to the Narromine pub, expecting to meet with Roger Bankes. He bought a schooner and drank slowly, although he yearned to gulp down half in one shot so the amber fluid could dull his worries. But he had little money, so had to take it easy. Quietly he was hoping that Roger might shout him, in reciprocation of their last meeting. Paddy wouldn't say nay to that.

Finally, at 5.30 Roger strolled in, dressed much the same as before, and like the previous occasion there were few other patrons at the bar. Times were tough, men couldn't afford to be spendthrifts, although the Lord knew they needed the alcohol to drown their woes. Maybe they were buying metho from the Gins... Paddy had been wondering about this, *and* the fact that Roger, as a newspaper publisher, seemed to be doing alright, but if fellers couldn't afford beer how could they afford to buy a newspaper? Bankes must have his fingers in every pot.

"Evening Mr. Bankes," Paddy greeted, trying to look and sound cheery.

"Evening, Paddy," Roger returned, taking the superior liberty to use his first name. "How'd it go in Warren?"

"Much as you said it be like, sir. Gee's as skint as a baked goanna. You should see 'em, place deserted, families eatin' boiled eggs with treacle. Someone could write a book 'bout their scrape."

"Aye. That's not a bad idea..." he mused. "You have another?" he nodded at Paddy's half empty glass.

"Aye, I will, thanks muchly. Been a hard two days."

Roger ordered two schooners, much to Paddy's delight.

While they waited Paddy came straight to the point; he had to. "You call yer sisters but, Mr. Bankes?" he led the way, leaving the field open for Roger to engage appropriately.

"Yes, I did." The beers were placed on the counter before the two men, and Roger took a hefty gulp before continuing. "They seemed interested, asked how old the girl be, I said five. I reckoned by the time she gets there she would be that age. Anyway, I told 'em your end of the story, missus dead, no relatives, and so forth. They asked to meet her..."

"Aye. So why they be keen to take her on?"

"Oh, they never had children, ya know. Never married. And one of the sisters died some time ago, so thinking.... When I told 'em her name was Lillian Mary, well, they jumped at it! Thought she might be a resurrection of their saintly lost sister." He gave a short chortle.

Paddy stopped at correcting Roger, that Lillian's middle name was *May*, not Mary. He thought anything that plays the narrative then he'd play it.

"Aye. Could be. She is a bit of a' angel. What's their situation, then, I mean, they got the ways to look after her?" meaning, did the three spinsters have enough money and a house and so on.

"Oh yeah. Educated. All of 'em teachers in the past, in fact. Think still do a bit of teaching. And, of course inheritance. Our father owned two properties in Parramatta, they got one of the houses. Quite comfortable, don't you worry about *that*."

"And school? They send her to school? She sorely in need of educating."

"Most certainly. As I said, they're school teachers themselves, so put a lot of store in education."

"Aye." Paddy was pleased to hear this. Then he changed tact. "Do I have to sign any papers for this, or what? Yer know, I ne'er done this sorta thing before."

"Nah. The sisters can take care of that. Maybe just a paper to give them guardianship."

"You mean adopt, like?"

"No, no. Adoption means they own the child, that you give 'er over forever. But if you make 'em guardians they're, like...Like a governess. You can take her home anytime."

"Aye."

"In any case, they can't adopt Mary," he called her, "because only one person can, and one sister on her own wouldn't have the means of raising the child. No, better just give them guardianship. There's an old fella there, Bayliss, used to work for the Sheriff in Wagga, he can witness it."

"Aye. And what about...?" Paddy needed to raise the issue of money, hoping both that he would not have to pay for this 'guardianship' and that maybe they would be paying *him* for the honour of having a child. "You see, I'm skint, I don't have a sixpence to pay 'em. Fact is, was hoping they could see their way to giving me a few bob, so I can be on me way. I planning to go to Bowral, get work there fer sure. Got a brother there."

"I don't know, Paddy. I'll give them a phone call tonight, again. You won't have to pay them anything, I'm sure. And I expect they can help you out to get to Bowral."

"Aye. Thank ye, Mr. Bankes. Ya, give 'em a call please, an' let me know."

"Done then." Roger put out a hand to shake, and Paddy gladly did so. "I'll let you know tomorrow morning. At Hilda's, right?"

"Aye. I be there. But... There one more thing," Paddy added. Roger raised his brow in query, although he suspected what was coming. "How I get to Parramatta? I'm a bit skint right now, ya see. 'Spect the train will cost a pretty penny."

"Ah. Yes. I see. I can lend you a quid, then my sisters can take that out of anything they might give you. How's that?"

"Mighty kind of yer, Mr. Bankes. We can do that. I can pay it back to yer sisters when I visit up from Bowral."

"All done then. I'll buy you another beer, before I head off."

Paddy was now pleased as punch, and not just with the two free beers. He had finally found a place with three women who wanted a child, and well-off enough to look after her, and teachers to boot. If they were anything like their brother then Lilly would be fine. And she'd be in Sydney, with lots of things to see and do, unlike the dry scrublands of midwest New South Wales.

Roger left for home, Paddy finished off his now third beer, and rattling some coins in his pocket, managed to buy two bottles of beer. Feeling better he trundled back to Hilda's boarding house. There he found Lilly again helping out in the kitchen and seemingly pleased to do so. Dinner wasn't quite ready yet, so he ambled out to the back verandah with a bottle of beer and made a rollie. Soon Lillian came to join him.

"Where we going dad?" she asked.

"Who said we goin' anywhere?"

"Aunt Hilda. She say you talking to the Bank."

"Roger Banks, sweetie, not *the bank*."

She just shrugged. "And...?"

"How'd you like to go to Sydney, Lilly? The city. The Big Smoke?"

"I don't like smoke, dad. Who Sydney?"

"Sydney, a big town, very big, lots of things to do and see."

"Oh. Lots animal eh?"

"No, not animals. Parks, streets, motor cars, schools, churches, trains..."

"We have dem in home, dad."

"Aye. But Sydney different. Many many. Not boring."

"We have train too, dad, in home."

"Aye, Lillian. Not just trains, but... Nice places. And places to eat." He began to wonder in fact what Sydney did have to offer over Junee. You only needed one pub, one grocery, one train... One of everything. "There be lots of people. And you can go to school."

"Wow dad. I like school. I like books. And the pee-yano."

"Well, you can have all that, and more. And there be the ocean."

"What oshun dad?"

"Water. Like a river or lake, but *very* big."

Lillian mouthed "wow" and her eyes were as big as plates.

He took a few hefty drafts of the beer and sucked heavily on his smoke. "You'll like it, girl. You will see and do things that kids back in Junee cannae do."

"Wow! Then I go back an' tell 'em what I sawed," she smiled triumphantly.

"Aye."

"C'mon you two. Dinner!" Hilda's shout from the back door startled them. "Better get it before the others come in."

Paddy and Lillian obediently returned to the kitchen table to have tea—rabbit Irish stew, Hilda called it, with fresh home baked bread. It was a quiet meal, as Hilda was busy with chores of running a boarding house; with four new lodgers, besides Paddy, she was kept busy.

After tea Paddy returned to the back verandah and finished off the remainder of bottle number one, while Lillian stayed to help Hilda. Soon four other blokes came in, ate quietly, then went down to the pub. It seemed they weren't interested in being congenial with Paddy, whom, they must have known, was also at the House.

He came back to the kitchen to get his second bottle, then resumed his backyard spot. Hilda said she would join him shortly and have a Sherry.

Twenty minutes later she and Lillian came out and joined him. Lillian traipsed around the backyard looking for something to do, as Hilda took a chair.

"You saw Roger again?"

"Aye. His sisters take the kid, might even pay me a few bob for 'spenses."

"You can get the train from here all the way to Sydney, goes through Dubbo."

"Aye. Might stop there tell me Da where I goin'."

"And where *are* you going?" she insisted. "After you dump the kid."

"I ain't dumpin' 'er, missus. Told yer, got no choice. She be well looked after. Roger says they teachers, can go to school, see the sights, maybe even the ocean. It's only fer awhile."

"Then you're going to Bowral?"

"Aye. Not far. Can visit on Sundays."

"I hope so. And take her to the beach, in Manly."

"Aye. She like that."

"Well, I hope she likes school, and can make new friends."

"Aye. She's a good looking girl, and polite. Sure t'make friends."

"I'll miss her, yer know…"

"Will ya now?" he smirked "Then you can keep her if ya want."

"No thanks. This no place. I couldn't give her what the Bankes can. And she needs kids her own age. Anyways, I'm a thinking of going back to Sydney. Nothing here for me, really."

"Aye. I stay meself, but no work, and cannae be bludging off yer ev'ry day."

"How ya gonna pay the train?" Hilda matter of factly enquired.

"Oh, Roger say he give me a quid, can pay him back when I visit the sisters."

Hilda finished off her Sherry in a gulp. "I'll get another drink." She was beginning to feel sad, and a little apprehensive that Lillian would be ok. She knew the girl would miss her dad.

When she returned she asked, "When you going?"

"Tomorrow. Roger say he will come by and tell me what's what. Then I get a train to Dubbo, tell Da, then be off again. Lillian likes trains," he added to distract from the growing uneasiness he and Hilda felt.

"Here." She handed him a slip of paper with an address: 44-46 Fairlight Street, Manly. "It's my sister-in-law's boarding house on the seaside, if you get a chance."

Paddy took the paper and slipped it into his pocket. "Bloody Nora!" he then exclaimed. "Roger ain't even given me the address of 'is sisters."

"I'm sure he will tomorrow."

Hilda left Paddy to finish off his beer, calling Lilly inside, and taking her to bed, tucking her in and talking to her, or rather, listening to the child babble on as four year olds do about her ramblings of the day. Maybe not having a child was one of the things

Hilda regretted. But, on the other hand, another person's child is one that an 'aunt' can walk away from at anytime, but she or he was the parents' child, *their* responsibility. She had cared for her young husband, Hugh McKinnon, and had been hurt by his loss. She didn't want any more pain. Maybe that's why she had returned to the isolation of Narromine....

Next morning, 9am sharp, Roger came to the boarding house. Finding Hilda and Paddy sitting about the kitchen, he joined them for a cuppa. He told them that his sisters had agreed for a trial period, maybe a few months, to take Lillian Mary, and would draw up a document for him to sign. They said they would provide Paddy with some recompense for his expenses only to get down to Sydney and then on to Bowral, but other than that they were already making an outlay to support Lillian, who was *his* responsibility. In short, neither party would need pay the other, except as above.

He then gave Paddy a slip of paper with the address, 'Loretto' as the name of the house, at 35 Iron Street, Parramatta North, and directions on how to walk there in ten minutes from the train station. He also added his sisters' names: Elaine Mary who was currently 43 years of age, Mary Madeline was 48, and Mary Mercedes at 50 was the eldest, although there was another non-resident sister, a nun, aged 42 years, Sister Mary.

'Bloody Nora!' Paddy silently thought, 'They all bloody hail Marys! No wonder they hopped when they heard Lillian was also a "Mary".'

Roger explained it was a simple 4-bedroom house, comfortable, with a large orchard out back, that Lillian no doubt would enjoy. He slipped Paddy a pound note, saying that should get him by for awhile.

"Thank you Hilda, for the tea. I be going now," he informed them, standing up. "Paddy...." He held out his hand to shake.

Paddy likewise stood up and shook hands vigorously with profuse words of gratitude.

"Ok, I be off! Good luck. Tell my sisters to telephone me when you arrive."

Paddy nodded.

After Rodger had left, Hilda turned to Paddy. "That's it then, Patrick," she teased. "All yer problems solved."

"Aye," he responded not wholly elated, still trying to comprehend how his luck had finally changed, and wondering of he really was doing the right thing. "I better go check the next train but."

He returned an hour later with news that the train was due at 2pm. He was going up stairs to pack, and clean up the room, then do a bit of laundry for Hilda. Lillian came in from playing out back and heard him.

"Where we go dad?"

"Sydney, Lilly! Ain't that excitin'!"

"Yayy! We see the oshun!" and she did a whirl around the table to Hilda's delight. "Are you coming aunt Hilda?" she asked with glee.

"No sweetie, I gotta stay here and run this hotel. You and yer dad go an' have fun, ok."

"Aww. But we coming back, aunty, ain't we dad?"

"Sure thing, in time. Just not straight away."

"Aww. But I like it here, dad. Can we stay here, dad?"

"No Lillian. You seem t'wanna stay every where we go. We be goin' t' Sydney, have fun, yer can stay at that for awhile, ok."

"It will be fun, Lillian," Hilda assured her, eyeing Paddy, thinking, 'It better be!' "Maybe there be some more cousins and aunts there for you to meet," she smiled.

It didn't take Paddy long to pack their swag, to strip the beds and take out the linen for washing. It was only 11 o'clock, so he did what laundry he could until noon, when Hilda called him for lunch.

It was a quiet midday meal, with both Hilda and Paddy thinking, and reflecting on the past and the future, and the welfare of Lillian. Hilda had been glad for the company the last few days, and maybe if things had been different Lillian and her dad could have stayed. But she told herself, it was for the best; she couldn't really cope with a new man in her life, and she certainly wasn't romantically attached to Paddy, nor want to be; and she was still unsure about having a kid about the place. What did Narromine have to offer a child at this time of economic depression? Once they had gone she knew she would get over their absence.

Paddy also wrestled not only with departing, but also with what he had to do for Lillian's sake. He liked Hilda, and would be prepared to settle down and work for his keep if nothing else until things got better. But failing that, the life of a swaggy, which he was of necessity, was not the future of a four year old *girl*. He had found a surrogate mother, or aunts for that matter, who luckily seemed keen to take Lilly and give her an education, which all were well beyond his means. But he couldn't foresee that even little girls grow up, and times change, and the social aftermath of the coming war of which most Australians had no inkling in 1932, would change everything.

Hilda gave Lillian a cheese and ham sandwich to take with her in case she got hungry, and some buttered scones and jam. Inside the wrapping paper she put a brooch that Lillian had admired. They set off at 1pm to walk the half mile to the train station, amidst hugs and endearments and gracious adieus, and promises amongst all three to write soonest. Lillian seemed in good spirits, perhaps by now used to coming then leaving, dawdling with imagination and excitement about train stations. Paddy reassured her they would be coming back, saying just as they had left grandpa and Ling at Dubbo they were going back there, or had gone to Warren but returned to Hilda at Narromine. He made no mention of old Ned they had left at Cootamundra, hoping she would have by now forgotten that.

Once again Lillian was soon excited to be on a nice carriage with sticky seats of cracked chocolate-coloured vinyl, quickly forgetting the past days, remembering what her dad had once said: "Life is all about coming then leaving, then coming back, then going again to a new place. Every one was a new adventure."

Yes, but in the case of Lillian it was always one way, a never coming back. She had not gone back to Cootamundra, or Gundagai, nor even Junee. She did not see old Ned again, nor aunt Mary, or Hilda. She did see grandpa and Ling again, of course, in Dubbo, although only for one afternoon and brief night, before they caught yet another train, this time all the way to Sydney town.

The train departed Dubbo at 7.30am, so they had awoken early, and had said their farewells to Anthony the night before. Ling of course was up and made them tea, and gave them food to take on the 12 hour trip. Even so, Lillian was sleepy and grumpy, but Paddy told her they could sleep on the train. With a pound in his pocket and the swag neatly packed they easily found a seat in a rather empty carriage. Again, it seemed people couldn't afford to travel much these days. But no doubt they would pick up a few more passengers at Wellington, Orange and Bathurst, and even go through Molong, a small dot on the map near where his father had been born in Carcoar, and 5 miles further on to an even smaller dot, to the nearest one-horse town of Cudal where Paddy himself had been born. It brought back vague memories, vague because it was all so long ago. Fifty or more years....

Map showing Warren, Nevertire, Narromine, Dubbo, and several of the train station towns down to Bathurst on the way to Sydney.

Although Lillian was a little excited about being on a train again, and going to the 'Big Smoke', she was also still sleepy, and Paddy managed to settle her down for an hour or two as the train shunted off on the first leg of a tiresome journey. He also stretched himself out as best he could on the opposite seat and snoozed, drifting between sleep and semi-consciousness.

Five

Perth 2021

A few days later Mark returned to Elizabeth's and Lillian's house, wanting to go over again the story of their mum being in Dubbo and Narromine. She had already told him and Elizabeth what she thought she knew, and Mark had written it up.

Elizabeth let him in at one o'clock, after Lillian had had lunch and a nap, so after a fresh cuppa they sat down in their customary places and he began to read the narrative to them, hoping to interrogate it to fill in gaps.

"So mum," he began, "you got to Dubbo and stayed at your grandfather's house, Anthony."

"Oh yes. I remember that. He was scary at first, big and hairy, like Santa Claus," she chuckled. "But after a few days I got used to him. He was actually quite nice. It was good to have another grandpa and go for a walk with him."

"A walk? Where? I guess there wasn't much to see or do in Dubbo at the time?"

"No. Just a matter of getting out of the house, I guess, talking...or rather me babbling, like kids do. Skipping along. There were no parks for kids, like with swings and slippery-dips, like what we have now. We just walked, not far, and to a park with grass and flowers, got some sunshine...."

"He must have been a bit slow, though?" Mark prompted to gauge his mother's recollection of his age and abilities.

"Oh yes. He had a buggered knee I think, slow, and couldn't go far. To me he was a hundred, but I don't know, maybe seventy-five or eighty. Just old. You don't understand that until you're old yourself, like me, now," she lightly laughed. "But always dressed up when he went out, not his best suit, but respectable."

"Ok, I got the picture, ma. Over-dressed by our standards. So, what about in Narromine? You met Hilda McKinnon, who ran the boarding house...?"

"Oh yes. Is that her name?! I had forgot. Yes, yes, Hilda. She was very young and nice. I think my dad had an eye for her," Lillian smiled.

"I suspect so. Maybe he was wanting to stay there, or leave you with Hilda for awhile?"

"Probably. I don't recall what they talked about. But it was a nice place, and I had things to do. I wanted to stay there."

"And you also met Roger Bankes?"

"Yes. Just once. He came to the house. He was young, too, and handsome. Neatly dressed, I remember, not like most people in the town or at the boarding house, always unshaven and daggy clothes. *He* was a professional."

"So you didn't know what he talked about?"

"Not really. I was only four! It was only later that it clicked, he was the brother of the three Bankes sisters in Parramatta, so he must have told dad to go there, and the ladies could look after me. What choice did I have?"

"I see. And you visited your cousins and uncle in Warren? Uncle Gee? Aunt Nellie's husband?"

"Yes. But I never met Nellie, she was gone from Junee before I was born, and she died before we got there, at Warren."

"And uncle Gee?"

"He was old, too. Everyone seemed old... Well, they would to a four year old. But dad later kept on saying he was stingy, couldn't even give us a decent cuppa tea. Glad I didn't stay *there!* But... It was an adventure, riding on the sidecar along the train line, then back to Narromine, I think, by horse and wagon. But, you know, wherever we went, it seemed we were always hungry, never knew when we might eat again, and what!"

"I can imagine, mum. It was the Depression... But I'm wondering... Narromine is not exactly a big town or tourist destination, even today. But you did mention it in one of your letters, or stories. So I have no doubt you went there."

"Of course we went there! I remember it like yesterday."

"Ok, but I'm wondering, why would your dad, Paddy, ever want to go there?"

"I didn't know at the time, he just said we had aunts and uncles and cousins there. It was only much later that I was told he used to live there, so I guess for him it was like visiting his old place. I can't think of why else, there was nothing there, it was just a station town on the railway going west."

"So that's why Hilda had the boarding house there? To catch travellers."

"Probably."

"So who told you that your dad used to live in Narromine?"

"Dunno. Marj I guess."

"Does it matter, Mark?" interrupted Elizabeth.

"Not really, I guess, at the moment. It just begs the question of how *she* knew.... But, regardless, it seems mum *did* go there, and so there must have been a reason for Paddy to visit. And there is some connection between Hilda, sister-in-law to Flora McKinnon who owned 44 Fairlight Street in Manly. But how do we figure the connection of the Bankes sisters and Walter Bayliss their sidekick ending up in Manly about five or six years later?"

"Isn't *that* the connection?" Elizabeth suggested. "Roger knew Hilda, who knew Flora, he told his three sisters, who then moved to Manly."

"Maybe... Except Roger died in 1933, and Flora lived in Junee; she wasn't exactly running the place herself. Unless... Maybe one of the Bankes sisters came up to Narromine for his funeral, met Hilda, who 'incidentally' told the Bankes sister about a boarding house in Manly...?" Mark suggested.

"That's a long shot! Assumes the sisters *did* come for the funeral, *did* meet Hilda, and oh, by the way... Hilda just happens to mention her sister-in-law, with whom she had had a falling-out, about the boarding house in Manly...."

"Well there you have it!" Mark somewhat insisted. "Maybe the sister or sisters stayed at Hilda's boarding house, and she told them in general conversation about the place in Manly, maybe even that her sis-in-law, Flora, was looking for someone to manage it. It was June nineteen-thirty-three. After all, she gave the address to Paddy, and told *him* about it, so why not mention it also to sister Bankes? Makes sense..."

"So the connection is two boarding-houses?" Elizabeth queried,

"Yup. Just luck, coincidence... But even if Hilda didn't mention it directly to the sisters, maybe they didn't need to come to Roger's funeral... He and Hilda were living in the same small town, would know each other, for sure, and she mentions to Roger that Flora, who maybe wrote to Hilda asking her to take care of the Fairlight property despite their falling-out, that if she couldn't, or could, Hilda mentions it to Roger, who mentions it to his sisters or Bayliss.... As we saw, Roger was the go-to-guy. The point is, someone must have told someone else, maybe Bayliss, maybe the Bankes."

"Well, let's deal with that when we get to it," Elizabeth asserted. "Besides, the problem then is, the Bankes didn't move there until about nineteen-thirty-eight, four or five years after Roger's death. Why wait so long...?"

"Yeah, I know. I mean, anything's possible, lots of scenarios. But just because Roger was dead doesn't mean that his wife, Nellie Dunstan, or his old man, couldn't continue to communicate with the three women. And don't forget, Mercedes died in 1936, in

Parramatta, so maybe Nellie and/or Percy, the father, went down for *her* funeral?

"Yeah yeah," Elizabeth condescended. "Meanwhile... Mum, what happened after Narromine? You got a train to Sydney?"

"Yes. Me and dad. Told you already. It was a long boring trip. I slept most of the way, so did dad."

Six

Dubbo 1880 — 1917

In his liminal slumber on the train to Parramatta Paddy recalled his dear mother, Ann Bridget Ryan, who was born in Rockley, another very small town, or rather, village, about 10 miles south of Bathurst.

It was a region of sheep farms and rolling green hills, just like Ireland, his older folk told him. His father, Anthony, much like himself later on, moved around quite a bit, to Carcoar in the same region, up to Molong, Dubbo, Narromine, and even Warren... Distances were generally not great, but given the antiquated means of transport and the poor roads it could take the best part of a day in travelling from one small spot to another.

Anthony never did tell Paddy how he met his mother, he just assumed it was at some country fair, or maybe by chance when Anthony had gone into town to get supplies. He may well have worked the sheep farms and by that way got to know Bridget, as she was commonly called. And, once having met her, Anthony may have readily travelled on horseback to see her, cutting across the rolling hills between Molong and Rockley, a much shorter route than the unpaved dusty or muddy roads.

Eventually Ann Bridget and Anthony married, in Orange, at the end of February 1880, she at age 17, he aged 25, their birth years being 1864 and 1855, respectively. Almost exactly nine months later George A. Egan was born in Cudal, close by to Molong. Nobody seemed quite sure what the 'A' stood for, but was assumed to be after his father, Anthony, and similarly he was called George after his uncle George Egan who died the same year in Molong. In any case, George didn't seem to like that name, and at whatever time or for whatever circumstance seemed to have adopted Patrick (Paddy) as his preferred name. A good Irish name, he thought.

The family shortly afterwards lived in Orange until about 1892, then moved to Dubbo, and at some time moved to Narromine, where Bridget eventually died in 1914. Several of their children were born in Orange, while the remaining were born in Dubbo or thereabouts. All together, Anthony and Bridget had 14 children, not an unusual number in those days; a few died shortly after birth, a few others dying at relatively young ages.

Apart from George A, the eldest, there were May, Eleanor Sarah, Teresa Agnes (= Green), Mary May (= Goodwin), Lilly M., John R., Arthur J., Walter J., Grace Lillian (= Herring), Lena, Margaret, Bertha A., and William David Egan.

After Bridget's death in 1914 Anthony moved back to Dubbo. He had been a general labourer all this time.

Some of George/Paddy's siblings married into such families as Goodwin, Herring, Green, and moved elsewhere in NSW, while two brothers, Arthur and William, eventually moved to Bowral with their own families, and even later William moved to Campsie, an inner western Sydney suburb.

As for George/Paddy, like any young lad of no particular skill, employed where and when ever as a labourer, and having sufficient education to be able to read and write at least, he roamed about the countryside close to Dubbo, preferring to get about by either jumping trains or riding horseback wherever fancy took him.

By 1899 the second Boar War in Africa had erupted, and being a horseman and for want of a lark and adventure George/Paddy soon signed up with the NSW Imperial Bushmen of the Australian and Colonial Military Forces, so he said, although he could never produce any documentation to prove it. He could vividly recall the day he came home with such adventurous excitement to tell his parents.

"Ahoy, Da, Ma!" he declared enthusiastically. "I just signed up!" His face was ruddy from hurrying home, and his smile showed ear to ear.

"What? What yer done now, boy?" Anthony demanded with exasperation born of Paddy's past exploits and misadventures.

"I joined up! The Army, Da. With Colon'al Milit'ry Forces. I'm gonna go t'Frica," he beamed.

His mother, Bridget, emerged from the kitchen upon hearing the ruckus. "What d'ya mean, the army? Cannae do that without ya Da's say-so!"

"Sure Ma I can, I nineteen now, Ma, I just signed in."

"Oh aye. Well, George, yer a damn fool, that be," his father retorted. "Why the feck ya join the *English* army? Why yer wanna fight *their* damn war, eh? My Da come all the way from Ireland to 'scape the bloody English, now ya wanna fight their feckin war!"

"Not just them's war, Da, it be the Afrikanas start it, Da. We been fighting 'em fer hundreds o' years. We gonna kick 'em outa 'Frica once and fer all. They bloody Hollander Boars."

"Oh Lord help us!" Bridget bemoaned. "Our son in a bloody war. Yer gonna get yerself killed, George! *Killed!* Ain't we had enough dead in the family wifout yer addin' t'it?"

"It's orright, Ma. I be with me mates, Australians too. We all goin'," he smiled. "I be wif the Bushmen, Ma, on horseback."

" 'Orse or na 'orse," Bridget retorted. "They still be shootin' at yer!"

"Geez Ma... Da, I thought yer be proud o' me, doin' me duty and all." Paddy looked perplexed.

"Oh aye, if ya didn't do som'in' stupid, but it *their* war, stay outa it is what I say!"

"Too late now, Da, it *is* our war, and I already sign. Wait till yer see me in uniform! I be looking like a right wallop."

The next week was one of dodging the simmering angst bred of misgivings in the household, as George/Paddy prepared himself for the adventure of his life. He knew his Da and Ma would quiet down, as his sibs and other relatives began to sing his praises of loyalty, duty and bravery, mixed with wonder and envy. His brothers no doubt were awed that George was going to *another* country, escaping the dull drudge and dreariness of rural NSW, and when he came home a few days later dressed in full military gear and carrying his *own* rifle, he looked like a real *man*, smart, handsome, almost suave.

There was nowt his parents could do about it other than silently worry and press upon him to be careful, not do foolish things or try to be a hero, and pray he would return, and return soon. Bridget prayed it would be only a few months. Anthony simmered with mixed attitudes of anti-colonialism and it being a *British* war, on one hand, while he also held quiet pride that his boy, his eldest, had become a real man, and looked professional in a drab khaki tunic, a brown sash across it, shiny new black boots, and his slouch hat.

Despite all the misgivings of some of his family, and some townsfolk, Paddy joined the march from central Dubbo to the train station, from where all 200 odd local volunteers would travel to Sydney to join thousands of others on a ship bound for South Africa.

By 1902 Paddy was on his way home. He had survived, with only a minor shot wound and having caught malaria, so he was to state later in 1917. But the fact was—other than that he never spoke of his sojourn to Africa, assuming he ever went—there was no official record of his enlistment. Perhaps he did go, perhaps under a different name, perhaps he managed to stay in the safe back-lines, or was simply lucky.

Whatever the truth, he did return to Dubbo and, even though uneducated, he knew how to play things, using his 'military record' to big-note himself when needed and leverage his war service to get a job or get a girlfriend when he returned. And that's exactly what he did. In 1903, shortly after his purported return from war, he married Emily Etta Oakley in Dubbo. She was almost a child at age 15-16, and an orphan, while young Paddy was 22. And no doubt such a young, adrift lass would be enamoured by a war 'hero'.

He came home once again to tell his family. Unlike his military enlistment this news was met with some warmth, although Bridget also had concerns about how he would support a wife.

"Da, Ma," he began one evening, as he walked into the Dubbo house, with Emily by his side. "This is my Emily," he introduced. "From Dubbo."

"Nice to meet you, Mister and Missus Egan," she acknowledged with a nervous smile and slight curtsy.

"I asked Emily to marry me, Ma, an' she say yes!" he beamed, and gave Emily a hug and a peck on the cheek.

"Oh aye. That be pleasin' then, son," Anthony affirmed, thinking this was far better than going off to an English war.

Bridget, taken more by the surprise, responded more awkwardly. "Nice to meet ya, then, Emily. I don't think I know of yer... Where in Dubbo you be?"

"Eulomoga, ma'am, just down the road abit. I staying with the Woodleys."

"Oh aye. The Woodleys. Church people, I know 'em. So yer not Catholic, then?" she quizzed.

"No, ma'am," Emily hesitatingly replied with a blush. "But I don't hold much for what religion, ma'am, just so long I'm a Christian."

"Aye, that be so?" Bridget frowned with a hint of suspicion. "And how old are ya miss?" she smiled trying to be pleasant, thinking this rather diminutive girl next to her six-foot fiancé looked all of only fifteen years old. That apart, she was quite attractive, still featuring a girlish look and stature about her, with a soft white complexion,

Irish-green eyes, a sharp nose, and long auburn hair that draped her shoulders with curls.

"Seventeen, ma'am, running to eighteen," she asserted with a slight giggle.

"Well yer cannae complain that, Annie, yer was just seventeen yerself when we got married," Anthony helpfully butted in.

"Indeedy. I know that, Da. So yer told yer folks, have ya?" she squarely eyed Emily.

"No ma," Paddy interceded. "She ain't got no blood folks, ma, she be a-orphaned. Her name is Oakley, ma. Emily Etta Oakley."

"Yes, ma'am. That be right. That why I'm living with the Woodleys, ma'am, helpin' on their farm."

"Oh aye. So ya told *em* then?"

Bridget was beginning to seem like an inquisitor, and Paddy made that known to her. "Golly Ma, we only now just decide, right Em?" Emily nodded, smiling. "You be the first we telled, get yer blessin' and all."

"Now George, we just wanting to know what's what, looking after this fair young lady. Of course yer have our blessing, but things gotta be done right."

"Yes, George," Bridget added, "yer Da's right. You just tol' us, so things to know, like, when? An' where yer gonna live, and 'bout work?"

"Aye to that," Anthony added. "How are yer gonna support a missus, George, and kids maybe?"

"I got work..., well, sometimes. But I can get more, don't yer worry 'bout that."

"When yer thinkin' of marryin' then?" Bridget pursued.

"Dunno, Ma. We gotta save up fer it, I guess..." Paddy answered with a little bewilderment. The couple barely had had time to think of practicalities.

"Then yer better get off wif yers and tell yer folk, I think," Anthony advised. "If they agreeable then 'spose we best meet up wif 'em."

On that note Paddy took his leave; Emily gave her gracious leave-takings to Anthony and Bridget, and they took a horse the four or so miles to Eulomoga.

It was nightfall by the time they arrived. Emily didn't tell her guardians of the proposed marriage, wanting them to meet Paddy first, as a possible suitor. He was invited in to have a meal so Mr. and Mrs. Woodley could get to know him a bit. They explained that Emily was originally from Newcastle, and moved up to Dubbo when her father died in an accident, then, just a few years past, her mother also had passed away. No doubt that because Mrs. Elizabeth Woodley was Emily's aunt, they took Emily on as part of their Christian and familial duty so she could help with the house, child raising and the farm work. They might be pleased to be unburdened with her, but didn't say so, although they might also regret not having her help. On the other hand, Paddy marrying-in might be able to help with some heavy farm work that always seemed to be needed done. Emily waited for Paddy to leave before any further discussion of him amongst the household, she wanting to gauge their opinion before suggesting she might marry him.

Over the next few weeks when Paddy was not working at odd jobs or casually labouring on the railways, or not at the pub with his mates, he made a point of visiting Emily and the Woodleys at their farm, not only to flirt with his beau but also to ingratiate himself to her guardians. Emily had already broached to them the subject of Paddy marrying her. It was her way of finally gaining adulthood and independence, a home and family of her own, as most girls of the times aspired. And no doubt Paddy was a good catch: young, handsome, strong, and from a good family, as far she knew.

But the Woodleys had been hesitant to agree, initially, saying they needed to know more about her prospective husband and, like the Egans, meet his kin-folk. Then there was the matter of paying for a wedding; most in the area were simple affairs with celebrations held in the groom's or bride's house, which in this case it would be more fitting at the Woodley's estate given the cramped and rather ramshackle house of the Egans. Then there was the matter of getting official approval from the *Guardian of Minors*, given that Emily was not 21. Add to these issues was the matter of a honeymoon; Emily wanted to go to Newcastle where she had kin, but Paddy doubted that could be afforded. He suggested they could get a train to Lithgow and see the mountains.

Eventually the Woodleys were convinced to meet with Bridget and Anthony Egan at their house in Dubbo, for which Bridget had to do much cleaning and preparation, and for which she commanded also her 3 eldest daughters, Eleanor, Teresa and Mary, aged between 17 and 20, to assist and make up a supportive party when Emily's guardians did arrive.

By all accounts the meeting went well. Although the Woodleys may have felt the Egans were below their own standard, they never held much aspiration for Emily, so marrying a handsome man who could read and write, from a family of good moral and Christian worth, was sufficient for them to approve the betrothed. Bridget's strategy to employ her daughters as messengers of good moral values paid off: they presented themselves as domesticated, unassuming, helpful, and regular Church attendees, who spoke supportively of their brother George in the same terms, and would be willingly available to teach Emily anything she didn't already know.

The wedding was set as a small, family affair, for January 1903, at the Holy Trinity Church of Dubbo, and according to the rites of the Church of England. This accommodated the Woodley's Protestant disposition and the ostensible Catholicism of the Egans, with the former hoping an infusion of Protestantism might engender a greater ethic of thrift on the part of Paddy and Emily.

Using the donations for the blessed couple they took a honeymoon as Paddy had suggested to Lithgow, Emily affirming that it had been a long time since she had left Newcastle and thus she was not sure if any of her own kin were still there. Upon their return three days later the couple were to discover that Paddy's family was moving to Narromine, very soon. Anthony considered that he could get more work up that way, with less competition, especially as the railway was planning to lay further tracks west. George/Paddy and his first new wife went with them.

Whether Paddy had actually gone off to the Boar War or not, or simply bummed around and worked as a labourer—like his dad had done and was still doing—until 1903, his immediate post-marriage working life was largely and similarly casual work, as well as getting somewhat drunk from time to time. But some 3 years later, by 1906 when his first child, a son, was born in Wellington a little way southeast of Dubbo, Paddy used his war service to land a steady job with the NSW railways, which somewhat surprisingly lasted through to 1912 (except for 1911). In 1908 his mother, Bridget, finally registered his birth of 1880 in Cudal at a Narromine office, because the Railways Department now required proof of birth place and date, especially if one were to become permanent. The railway job seemed to take him out from Narromine to Warren, Nyngan, and as far as Cobar if not beyond. Indeed, he moved around quite a bit, either for work, or just living in various towns, for his second child, also Emily, was born in 1909 in Warren, about 50 miles from Narromine, the former serviced at that time by a spur line. And in 1913 another daughter was born in Cobar. Unfortunately she died the same year, as did his first-born son also die in 1913, at age 7.

Thus Paddy moved around quite a bit, although within the same region, but seemingly based more in Warren, a very small, out of the way township. In these few years he could be away from home for days or even weeks at a time, working the railways or mustering sheep and cattle, or whatever else came his way.

It might seem, then, that with a wife and especially with children, Paddy may have taken his paternal responsibilities seriously, but the record might suggest otherwise.

Indeed, having a family to support, yet frequently spending money at the pub more than he brought home, might be suggestive as to why he did not work for the railways, or elsewhere perhaps in 1911. However, by April the following year, 1912, he was back working on the railways as a fettler, but on 30 November was dismissed.

Matters would only get worse: two of his children died in 1913, not an uncommon occurrence, as many died from diphtheria, influenza, TB, whooping cough, measles, mumps, polio, and scarlet fever. But it was nevertheless a devastating turn of events.

What Emily may have thought of this, and done to survive through the double-trauma and to support her remaining namesake daughter, one can only surmise. She may have asked for help from Paddy's family or the Woodleys, or now at about age 26 she may have done what many young destitute women might do—Emily Etta Oakley-Egan took a lover.

George Arthur Sands, one year younger than Emily, also worked on the railways, quite consistently from 1908 to 1941, based primarily in the Orange District, but also worked the lines to Newcastle, Goulburn and even Sydney and Junee. His employ varied between shunter, guard and often a porter, which would pay somewhat more than what Paddy as a labourer would have earned.

George Sands was born in Kogarah, a southern coastal area of Sydney, in 1887. His family, however, was rather dysfunctional, with his parents often involved in domestic turbulence of sorts. When he was 2 years old George Sands was placed in a Sydney asylum for orphaned children, then when his father died his mother retook custody of George. When he was 21 his mother, Helena, also died. It was at this time he took a job in the Railways Department, which no doubt brought him in contact with Emily either in the Orange-Dubbo-Warren area where she lived, or perhaps through her connection with Newcastle which George Sands often frequented and Emily visited. Regardless of how, but more likely through their mutual travels, George Arthur Sands had by 1915, at age 28, courted Emily. There could be little doubt for Emily that George Sands was more hardworking and probably more sober and honest and 7 years younger than Paddy, and she may have had a degree of empathy with him due to both their fractured childhoods. But it would take 3 years, to 1918, before George Sands took up a permanent base in Newcastle, still with the Railways, and take Emily with him.

Meanwhile, by September 1915 Paddy had hung around Warren, where Emily still lived, but the marriage was by now, if not before, tumultuous. Again Paddy took to working where and when he could, and to drinking. Since many of the young Australian men were signing on for the War, he was well placed to find work in replacing the labour shortages. But by early 1917 his life and marriage came to a head.

In February of 1917, running to 37 years of age, he enlisted in the Australian Imperial Forces to serve abroad for WW1, oddly stating on his application under 'next of kin' a Mrs. Annie Taylor, a friend, c/- Dubbo Police Station, and that he had no criminal offences against his name, that he had been in the Boar War, and was *not* married—perhaps saying so in order to ensure half his pay didn't go to Emily but into his own pocket for grog. The only truth he seems to have affirmed was his occupation as 'labourer'.

Well, all this was to come unstuck when, in May of 1917, he was arrested at the *Railway Hotel* in Warren, charged with desertion, and escorted to Victoria Barracks, Sydney. There he made a true statement, perhaps one of the few he ever made:

'I did at Dubbo on or about 28th February [1917] *enlist and did not report back to camp, being at the time on a drinking bout and in a bit of family trouble and I did also enlist as a single man. But I am a married man and was married at Dubbo 31-1-1902. My wife is still loving and have one child. I am willing to admit that the Dubbo statement* [his enlistment declaration] *is not true.'*

Indeed, he was still legally married, and unable to divorce because he and Emily both were Catholics; and he did in fact have only one child remaining alive: Emily Etta Junior.

No doubt the Army took some sympathy on him, given his age, that he had a family, and had, according to him—but which may also have been a lie—been in the Boar War. Such sympathy may have been cloaked in his medical examination which listed him as unfit due to having contracted malaria in Africa, having sciatica, and that his right-hand 1st metacarpal (thumb) was missing.

He was discharged in June 1917 as unfit, and for a few years was never seen or heard from again.... Well, not exactly, as in keeping with Paddy's/George's apparent wandering character.

Seven

Parramatta: Arrival 1932

Paddy was awoken an hour later by the train braking, jolting and hissing as it came into Wellington, the first brief stop about 40 miles from Dubbo. It very soon shunted on, heading for Orange, now a big town, some 60 miles further south. He hoped Lillian would be awake and chirpy soon so he could point out Molong as they passed by.

The jolting and noise had indeed also awoken Lillian, who sat up and rubbed her eyes, looked about and asked, "Are we there?"

"No," Paddy replied, "it's a long way to go yet. Have something to eat. We be passing Molong soon."

"What moo long?"

"It's where yer gran'da was borned, and just down the way I was borned. Cudal."

Lillian just shrugged, the names and places having no meaning for her. She rummaged in the swag and pulled out a sandwich Hilda had made. Just as she finished Paddy excitedly pointed out the window.

"There! It's coming right up now," he pointed.

The train slowed a little as it approached a bend, at which stood a tiny wooden shed with the name *Euchareena* etched on a board and a timber platform not even half the length of a carriage.

On the other side a dirt road went off into a valley, and a dilapidated white wooden signpost pointed to 'Molong 5M'.

Lillian craned her neck to see, but not seeing anything larger than an empty shed with a rusty tin roof, she looked at her dad and shrugged dismissively. But for Paddy it brought back fond memories of his youth, beginning for him in 1880 and for his Da in 1855. 'Time flies,' he pondered. 'Almost fifty-two years. Where it all gone...?'

Lillian had a drink of water then curled up again, bored, and eventually fell back to sleep. After another hour they reached Orange. Paddy woke Lillian, telling her to come for a walk, so she can go to the loo and they'd get something to eat, since the train stopped for a half hour. They left the swag on the seat and stepped out to the cool air. He found a Station toilet for Lillian, and while she went inside he again looked about, remembering this town. He had spent a good number of his first years here in the '80s with some of his siblings, and even now had a sister living in the town—well, she might still be there... Anyway, he had no time to go see her.

Lilly came out, having washed her face with cold water, and Paddy went in to the 'Mens'. Afterwards they strolled along the platform to a refreshment stand and bought a large mug of tea to share and a pan of bubble-and-squeak with bread. They found a sunny bench on which to indulge in what Paddy knew might be their only midday meal, and possibly last bit before Parramatta. They still had maybe six or seven hours to go.

Suddenly steam swirled and churned along the platform. A shrill whistle sounded. Paddy and Lillian hastily boarded at the nearest carriage just as the giant wheels gave a mighty heave. The train quickly picked up speed on the downhill, the compartments rattled and banged and strained from left to right then settled into a steady movement, the wheels clickety-clacking on the tracks. Father and daughter slopped into their seats. For the first half hour of this leg of the journey Lillian stared out of the window content to look at the scenery of dry grass and bush, of cows and sheep. Then she yanked down the window almost falling out as they crossed a rickety bridge. Her reward was nothing but an eye full of sooty smoke. Twenty minutes later Lilly's patience had come to an end.

"We there yet dad?"

"Nah. Still a longs way to go. Bathurst town the next stop. Just look out the window awhile, Lilly."

Another twenty minutes passed by, as did the train across the monotonous scenery. Lillian became bored again. She retrieved a new book that Hilda had given her, and was happy for a while to flip through that until once again she fell asleep.

'Bathurst,' he reminisced. 'That where me ma was borned.' He had never been to Bathurst; it seemed that his mother, Ann Bridget Ryan, didn't want to go back there, even to visit. Maybe she had a falling-out over her marriage to Anthony. Like his own Emily, Bridget had been only 17, so maybe she ran away, or somehow went against her folks' wishes, unlike Emily who got the Woodleys' blessing. He didn't know....

An hour later the train stopped at Bathurst, which resulted in more people boarding, not surprising since it was a common commuter station, only 130 miles from Sydney. All the hubbub woke Lillian who sat up and wondered what was happening.

"Are we there yet dad?" she asked for the third time.

"No, Lilly. Getting there. Two more stops."

Lillian huffed. She liked travelling on the train, but she also liked getting to a destination.

The train moved out, and onward. Another hour it reached Lithgow, which Paddy fondly recalled as his and Emily's honeymoon destination. "Geez," he muttered to himself. "When that be?" He rubbed his chin in thought. "O-three.... Near thirty year ago..."

Even more people boarded, then the train steamed its way down the mountains to Penrith. Paddy told Lillian to look out the window, the countryside had changed to lush bushy vistas and high mountains. She appreciated this scenery more than the dry scrublands and paddocks further west, but she refrained from opening the window, especially now it was getting cold in the Blue Mountains.

Another hour and they reached Katoomba where more passengers boarded, many holiday makers so Paddy seemed to think. The carriage was getting crowded, and Lilly and Paddy were now confined to just their own two seats.

"Are we there yet?"

"Not much longer," Paddy answered. "We nearin' Penrith now."

"Is that where we get off?"

"No. We go on t' Parramatta, that be where we get off, and then walk a short way."

Another hour, as the train had to go slow down the mountains and around many winding curves, before they reached Penrith.

Many people now got off, but it seemed just as many also got on, probably going to Parramatta or Sydney.

"Next stop Lilly," Paddy tried to placate her, sensing she was getting very impatient, bored, hungry and tired.

One more, final, stop. He closed his eyes as Lilly was content now to look out upon the growing suburbs beginning to sprawl out from the coast.

Paddy reflected he had not been to Sydney since 1917, the first time, when he had been taken to Victoria Barracks in Paddington, charged with AWOL. After being discharged he was too ashamed to go back to Dubbo, and the shame was double because his own wife had already abandoned him, shacking up with that bastard George Sands. There was nothing to go home to. He figured he'd stay in Sydney awhile, maybe even until the war ended, whenever that was going to be, and get a job. His folks would think he'd either gone off to war and got himself killed, or whatever they wanted to think. He didn't have to face them, not at least for some time. He would get a job in Sydney, he had planned, easy, since so many young blokes had gone off to war; labour was short.

He was jolted from his thoughts by the conductor coming through repeatedly bellowing "Next stop, Parramatta!" Lilly jumped up and pulled at her dad.

"We here dad! Par'matter, dad."

"Aye. Ok ok, put yer stuff in the swag," he directed as he picked up the kit and straitened his dress and Lillian's. "C'mon. Hold me han."

Paddy waited for the train to completely stop before stepping onto the platform then lifting Lillian down from the high step. He led the way to the signposted exit. They were on the north side of the line, so didn't have to cross any platforms or lines, but what the feck, he had no idea where Iron Street, North Parramatta, was. It was already late, 7.30, the train was late, and getting dark quick.

He asked the Station Master, who luckily had a map, but it took some time to find the street. Paddy was directed that the simplest way was to follow O'Connell Street—a good Irish name, Paddy thought, couldn't go wrong—go across the bridge and keep going, then turn right at Dunlop Street, that'd take him to Iron Street.

"But might be an 'our, walking," the Master told him, " 'specially with a youngin."

"Aye. How much a cab might be, then?"

"Oh, can't say, rightly," the man said, rubbing his chin in thought. "Maybe two, three, bob. The rank's right outside, you best ask *'em*."

"Aye. Thank yea, sir. C'mon Lillian."

He took her hand again; there were too many people, he didn't want to risk losing her in the crowd. He found the horse-drawn cabbies and asked. The quid that Roger Bankes had given him was fast running out—and he hadn't even had a drink for almost two days. He would need money to get about Sydney, find a place to sleep and eat, and to get down to Bowral.

He took up the offer of two bob for the cab, loaded Lillian on and clambered aboard. Lilly had never been on a hansom cab before, so she felt very much like a lady, and beamed at the traffic and people walking on the footpaths as they set off.

Now the time had finally come, thought Paddy. To off-load Lillian so he could get on with earning some money, and doing what he had always done, and getting Lilly settled into a nice house and at school. He didn't know these three women, the Bankes sisters, so wasn't sure how to deal with them, hoping he could extract some recompense for the privilege of them taking Lillian. He hoped that Roger had not told them, either, that he had given Paddy a pound.

And, more immediately, if they would be hospitable enough to feed him and Lilly and give them a bed for the night. This was the city, and people here, he knew, were not as hospitable as country folk.

The cabbie dropped them off at the end of the street, so they began to walk, looking for number 36. Many of the houses didn't have numbers displayed, or it was too dark to see them. But finally, more than three-quarters up the quiet, narrow roadway, just over from Prince Street that intersected with Iron Street, they found it.

The number was clearly presented next to a black front door that stood in the centre of a brown-brick façade that walled a neat smallish bungalow in the colonial style. There were two barred windows on either side, but no light shone from within. Paddy thought this house would be rather small inside, unless it stretched out back aways. A neat path ran up the centre of a small front yard to 5 steps that reached an equally smallish and bare front verandah. He wondered if anyone was awake inside. It wasn't so late, 8pm, he figured, but what if the three ladies were asleep, or unwilling to open the door to an unexpected visitor? The black door. He stared at it, loathing to tap-tap at it with the brass knocker. It was foreboding not just of what kind of reception he might get, but of what lay in the future behind it.

"Is this it dad?" Lillian interrupted his thoughts.

"Aye. But maybe them's asleep already. C'mon we nosey 'round the back."

Another gravel path led to a side passage on the right. Half way up the side of the house a wooden gateway sat squarely in a tall fence of cream. Paddy put his hand through a small opening and found the bolt on the other side. Slipping the bolt back with a clang he pushed open the squeaking gate and stepped through, with Lillian tightly holding onto his leg. The noise from these actions echoed in the stillness of the night. But he could now see a dim light shining from the back of the house. He hoped they didn't have a dog, but figured if there was such a bloody mongrel it would have been barking by now. He stepped forward, with Lillian frightened but still in tow, until they reached the corner. Poking his head around he saw a man, rather old, he thought, and a bit fat, sitting on a wicker chair smoking a pipe. A cup of what might be rum sat on an old wooden table next to him. Paddy stepped around into the dim light.

"Good evening, sir," he said with confidence.

The man jumped up, surprisingly quickly given his corpulence and stature, almost knocking the table and cup over. For the slightest moment he stared, before letting out some expletives.

"What!? Who the feck are you?!"

"Paddy Egan, sir. Good evening. An' this my daughter, Lillian," Paddy calmly answered without apparent threat.

Lilly poked her head around her father's leg, which drew the man's eyes, giving him reason now to believe that the strangers were not robbers or murderers.

"Eh? Egan? What the feck you doing sneaking 'round here at this time o' night? You give me a bloody 'eart attack."

"Sorry sir," Paddy said in an attempt to placate. "We be looking for the three sisters, Bankes, by name, I believe."

"Bankes? Yes, yes, This is their house. But what you be wantin' wif *them*? And at this time o' night?"

The man assertively stood his ground.

"Roger Bankes, sir, in Narromine, told me to come here. I have some business with the ladies."

"At this time of night? The ladies retired already. What business?"

"About my daughter, 'ere, sir."

"Then you better come up, take a pew. There be a chair there."

Paddy moved forward with Lillian almost trembling at the sight of this old, short man with a pot-belly stomach, standing in just his shirt and trousers with braces.

"Keep yer voice down. The ladies be asleep by now, I reckon. Me name's Walter. Walter Bayliss. At the Sherriff's office 'ere in Parramatta."

'Crikey!' Paddy thought, 'A bloody copper...'

He climbed the two stone steps to the verandah, with Lillian still clinging tightly to him, and took the rickety wood chair offered.

"Thank ye," he acknowledged. Yearning for a sedative for his cranium and some Dutch courage, he said, "That be a nice drop of rum you got there."

"Aye. Take a swig if yer like. Only one mug I got but."

Paddy didn't need a second invite. He picked up the cup and took a hefty swig, almost immediately feeling the calming balm course through his veins, his muscles relaxing, and his brain cells enlivened.

"What d'ya want with the women?" Bayliss pursued.

"Oh that be Roger Bankes, he 'ranged for the sisters t'look after me girl, here, awhile."

"Ahhh," Bayliss exhaled. "Yea, I 'member now, they mention'd it few days back. Egan, eh. Where you from?"

"Junee..."

"Ahh. Junee.... I was stationed at Wagga, 'bout thirty years."

"Oh aye. But we come from Narromine, been up there visiting kin." Paddy rolled a smoke and lit up, waiting for Mr. Bayliss to say something.

"Ya better have 'nother swig then. Seems like you need it. Goes wif t'smoke."

"Aye. Thank ye," he graciously responded, and picked up the cup and almost drained it.

No sooner had he put the cup down than the back door squeaked open a crack, and a female voice, quite raspy, was heard. "Who's there? Is that you Walter?"

"Aye Miss Elaine. There's a fella 'ere, from Narromine. Says Roger sent 'im."

Elaine, one of the three sisters Paddy assumed, opened the door another 2 inches, holding her dressing gown tight in modesty.

"Narromine? Roger? What's his name, Mr. Bayliss?"

Paddy stood up and turned toward the darkened doorway, Lillian peering from behind his leg where she cringed.

"Paddy Egan, ma'am," he informed her. "Your brother, I believe, Roger Bankes, 'e send me down 'ere, says you can look afta me kid awhile."

"Oh. Yes. You have to speak with my sisters on that. They be asleep now. Tomorrow morning if you please."

"Thank yea ma'am," he replied almost at the same time she shut the door.

Walter Bayliss poured more rum. "You have a place t'stay, then?" he enquired.

"No sir. We just got 'ere. Train t'was late."

"Aye, I see. Then we better finish this rum, don't want the women seeing no empty bottle 'bout. You can sleep in the kitchen. I see yer got a swag. Stove's going, should be warm enough."

"Thank ye, again, sir. There wouldn't be a slice of bread and cheese for the wain with a bit o' Irish luck?" he boldly ventured.

"Oh aye. Can manage that. Pumpkin soup on t'stove, and bread. How that suit?"

"That be grand, Mr. Bayliss. Thank ye."

After some food of soup and plain bread, not nearly as good as Hilda used to serve so Lillian thought, she and Paddy bedded down on the kitchen floor of timber, using his swag as an underlay; the wood stove was on, so Paddy stoked it with a few more pieces of coal that should keep it going most of the night. Bayliss gave them an additional blanket should they need it, then he went off to bed in a small room adjacent, saying he would be up at six to make tea and stoke the fire.

Eight

Perth 2021

Almost daily Mark visited his mother at Elizabeth's house, and the three of them sat together for hopefully an hour, at least, to extract from Lillian more details and a more precise timeline.

After settling in to their usual spots, Mark asked of his mum: "Ma, you wrote in one of your stories that you came down by train with your dad; from where?"

"I'm not sure. Junee I guess. That's where we lived, remember?"

"Yes mum, but you said he took you to Narromine. So maybe that's where you came from, not Junee? Roger Bankes was living in Narromine at the time, nineteen-thirties."

"Oh. Then it might have been. I know I saw Roger Bankes. Dad said he met him at the pub, then later he came to the house."

"What house was that?"

"A boarding house. We were staying there. Ran by a nice woman, can't recall her name now, but I know she owned the place in Fairlight, in Manly, because she kept on telling dad to take me there to the seaside."

"So, what did Roger say?"

"Oh I don't know, I was only four, or five. Something about his sisters, in Parramatta I realized later. I know their names, because I lived with them for over ten years: Madeline, Elaine, and Mercedes." She smiled, having shown she could remember things.

"Spinsters?"

"Yes. They never married. Very religious. Wanted me to be a nun. Maddie was the nicest one, the middle one."

"Anyone else there?"

"Oh yes, an old fat man. Very old he looked, to me then, at my age. Bayliss. Walter Bayliss. I remember *him*, I was scared of him, just the way he *looked*, even though he had nothing to do with me."

"So what was he doing there?"

"I don't know. A boarder, I think. Had a room out the back."

"Do you know how he came to be there? I mean, what was his connection with the Bankes sisters?"

"No idea. All I know is that he was a Sherriff."

"You don't think one of the sisters was his girlfriend?"

"Oh no, no. They were not interested in men."

"Ok, so going back to Roger Bankes in Narromine. He told your dad to go to Parramatta? Then what?"

"Well, we got a train of course, down to Sydney, Central, then another train to Parramatta. A red train. They called them red rattlers in those days. We went all the way out, I remember going across a river..."

"Why would you go all the way into Central, when the train from Narromine would stop at Parramatta?"

"I have no idea, Mark. It's all fuzzy. I just remember getting trains."

"Oh, ok. So you got to Parramatta, the three sisters, then what?"

"That's it. Dad told me to stay with them, they would send me to school, which I really loved, they would look after me for awhile, he said. He had to go find a job, and would come back soon, maybe a few days."

"How long before he came back...?"

"I need a rest. Elizabeth, can you put the kettle on, please."

Lillian rose from her chair, using her walker to help lift her to her legs, then hobbled out to the sun in the backyard. Mention of her dad leaving her at Parramatta had clearly upset Lillian; her eyes glazed over, she didn't look at Mark or Elizabeth, an action they knew to indicate she was angry, ignoring them. Perhaps not angry at her two children, but angry because of what her father did and that Mark and Elizabeth had resurrected it.

Mark realized they might have to leave that topic for a while, and later try to approach it obliquely.

Elizabeth put the kettle on and got some cups, as usual with enough clattering to wake the dead. Then returned to Mark, as they waited for the tea to draw.

"You upset her."

"I know," Mark defended. "So long ago, what, ninety years. Almost a century!"

"Memories have no time limit," she unnecessarily pointed out.

"Ok ok, I've got the message. Maybe we skip the Parramatta bit for a while, jump to Fairlight, happier times, then work into that narrative, backwards, how she came to be at Manly..."

"Yeah. I'd like to know what her life was like, if she was happy, before she met dad," Elizabeth declared with some bitterness.

"Did she ever have a best friend? I'd like to know if she had friends her own age, who she could talk to, do things with."

"I think so. She does mention a friend, or maybe two, one that she worked with, I think."

"Good. Dig out anything she wrote about that, can you?"

Elizabeth went off to pour the tea and serve it to their mum outside. Mark joined them. He didn't know whether or not to say 'sorry', so just left it as unspoken, hoping ma would get over it soon. He *was* sorry, no doubt. Like Elizabeth, he also yearned to know of their mother's happier times, that her life had also happy times, instead of the drudgery he saw of her raising 4 rambunctious kids when he and his sibs were growing up.

Thirty minutes later, without any further mention of mum's history, but rather their mother talking about the house, the garden, flowers, he bade farewell, saying he would be back in perhaps two days, thinking that mum would need some respite from his insensitive probing. Elizabeth walked him to the door.

"By the way, there's no major river between Sydney and Parramatta on the train, none that you would notice," he whispered as he stepped onto the threshold.

"Are you sure?"

"Yep. Doesn't even cross the Georges River. But... There *is* the Nepean river at Penrith you cross coming into Parra' from Dubbo-Narromine."

"Oh well, maybe she's just confused. Maybe she got trains at other times, and is just blurring them all together...?"

"However, red-rattlers were certainly around in nineteen-thirty-two, they were introduced in nineteen-twenty-five or six."

"So that's no help..."

"She wrote this down? About the train?" Mark asked. Elizabeth nodded. "Poetic licence then..."

"Speaking of which.... I'm still not convinced George Egan in Dubbo is Patrick, mum's father. We need evidence. *Ancestry*, I think, or some other place I read, says we need three pieces of evidence for each person or claim."

Mark looked at his sister. He was an academic, he had a PHD, had taught many Courses over thirty years, including Research Methods, and had undertaken many research projects himself. He knew all about 'evidence'. Evidence was not proof. Evidence was always subject to interpretation, until such time there could be only one interpretation. And when that one interpretation was the only possible one, he would fondly cite Detective Foyle: *'I can't think of any other way, can you?'*

And for Elizabeth the answer was of course, No.

"Ok, let me try to explain it. Heat up the tea, we'll sit in the lounge."

Elizabeth refilled two cups of tea and nuked them. Settling in the lounge to which they now returned, where hopefully nothing would distract them, he began to try to simplify the discourses of Research.

"I know what you're saying. Some 'expert' says you need three pieces of evidence, such as a birth certificate, census record, marriage or death record, or whatever. But who is this so-called expert? Who gives him or her a right to declare the Trinity of Proof? In any case, it's not proof, it's only evidence."

"But they're registered documents....," she protested. "And the expert should know what he's talking about."

"*Should*, but not necessarily does. And who says I must follow his or her rules? As for registered documents, well, let me give you an example, or two: Paddy's death registration says he was born in Ireland. Who told the attending Doctor that? His last wife. How did she know? She didn't. She may have *assumed* that, because he had an Irish accent and therefore he was born in Ireland, or, *he* told her that. She's only repeating what she has been told, and the Doctor jots that down. If it was today the Doc might ask for a passport, Drivers Licence, Medicare Card, Birth Certificate, whatever, but they didn't have these things in eighteen-eighty or even nineteen-fifty-two, and no one asked for them. People relied on the honesty, if not factual truthfulness, of the informant."

"But it also said he was seventy-three when he died..." Elizabeth still protested.

"Yes. And the point is? Again, she, Adele Moore, his fourth wife, told the Doc that, and *Paddy* told her how old he was. If he was lying...."

"So he wasn't seventy-three? Which means he wouldn't be born in eighteen-eighty, and therefore he's not Dubbo George!"

"Well, *maybe* he isn't. But if he's not, then who is he? Where is the evidence of *his* identity? Let's take another example: Dubbo George's mother, Bridget, registered George's birthdate; she did that in nineteen-o-eight, twenty-eight years after he was born, supposedly in eighteen-eighty. How do we know *she* wasn't lying?"

"Well, I guess she was there at the time, bit hard to give birth if the mother is not present."

"*But*, she married Anthony in eighteen-eighty. Maybe, just maybe, he was born earlier, say eighteen-seventy-nine, out of wedlock, but she didn't want to admit that, so registers his birth nine months after her marriage... And registers the birth not only twenty-eight years late, but also in Narromine, when George was born in Cudal. Why? Where's the *original* birth record, if there is one? Here I'm making the point not about dates or ages, but whether or not we can rely on those documents, which your so-called expert says are 'proof'."

Elizabeth shrugged.

"Well, the simple answer is Bridget lost the original, or never had it, not uncommon in those days, and-or memory failed her. My point is, yes, according to your 'expert' we have a 'solid' piece of evidence, a document, but which itself could be false, unreliable."

"That's why you need *three* pieces of evidence."

"Fine, we have three: birth certificate of George, marriage certificate of George/Paddy, death certificate of Paddy—all unreliable because they themselves rely on unreliable information. The alternative is to consider a narrative that can possibly reconcile the differences, similarities or problems—and explain their unreliability!"

"So what then? Rely on mum's memory?"

"Yes and no. We coordinate the evidence, hypothesize, if some of the evidence is true, then how can the pieces fit together to make a whole identity of one person? For example, let's assume Bridget is correct: George was born in eighteen-eighty, died in nineteen-fifty-two according to Moore, makes him seventy-two, seventy-three,....give or take. So same ages for both guys. Or, how else might we account for Dubbo George disappearing from the face of the Earth in nineteen-seventeen, and suddenly outa nowhere Paddy-George turns up in Junee a few years later, *ostensibly* nineteen-twenty-six?

"Or would you really like to suggest that two guys, same name, born same year, parents with the same names, both with buggered hands, and even same signatures, existed at the same time?"

"Then we have no proof," Elizabeth partly conceded in exasperation.

"Right, we have no *proof*. But we have *evidence*. There is more than one type of evidence *à l'encontre* your *Ancestry* expert. The very lack of evidence, or the contradictions of evidence, or a pattern of whatever evidence there is that can be harnessed, are all forms of evidence. Add to that, we have an eye-witness!"

"Ha! Mum!? She's unreliable, just like your documents."

"Yes! Of course, like any witness to a murder. But nevertheless a witness, and one who can be interrogated."

"Oh, so now you're gonna torture mum?"

"Worse than that! I'm gonna throw her under the bus!—metaphorically.

"Just think for a moment: with what little documentation we have, as unreliable as it is, our key witness says she went with granddad to Narromine. C'mon, who would even know that place existed! I had never heard of it until now. So, why would Paddy-George go there!? Unless he knew the place, somehow, for some reason. And guess who lived there in the eighteen-eighties, and the nineteen-thirties, even? George and his kin! Plus, Roger Bankes lived there, who, more than coincidentally, was the brother of the Parramatta sisters where mum ended up. All we have to do is put Paddy-George in the picture, in Narromine, too meet with Roger, and Bob's your uncle. All fits. And why wouldn't Paddy-George go there if he didn't have kin or history in the place? Add to that, mum keeps mentioning having met Roger. So, add that to all the dates and mis-dates, and names and ages, and we have a jigsaw puzzle, the pieces of which begin to fit together if you flesh them out, indeed flush them out, step back, look at the bigger picture, think outside the box. It's called imagination."

"Still no proof."

"But *evidence* that fits the crime scene. Sure mum's unreliable, but she was *there*, she can flesh things out, that makes a narrative *that makes sense*. I can't think of any other possibility, can you?"

"So we need DNA, and some photos would be helpful," Elizabeth lamented.

"You've done the DNA test, chase it up. Meanwhile, I see you and mum tomorrow, and we'll move on to mum's arrival at Parramatta."

Nine

Parramatta: Departure 1932

True to his word, Walter Mason Bayliss stumbled into the small kitchen at a little after six. He hadn't changed his clothes, still dressed in dirty grey pants with the suspenders hanging down, and an undershirt that was part of his long-johns. He stepped around Lillian who was still asleep, while Paddy gave a sleepy stir and rubbed his face awake.

"I'll just get t'stove runnin' agin, and put 'kettle on," Walter told him. "You might wake the wain, so we can have a cuppa."

"Aye." Paddy shook Lillian gently, whispering for her to wake up.

"I need pee, dad," she whimpered, rubbing her eyes and protesting against being awakened.

"There be an out-house down back," Walter told them.

Paddy rose to his feet and lifted Lillian up, then took her out the back door to the toilet ten yards down the backyard. While she went inside to do her business Paddy looked about the property, that he could now see clearly in the daylight. There was an old paling fence a further ten feet on, with a gate that led to an orchard about as large as one could see. He walked to the corner of the yard, and did his own wee behind a fruit tree, unable to wait for Lillian.

A minute later they sauntered back into the kitchen.

"You can wash up here, in the sink, if you like," Walter told them. "No hot water but. Tea'll be ready in a jiff."

"Aye. Thank you. What time the sisters be up?" he asked, now contemplating the next step in his passing visit.

"I 'spect they be up already," he informed Paddy. "Early risers. Say their mornin' prayers, then have breakfast. I'm acooking it now. Eggs and corn beef."

"I see." Paddy packed up his belongings, giving more floor space to Walter to do what he seemed to routinely do every morning. "You off t'work this morning?" he asked, partly to make idle conversation, but also to probe Bayliss about his role in the household.

"Not t'day, it Saturday. No Court Saturday."

"Oh, yeah, I forgot. So what do you do at the Court?"

"Odd jobs, mostly. Clerk, keep records, direct people, clean up, that sort of thing."

"Aye. Sounds like a winner. And yer a relative to the sisters, then?" he probed.

"Oh no no. I transferred up to Parramatta. 'Bout to retire, needed a place to stay. Roger Bankes told me some time ago his sisters might have a room."

"Ah. That be lucky."

"Sure as beans. Cheap rent and just help out. Between you and me, they appreciate a man in the house, do odd jobs, watch over things."

"Aye and what better than a sheriff, eh."

"Oh no, I ain't no sheriff, just work at the sheriff's office."

"Oh aye. Still, a' 'portant job," he added to endear himself to Walter.

"Yup. Very important, if I don't mind saying so. Meet all sorts of folk in that job."

"Aye. Is that how yer met Roger?"

"Sure as. Awhile ago now. Newspaper man, doing the rounds of the Courts. Anyway, tea's ready. There's mugs there, and sugar. I'll take this lot into the dining room." And with that he picked up a tray decked with a large porcelain teapot in a cozy, three cups and saucers, a small jug of milk, and a container of sugar.

The three women had just ambled in and were getting settled in the dining room. Elaine had already informed her two sisters that a visitor had arrived 'late' last night.

"Who came last night, Mr. Bayliss?" Mercedes, the eldest, enquired as she poured the tea.

"A Mr. Egan, ma'am, with his wain. Five year old, I believe."

"Ahh. Egan. Yes. Roger told us about him. We shall speak with him after breakfast, in the drawing room, thank you."

"Yes ma'am. I just give 'em some toast and eggs then?" he thought to check.

"Very well," Mercedes agreed. "And breakfast as soon as you're able, please, Mr. Bayliss." When Walter left them, she turned to the youngest sister. "So you met them last night, Elaine?"

"Only for a moment. And it was dark."

"And? How old is he?" she pursued, not because she was interested in men, far from it; she did not trust men, and did not want to have to deal with some young, lay-about galah. Nor did she trust Elaine, or think highly of her; Mercedes had always found her, as the youngest, annoying at best, clumsy, forgetful, or deliberately withholding information.

"Can't say, rightly. *Not* young."

"And the child?"

"Presentable, I should think. Perhaps needs a bath and new clothes. But attractive enough, I suppose."

"Where shall she sleep, assuming she stays?" Madeline, the middle sister, raised.

"Mmm. Not in *my* room. You know I like my privacy. And she may well snore!" Mercedes declared.

"And *we* do not have the space," Elaine equally asserted.

"Then we shall have a cot of some sort placed in the dining room, or kitchen perhaps. One that can be put out of the way," Mercedes calmly directed with quiet authority.

As Paddy had surmised when he first saw the house from the outside the night before, it was rather small. Mercedes, the eldest at age 50, had a room to herself at the front of the double-brick dwelling. The next room, of equal size, was shared by Madeline who was 48, and Elaine, five years younger. On the other side of the hallway that ran down the building's centre was a formal sitting room at the front, and then a dining room that doubled as an informal social space. Beyond that was a much smaller room, barely 6 feet across, that Mr. Bayliss occupied, and across the hall a kitchen of equal size. Overall, the house was quite symmetrical. A laundry-cum-bathroom with two wash tubs was located adjacent to the toilet out back. Beyond the forty or so feet of back garden was an extensive orchard, as Paddy had noted, replete with apple, apricot and cherry trees.

Walter returned to the kitchen to retrieve the three sisters' food that had been warming on the stove. Laying it on a large plate along with other plates and cutlery next to three slices of toast and butter, he delivered another tray to the ladies, also. Having then returned, he cooked up some fried eggs and a slice of corn beef each for Paddy and Lilly.

"The sisters will see you in the sitting room at front, after breakfast," he told the visitors.

"Aye. Thank ye. What will be their names, if I may ask?"

"Mercedes, or Dollie; she's the eldest. Then Madeline, or Maddie she likes to be called; and the youngest is Elaine. I should forewarn you they all dress in black."

"Mourning?"

"Only for Jesus," Walter chuckled quietly. "Very religious these women. Rather than become nuns they do Church work and devote themself to Jesus who, as you know, died."

"Ah aye, some time ago I should think... So they mourning *Him?*" Paddy sought to clarify.

"Indeed. And to add... The parents named them all 'Mary', so you have the three Hail Marys," he again chuckled.

Paddy looked quite bewildered at this configuration. Walter could see the effect his description had had, so continued, as he dished out the food to a small wood table where Paddy and Lillian sat.

"There be a fourth sister, but you won't see her, 'cause she *is* a nun! Florence her name, but now Sister *Mary* Dara."

"Another Mary?" Paddy exclaimed.

"Oh, there be more. There be 'nother sister, May Monica, but might also be a Mary. But she died when still a wain, bless her soul."

"Amen."

"Then there be two brothers, one be training as a Priest in Manly."

"Good Lord!" Paddy declared in wonderment.

"You Catholic?" Walter asked.

"Aye, as sure as I'm Irish."

"Then that'll hold yer in good standin'."

"They own this house, I 'spect?" Paddy queried as he helped himself and Lillian with the eggs and beef and toast.

"Family does, at least. They Da and Ma used to live 'ere. But when she die—just last year, it be, nineteen-thirty-one—he, Walter Senior that be, went t'live with Roger in Narromine. Yer didn't meet up with him?"

"No. Just Roger. And he seem'd well-to-do."

"Aye. Not short of a quid. But not so much now, as before."

"How's that?" Paddy was curious to know.

"Well, let me see," he pondered, rubbing his chin with one hand while picking up a second cup of tea. "If I got it right, the father, Walter, he marry Mary Eccleston..."

"Another Mary!" Paddy couldn't help but exclaim again with incredulity.

"Aye. And her mother was Mary, and her grand ma before 'er."

"Holy Mary of God!"

"Aye. But the thing is, she an Eccleston...by marriage. That meaning the three sisters 'ere, their granddaddy and great grand daddies was Eccelstons."

"I know that name, somewhere..." Paddy pondered, hoping Bayliss would jog his memory.

"Aye. Big family, landowners, up Bourke way. The granddaddy go back to near the first fleet. Bought some land down 'ere, too. Fact is, they got 'nother 'ouse just 'round the corner, Prince street. And yer seen the orchard outback? That just part of what used to be. Come the depression o' the nineties, they mostly went bust."

"Aye. But still be Eccelstons in Bourke, I knows it."

"Sure. But not so big these days. Bad crops and drought, kids to marry off... Lucky Bankes inherit this property through their ma."

The conversation was interrupted by Lillian who asked when they were going, looking at Mr. Walter Bayliss with some fearful distaste.

"We gonna see these ladies, first, darling. Maybe they send yer to school. Yer like that, wouldn't yer?"

She nodded and yawned.

"I go see if they ready, Mr. Egan." Walter went out to the dining room.

"I don't like him, dad. He fat and mean. Can we go?"

"Don't say that Lilly, he's an ok fella. Sure he look better when he be in uniform."

"He a soldier dad?"

"No. Policeman."

Lillian knew enough about policemen, but thought Bayliss didn't at all look like a policeman. Just then Bayliss returned with the tray of tea things. "They see you now. Let me get t'other tray, then I take yer."

Bayliss warbled out again, and shortly returned again with the second tray, which he put down on the table. "C'mon then." He looked the pair up and down. "Straighten yerselfs up abit."

Paddy tried to unruffle his shirt and trousers, and brushed his hair back with his hand. Then he checked Lillian. She looked about as bedraggled as he, but what could he do? She had only two skimpy cotton dresses, one pair of well worn shoes, and a cardigan. All were in need of cleaning, repair or replacement.

As presentable as they ever could be they followed Bayliss to the front room. Entering, the three ladies sat stony faced, staring at the spectacle. While they were somewhat used to seeing the squalor of the working class when they were governesses or teachers throughput NSW, to have such a father and daughter in their living room they found quite intrusive, almost offensive. Only Elaine smiled a little, but more in mockery.

They were not asked to sit down, but stood awkwardly, like show pieces, with Walter Bayliss hovering behind them, as if he might be needed to put down any disturbance.

"Morning ladies," Paddy greeted with feigned platitude. "I'm Patrick Egan, from Junee. This my daughter, Lillian Mary," he said, deliberately misnaming her real 'May' to 'Mary' as Roger had done. Of course now he realized Lillian could be a 'May', as the younger deceased sister of the three ladies had been called.

It was Mercedes, the eldest, who led the conversation: "Our brother, Roger, told us that you needed someone to take care of your daughter for awhile, Mr. Egan."

"Yes ma'am, if that be possible."

"And why is that? Where is her mother?"

"She passed over ma'am," he said quietly, not wanting to use the usual terms of death for fear of upsetting Lillian, "last year, nineteen-thirty-one." He tried to look forlorn.

Elaine, always in a flutter, gave a gasp, realizing it was the same year as their own mother passing, but a sharp look of rebuke from Mercedes dictated silence.

"That's most unfortunate, I'm sure," Mercedes calmly continued. "She doesn't have aunts, grandmothers, other family?"

"No ma'am. My own mother, she went many a year ago. My Da, he be getting on. And my sisters got their own family. Her gran also passed," he lied, not wanting to have to explain why Rachael Keough could not, would not, take Lillian.

"I see. And she's the only one?"

"She is ma'am," again he lied, not wanting to explain his past complicated life.

"I imagine, then, you must work, and so there is no one else who can supervise her?"

"That be correct ma'am."

"And just how long were you thinking of her staying with us, Mr. Egan?"

"I don't rightly know, ma'am. Until I get things sorted. Maybe a month....?" He tested.

"What is her full name, Mr. Egan?" Elaine dared speak out.

"We just call her Lillian, or Lilly for short. But her full name is Lillian Mary May Egan, ma'am."

All the sisters looked at one another, with a thousand thoughts swirling amongst them, but each focused on one possibility: 'Could it be....?'

"She needs a bath," Mercedes declared to give a halt to the fantasies the ladies were mentally entertaining.

"Yes ma'am. We bin travelling two days."

"Very well. I think it best, Mr. Egan, if we can speak confidentially. Even four year olds can have large ears. Elaine," Mercedes commanded quietly, "can you please take Lillian Mary to the dining room, perhaps find something for her to play with. Then hurry back."

"Yes sister. Come along, Lillian." Elaine feigned a smile, taking Lilly's hand. "Let's see what's in the other room."

"Take a seat Mr. Egan," Mercedes continued after Lillian and Elaine had left together. "We need to be clear about the arrangement."

"Yes ma'am," he agreed, as he took a place on the sofa.

They all waited in silence until Elaine returned and resumed her seat, Paddy pretending not to be nosey but nonetheless looking about the sophisticated room, as he thought of it. This was not so large, but a square of polished floorboards, a barred window looking out over the street, and curtained by white lace drapes. The walls were papered in an olive green that fitted well with the dark wooden furniture, wall trims and mouldings that were almost churchy. A similar green settee on which he sat took up almost one wall, and opposite in a semi-circle were the three ladies occupying wing-back chairs of different colours—mauve, a soft pink, and royal blue for Mercedes. A mantel crossed an open fireplace, on which were photographs and other homely decoratives, and, of course as he expected by now, a medium size crucifix and portrait of Jesus. An empty centre table separated Paddy from his hostesses.

"Now Mr. Egan," Mercedes continued when Elaine had settled upon her harried return, "our dear sister, the youngest, only a child, passed away some time ago, and we miss her greatly, but even more so is that she never had an opportunity to live a devout life. Your daughter might, let us say, living here, compensate for that loss. So, we could be prepared to give Lillian Mary a trial period, for several months, if you are agreeable. This should be sufficient time for you to get settled in work, and perhaps even find a new wife. We would need to consider options in due time."

Paddy wasn't quite understanding of what the lead sister was suggesting, but thought that somehow Lilly would replace for a time their lost wain, and he would come back for Lilly, if circumstances allowed.

"Aye ma'am, that be fine with me. But..."

"But what, Mr. Egan?"

"But, what if my work and situation don't work out as we plan, and I cannae get back 'ere in due time."

"Then let us keep in touch, Mr. Egan," she answered, assuming Paddy could read and write, but refrained from asking and thereby risk insulting him. "And set a period of six months at which end we shall make adjustments."

Paddy thought that six months would be a good time for him to sort out work, a place to live, and anything else. It was long enough for him, and not so long for Lillian.

"What will she do here, ma'am, if you don't mind me askin'?"

"She will go to school, Mr. Egan," Mercedes flatly but firmly declared. "We all used to be teachers, we can teach Lillian basics until she is ready to attend elementary school."

"Thank yea ma'am, but I cannae afford her schooling," Paddy hinted about money matters.

"We don't expect you to."

"An' she be working 'ere, I mean, in the 'ouse?"

"Oh no, Mr. Egan, not really. She will have responsibilities to learn as she grows like any child in any home—helping with cleaning according to her ability, dusting,...."

"Making the beds, also," Madeline added.

"Yes Mr. Egan, simple household chores according to her ability, and hence able to learn good housekeeping."

"Aye, that be useful, I dare say. And cost ma'am? I cannae affor' boardin' fees ma'am, I no work at this time, and just a simple man."

"There are no costs to you Mr. Egan. She will earn her keep in the house and in the House of the Lord. So we expect her to attend a Catholic School and Church regularly, and, who knows, she may wish to take vows when she is old enough."

Paddy wasn't sure what Mercedes meant by 'vows', nor at what age she was referring, but thought he would keep in contact with the three sisters and write regularly to Lillian to see how things were going, then act accordingly.

"Aye. Sounds fine to me, then. When she start 'ere?"

"Today I should think, after she has had a bath."

"Oh aye. But...." Paddy furrowed his brow with consternation. "But, I thinkin' she might be a bit upset with me leavin' so might I suggest I stay 'ere a day or two, get her settled, you know...? Then when I go I leave me swag in the shed outback, so she think I'm acoming back. She be happy with that."

"I see. Very well. Perhaps two days?"

"Aye. That should do it."

"Then all is final. I will have Mr. Bayliss draw up a paper to the agreement."

"Aye."

"Anything else?" Mercedes asked of her sisters, who silently acquiesced to the arrangement. "Then, Elaine, Maddie, you might like to take Mary Lillian for a bath... And find some dress more fitting."

With that the younger women rose and proceeded out to undertake the tasks as directed. Paddy thanked Mercedes and followed them.

It didn't take much to convince Lillian she needed a bath, she loved water. Subsequently she was ever so pleased to have a new dress, which Paddy suspected had belonged to their long lost wain sister. He stood by as the two ladies, Elaine and Maddie, almost played with Lillian as though she were a doll. Then they showed her the remainder of the house, and the adornments of which she was awed, but also commanding she was not to touch anything. The strategy of enticing her to be comfortable in the place and *wanting* to stay seemed to be working.

Nearing noon Paddy coaxed her away for a walk in the orchard behind the house, so he could talk to her gently, and probe how she might feel about staying at Iron Street for a 'little while', he was careful to unspecify. While she was happy to do so at first, when he told her he would go off 'for a few days' to get work, she was a little apprehensive, but he assured her that he would be gone for only a few days, and would not go until Monday, two days hence, and would leave his swag so she would know he was returning. She acquiesced for the moment, quickly dismissing her concerns as she romped in the orchard, picking cherries.

One o'clock was lunch, which the ladies took in the dining room, leaving Paddy, Lillian and Mr. Bayliss to have theirs in the kitchen. Mercedes thought it best that way, not only because she did not want to indulge with Mr. Egan, nor with Mr. Bayliss for that matter, but also to allow Lillian to be lulled into a sense of security with her father.

In the afternoon Paddy took Lillian for a walk around the streets, and even up to O'Connell Street to watch the trams go by. His other, not totally ulterior motive, was to buy a few bottles of beer for the evening; he suspected that by the way Walter secluded himself and his rum out back that the ladies would not be too open to any alcohol in the house. 'Devil's poison, I dare say they would think it,' he silently thought.

At six o'clock the sisters called for Lillian to join them in an evening prayer in the drawing room, in front of the fireplace and adorned mantel. Paddy and Mr. Bayliss were excused. Thankfully it was a short religious meditation, for while Lillian was initially enthusiastic at the novelty, she quickly became fidgety.

By six-thirty, as it grew dark, dinner was served, again cooked and served by Mr. Bayliss, while he, Paddy and Lillian again ate in the kitchen. It was an opportunity for both parties to separately discuss the events of the day.

Walter began by enquiring of Paddy if he was happy with the arrangement, as he called it, vouchsafing that the ladies were benign god-fearing women, and had found solace in the arrival of Mary Lillian, as though she were some reincarnation—a word of which Paddy had only a vague notion and did not pursue. They couldn't say much in front of Lillian but in general terms Bayliss approved of the arrangement, saying it was a grand opportunity given his, Paddy's, circumstances, and the alternative of dragging a wain about the countryside was not agreeable.

As for the three spinsters, the conversation similarly focused on what had been achieved, and the future. All three quietly felt they had been blessed, that the deliverance of Mary Lillian, as they know referred to the child, was somehow divinely ordained. It was not so much as though Mary Lillian was an angel, or their wain's spirit per se, but that they had been given an opportunity to care for, educate and love in a spiritual way their much younger sister, her life, had she lived beyond the age of five. Somehow, perhaps because of their devotion, and because it was not their place to question the mysterious ways in which the Lord worked, they now had been able to give May Mary Monica's spirit a life as they, the elder sisters, would have deemed it.

To consume the evening hour remaining before retiring, Maddie sat with Mary Lillian in the dining room with several books, gauging what the child liked, and what she might be capable of in terms of reading and writing at this time. Mary Lillian liked books with pictures, especially of animals and farmyards and the like, which spurred Maddie to take notes and draw up some lesson plans for the future, which no doubt she would have approved by Mercedes.

By 7.30 Mercedes came in and directed that it was time for bed; Mary Lillian would sleep in a cot crammed into the room of the two younger sisters, until something else more suitable could be arranged.

Mr. Bayliss shut down and locked up the house, then discreetly ambled out to the back verandah and took his usual seat. He lit his pipe and poured some rum. Paddy joined him with a tall bottle of beer that he had managed to keep cool in a bucket of water hidden under the kitchen table.

After settling in and a few gulps of rum or beer, respectively, Walter turned to Paddy to ask, "So do yer 'ave any plans, then?"

"Aye. I got a brother or two down Bowral, I head for that. Hope they can 'elp me out with gettin' a job."

"Promising, promising..."

"Aye. Best I can do, given the times. There be thousands men 'ere in Sydney lookin' fer work, and I don't knows me way around the city so much. I'm born'd t'country, that what I know, and best fer me, I think."

"Aye, seems it. Least you got kin yer know."

"What about yerself, Mr. Bayliss? Yer say yer come in from Wagga t' big smoke? Why that be?"

"Oh, nothing really. Due to retire soon, got a transfer up here, got a bit put away... Was thinking of visiting the seaside. I used to live near the sea. Enough red dust for *my* lifetime, I reckon," he asserted with emphasis.

"Aye. But for me, I tied t'land, till I die, I reckon. Not one for city or sea."

"When yer heading off?" Bayliss asked.

"Mondee, I reckin, but bit o'problem with that."

Walter gave him an enquiring look, before taking another slug of rum, and just waited for Paddy to explain. He had heard so many problems in his profession over the last 30-odd years, he wasn't about to invite any more.

"Yeah, need leave me swag 'ere so Lilly don't fret, she think I coming back."

"But yer *are* coming back, ain't yer?"

"*Sure* I am. Just not sure when. Could be weeks..."

"I got a' old swag, make it dapper a bit, roll it, yer know, make it look like yers, stick it in a dark corner. She won't know the difference."

"Oh aye, that's a thought."

"We do it tomorrow, when they all at Church."

"Church? Oh Lordy! I ain't set inside a Church for as long as I remembers...."

"Not to worry. It be the ladies go. Early Mass six o'clock, then come 'ome and read the Bible, then eve'nin' Mass, six o'clock agin."

" 'Spect Lilly go wif 'em, then."

" 'Spect so, least the eve'nin' one. Wouldn't wanna wake the mite at five in the mornin'."

Paddy would wait to see what evolved the next day, so long as *he* didn't have to sit in a drafty Church for hours first thing in the morning. So he changed tack.

"The ladies," he broached, "you think they got a few quid?"

Bayliss gave him a look of consternation. "Why you ask that?" wondering if Paddy was planning on stealing something.

"Just that... Not sure I got 'nuff coin to get me down t'Bowral. Thought maybe they could lend me a quid."

"Oh, I see," Bayliss responded with some relief.

"The way I sees it, I givin' me daughter, yer know, t'make 'em happy, maybe they could help me out a bit, just a short loan, yer know..."

"Aye. I know what yer mean. Bit delicate that, I dare say. They a bit skint. Oh they give t'charity an' all, but only to do God's work, ya know what I mean."

"Aye. But it *is* God's work, aint it? My Mary Lillian being God's gift to 'em 'n all."

Bayliss rubbed his chin in thought, and took another gulp of rum. "Best I ask 'em 'bout it. Not sure how, that all."

"Maybe… Maybe say it be hard for me to leave if I skint, and if I cannae leave no reason to keep Lillian 'ere," he presented with spurious logic.

With that he got up to retrieve his second bottle of beer, leaving Bayliss to ponder how and when he might broach the subject with the spinsters the next day, Sunday. Being a Sunday, he thought, they might be more charitable.

Paddy returned after a short moment and resumed his seat, taking a hefty swig from the long-neck.

"Maybe yer best chop some wood for the ladies tomorrow, when they out," Bayliss suggested. It was a job he was supposed to do, but he felt too old to do a lot. "They might 'preciate that."

"Aye. Can do that."

"And you an' the kid pick some fruit out t'orchard. Ten bob's worth o' work."

"Aye. I not afraid of work," Paddy affirmed, then took another large swig.

"Righto! I'm off to the flea pit," he declared, gulping the last of his rum. "Leave you t'lock the door on the way in."

"Aye. Night."

The following morning Mr. Bayliss was, of necessity, up very early, at 5am. He had to make the tea for the three ladies as they readied themselves for Church at six. Fortunately for them the Church, St. *Mary's* no less, was only a few blocks away, so they had no difficulty in being served only tea in the dining room and then slipping out the front door just past 5.30am. Both Mr. Bayliss and Paddy resumed their disturbed slumber, while Lillian had not awoken at all amongst the bustle.

By 7.30 Bayliss once again had the stove going and was preparing another pot of tea for the ladies upon their imminent return, as well as for himself, Paddy and Lillian. On the table he also had the makings for scrambled eggs and toast bread, as the three spinsters did not eat meat on Sundays, nor on Fridays.

They arrived home in due time, their blessedness again having been renewed, and going to their respective rooms changed from their black Church clothes to their black house wear. After breakfast they retired to the living room to read Verses for half an hour, chat, knit, read the newspaper, and discuss Mr. Egan and Mary May Lillian, as they had unilaterally decided to officially call her.

Mr. Bayliss, having had his own breakfast of eggs in the kitchen in the company of Paddy and Lillian, was called for. Mercedes told him to shut the door as he entered.

"Mr. Egan is leaving tomorrow, Mr. Bayliss?" she initiated.

"Yes ma'am. I do believe so. But… He did mention that he might not have sufficient funds to get to Bowral or sustain himself until he found work."

Mercedes gave a haughty scoff. "And why would that concern us, Mr. Bayliss?"

"If I may be direct, ma'am, he was hoping you ladies might see fit to lend him a pound to see him through. He's out now in the orchard with Mary Lillian," Walter was careful to name her, "picking fruit. And is keen to chop some wood for the fires, ma'am."

"That seems like about ten shillings worth of work," Maddie suggested.

"It may," retorted Mercedes. "For as you know, my sisters, we are not in the business of providing charity to strangers."

"That is so, Mercy," Maddie rejoined, "but it is nevertheless Christian to be charitable. *And,* I may add, sister, he has delivered to us so much delight."

"Well, as for the latter, that shall need to be seen."

"Mr. Egan, ma'am," Bayliss interceded, "insists it be a loan until his return to visit Mary May."

"Then you shall add that to the agreement, Mr. Bayliss, if you will," Mercedes affirmed with the quiet although insignificant acknowledgement of her two junior sisters. "Ten shillings for the work, and ten on loan, shall we say?"

"Yes ma'am. He will leave after breakfast, tomorrow, then. And, if I may suggest, one of you kind ladies might take Mary May for a walk in the park or some such when he goes, to take her mind off her father's leaving?"

"I do hope we don't have a scene, Mr. Bayliss," Mercedes answered. "We *do* expect the child to be well behaved."

"I will make a point of informing Mr. Egan to stress that point to his daughter, ma'am."

"Perhaps, Mercy," now Elaine interrupted, "we could take her to the Church charity shop, she is in dire need of some clothes, and shoes."

"Very well," Mercedes agreed. "We may also take some of the picked fruit for a donation, and the remainder to the greengrocer for purchase."

With that decided Mr. Bayliss politely bid his adieu and joined Paddy and Lillian in the orchard to tell them of the arrangements.

"Come ladies," Mercedes directed, when Bayliss had left them. "We have much to do this afternoon."

The rest of the day was spent with Lillian picking fruit, Paddy chopping wood and stacking it conveniently near the back door, and the ladies having a nap after their lunch, then organizing where Mary

May Lillian was to sleep for the duration of her stay....However long that might turn out to be.

Come 5pm Elaine called for Mary May to have a bath, then dress in something fitting for Church: a clean cotton dress of subdued gray, and a black coat that enveloped her was decided for her. A black scarf, something that was quite a novelty for Lillian, was added. By 5.45 they set off for St. Mary's.

Immediately Walter and Paddy arranged a look-a-like swag in the laundry outback, placing it under the troughs in the dark so Lilly would have difficulty discerning the fake, and stored the real McCoy in Walter's room.

In the meantime Mary May Lillian was awed by the large and gothic nature of St. Mary's, and enjoyed the choral singing, much more than the constant kneeling in the pew that played havoc on her boney knees. But an hour into this increasingly boring scenario Lillian became fidgety, eventually whispering to Elaine next to her that she needed to 'pee'. The ladies were thunder-struck by Lillian's language as much as the need to disrupt the current reverence. Elaine was 'elected' to take Mary May Lillian outside to do her ablutions, and they remained outside in the gardens for the next thirty minutes for fear of Elaine and her ward again disrupting the congregation. Mercedes was none too pleased when the Service finished, and she and Maddie streamed out with the others. Mercedes was quite haughty, but said nothing: reckoning may have to wait for another day.

Arriving home, the same dinner routine as previous nights was enacted, with the women retiring by 8pm and insisting Mary May Lillian follow suit. And as was now common, Bayliss and Egan sat out the back imbibing of alcohol and tobacco. Being a Sunday Paddy had been unable to buy any beer, but happily Walter was able to sell him a flask of rum for two bob, and with that taking effect the conversation was subdued and intermittent until they each retired at 9pm.

Bayliss was again up quite early, stoking the coal and wood stove, making tea, serving the ladies waiting in the dining room by 8am. He then rustled up some eggs and sausages for everyone, although of course as usual served separately to the two groups.

It was now Monday, and Sheriff's Clerk Bayliss had to be at the Courthouse by ten o'clock, so with appropriate adieus left the house for the day. Paddy took Lillian for a walk in the orchard, her favourite place it seemed, and explained that he was going into town to find work, just like he had done several weeks ago in Dubbo. Of course she was hesitant to let him go, but he assured her he would be back, that night or the next.... And he showed her his swag in the laundry room.

That organized, he paid his thanks to the three women, received a pound note, and asked them to occupy Lillian. As arranged they enticed Mary May Lillian to go shopping for 'new' clothes at the Church shop, so that while they were gone he slipped out with his real swag.

Paddy headed off without further incident, or concern, toward the Parramatta train station. He hoped to change trains at Central Station to Bowral where, he knew, he had two younger brothers, Arthur and William. The former was ten years younger than Paddy, born in 1890, and before had been working on building a dam or some such, and William was the baby of the family, born in 1902, and so 22 years younger. Each were married now and had their own families, Paddy having met only Arthur's way back in 1917. 'Ah yes, memories...' he reminisced.

'They were a few good years in Bowral, helping Arthur and William on their farm.' "When that be?" he muttered to himself as he walked toward the station. "I seem lost track o' time...late 'seventeen, or maybe early 'eighteen...?" He began to calculate...

Having been discharged from the army in June 1917 he buggered around Sydney for a short while, doing odd jobs, but didn't feel the city suited him, so as soon as he had a few quid he hightailed it down to Bowral. 'Musta been 'eighteen,' he silently decided for himself. 'That be where it all started...'

The red rattler suburban train from Parramatta rambled into Central and stopped with a jolt, stirring Paddy from his liminal state. He moved across the concourse to locate the Country Trains, finding an old steamer to Bowral sitting at Platform Seven and scheduled to depart at noon, an hour hence. Having bought a one-way ticket for 3/6, he returned to the train and took a seat, dropping off into a slumber almost immediately.

'Bowral... Memories, ah yes, they were the good ol' days, after I got outa that bloody army. And Emily.... Left that two-timing bitch behind, everything behind. Start fresh....'

In a slumbering daze Paddy romanticized back to 1917....

Ten

Bowral 1917 — 1920

'...Emily. Emily Oakley... That was when it all began', he mused.

She had found another man, or *he*, that bloody Sands fella, leastways had found *her*, largely abandoned, having lost two kids already, and a third barely surviving on the scraps she could get while Paddy was off gallivanting the rail lines or somewhere else for all she knew, and maybe with some other woman, or in jail... She didn't know where Paddy got to, when he'd be home, and no wages coming in from him for weeks on end. And when he *was* home, always drinking, drinking down the pub or drinking at home. Always drinking.

And why not?—Paddy often had thought. She was too young and inexperienced when he married her, didn't know how to cook or clean, just expected him to be home every night. And three kids already, until two died in 1913, one after the other. She was distraught, blamed him. If he'd been home, brought in his wages instead of his drink, the kids could have had more to eat, they could have got medicine. But what medicine or doctor, stuck out in the one horse town of Warren?

She blamed him, for the death of her kids, for their poverty, for everything. She and her guardians, the Woodleys, had thought he was a steady worker back in 1903, but now, almost ten years on... What had happened to him? Things were not going so well, married life and work wise, he couldn't make ends meet, give Emily the things she demanded, such as a decent house, food, and maybe even some small luxuries such as clothes for herself and their kids. Not surprising, given half his wages went on grog and tobacco. But what else was a man to do stuck in the backwoods of nowhere?

During 1911 he was either too drunk or drunk too often to work the railways; instead of earning a quid he earned a bad reputation. When he could work he scrounged around for bits of labouring work, cash in hand, quick 'easy' money to gratify his and Emily's demands and needs. Then in 1912 he went back to work on the trains, until November 1912, when he was dismissed, for good. No reason given. Just they had had enough of his intermittency.

He bummed around once again, barely keeping flesh on bones, then would take off for weeks at a time, telling Emily he was going on the swag, a roustabout, getting a good job shearing or herding, whatever he could imagine. Then, in late 1915, having been absent on and off over 2 years from Emily and his fractured family, with no work prospects, he returned to Warren.

That was when he discovered Emily and Sands, George Sands. He worked the lines also, had a cushy job most of the time, nice uniform, well kempt. Train guard, he was. Must have been going on behind his back for years, whenever he was away, he figured.

She didn't admit it, nor deny it. But didn't want *him*, Paddy, coming back either. He went off again, here and there, doing odd jobs, for almost another two years...

'I'll show her...and *him!*—that bloody Sands feller!' he finally decided. 'I'll get a regular wage, and a uniform *too*. Join the army, that's what I'll do. They'll take me, I done it before. Experience counts. And they need all the men they can get.'

It was by now 1917, February. Without telling Emily or anyone else he enlisted at the Dubbo office. He thought he'd surprise her, but when he turned up all swell and dandy in an army uniform at their house in Warren a few weeks later, all she could ask was when he got paid, if he had any money. Without money she didn't need him, or want him.

He went to the pub to drown his sorrows, as the cliché goes, and make a nuisance of himself in Warren. That's where the Military

Police found him, AWOL, desertion. At first when he had enlisted he had lied about his circumstances, saying he was single, but now, taken to Victoria Barracks in Sydney, he admitted to being married with one remaining child, and was having family problems—to put it mildly. Luckily for him, perhaps out of sympathy, he was discharged in June 1917 after a medical examination found him to be unfit. He was then almost 37 years of age.

He couldn't go back to Emily, she wouldn't have him, and she was preparing to live with George Sands in Newcastle. He couldn't go back to his Da in Dubbo, or his sisters in the area, they would have heard about his irresponsible activities and his marriage problems. Despite his past transgressions he did have some shame. He figured everyone now might think he was again in the army and had gone to Europe, perhaps eventually thinking he was wounded or killed there. He also knew his two younger brothers would keep his secret, so he would head for Bowral as soon as he could get some coins together.

Discharged from Victoria Barracks with barely a pound in his kit from Army back pay, he found work on and off in Sydney; it was easy with the War still raging and thousands of blokes away. But his wages went mostly on rent in a doss house, tobacco, and most especially grog.

After the Armistice of 1918 and the beginning of the return of servicemen, work became more difficult. Ex-soldiers were given priority. And, by 1919, they brought with them the Spanish flu, which was knocking people over like blind flies. He would be bound to catch that! All things considered it was time to cut and run.

It was easy to get to Central Railway Station and board a train going through to Bowral, where he would gladly get off.

It was past two o'clock when the train pulled into Mittagong station with a jolt that awoke Paddy from his dreamful slumber. He looked about, realizing the next stop, Bowral, about 15 minutes hence, would be his. As the train pulled out he stood up and stretched, gathered his scarce belongings, and looked out the window.

"Ah, the fresh green hills," he murmured to himself, "so much like Ireland me grand-da had told me 'bout." Not like the dry brown paddocks he knew of the northwest. One day he would return to his Irish roots, to pay homage to whence he came. But for now, New South Wales was his home.

Once again the train soon came to a jolting halt, and he stepped onto the small platform into the warm sunshine. He could feel the crisp country air imbued with the smell of fresh green fields. He looked about. It was awfully quiet.

Bowral Train Station

He had Arthur's address, but being his first time in the town he hadn't a clue where it might be. He had to find the station master, if there was one, or a map, or maybe someone who knew their way about. If it was far, and he had to pay a cab, it'd probably cost him a fortune. Also, even though he had his swag and could sleep under the stars, he had no food, and worst of all, no grog to dull his misery. And he rightly expected the nights could get cold down in the Southern Highlands.

He went in search of someone to ask and encountered an old man, past his working prime so Paddy thought, shuffling around the station. He looked up as Paddy entered the station rooms.

"That the last train, lad, if yer gonna ask," the old fella said.

"Aye. But not, not askin' that, just got off it. Looking for me brother, Arthur Egan. I got this address, 'ere." Paddy handed him the slip of dirty paper with Arthur's address, '*Greentrees*'.

"Ya, I know that place. A bit far. You plan on walking?" the old feller queried with a skeptical look.

"How far?"

"Ya can't walk it, lad, take yer half a day...if ya don't get lost," he chuckled. "Yer better off going over t'pub, there, 'cross the line," he pointed as he shuffled back onto the platform. "All the drays and sales blokes stop there. Maybe yer can 'itch a ride from one o' 'em, but that most likely be t'morra, son."

"Tomorrow...?" Paddy quizzed.

"Yup. They be coming in soon, close t' four o'clock, and bed down, then get an early start t'morra. No point deliverin' at night time."

"Aye. Thanks. I'll go over and see what be had."

With that Paddy retrieved Arthur's address from the old timer, shoved it in a pocket, then jumped down and across the twin lines, and up the other side. He crossed the road and went into the hotel, *Royal Bowral*.

It was empty, except for the barman tidying up the little to tidy up.

With only 10 shillings left in his kit he asked for a cheap room. Four bob, he was told, with breakfast. He had no choice. He'd have to hang about until some travellers came in and try to scrounge a lift the next day. The barman told him that there was a real chance of that, at least part of the way, the folks passing through didn't mind a bit of travelling company, and that he should hang about at the bar after four or five o'clock, and he'd try to steer Paddy straight. It was too early to have a beer, he thought, and better to keep his coins to buy a fella a beer later in order to scab a ride; so he laid down in his room for a snooze.

At five he was woken by the increased noise downstairs, so he had a wash and wandered down. Men were coming in to the bar by the truckload, it seemed, dressed in an array of old suits and soft hats, to dungarees and flannelette shirts. He wiggled his way amongst the throng at the bar and ordered a schooner, tipping his hat to a few blokes either side.

One feller seemed to be on his own, so Paddy struck up a conversation with him, Harry by name. He was a travelling salesman, down from Sydney, doing all the towns in the southern highlands: Mittagong, Bowral, Moss Vale, Berrima, and as far south as Goulburn. That was his territory, and he sold anything and everything, from clothes to plates and cutlery and shoes. If he didn't have it he'd take an order and deliver the next month. His next stop was Moss Vale, and he was happy to take Paddy that far, but it was still aways from *Greentrees*, which was more east near Robertson and Glenquarry. Harry yelled out to a mate, Mike, along the bar, who sidled up. Harry told him that Paddy was heading down Glenquarry way, and if he had room for some company. Luckily Mike agreed, saying he was leaving 7am sharp to beat the heat, and Paddy could find his truck out front, with *Mike Merchant* painted on the side. Like Harry he carried all sorts of odds and ends, especially farm tools, going to Robertson via Glenquarry then on east to Albion Park, then the coast.

Paddy thanked Mike, and vowed to be at the truck by seven, then bought him a beer and chatted awhile. After his second beer Paddy was feeling a bit queasy, not having had any food since morning, so he wandered out back where he suspected was a kitchen. He wasn't wrong. He managed to scrounge a few sausages and vege, for a price of course, then returned to the bar for a third schooner. The place had quieted down by then. Getting on half-seven he thought it best to call it quits; he had to be up early and his dosh was getting perilously low.

Now Thursday, it was the first day of a new life, he hoped. He would bunk with his two younger brothers, work, save some money, and maybe see what developed. But first he had to get to *Greentrees*, to Arthur's house, without any notion of how his brother was set up.

About all he knew was that Arthur was married, but he wasn't even sure of Billy, the youngest, if he was still with him.

He waited at Mike's truck, and true to his word they drove off into the morning sun. They stopped briefly at a few farms on the way, with Paddy helping to load or unload whatever Mike directed, glad of the help. With the stops, it took 2 hours to get to Glenquarry, which was not so much a town but a scattering of farm houses. They drove through, passing by the north end of Wingecarribee River and dam, finally seeing a sign pointing up a dirt road to *Greentrees Farm*. Paddy jumped out with his swag and thanked Mike, who told him if he ever got to Sydney to look him up, he might have a job for Paddy from time to time.

Mike drove off in a cloud of dust as Paddy looked at the dirt track leading up to *Greentrees*. He couldn't see any house from where he stood, so figured it might be another mile or so up the road. He set off, full of hope.

At a brisk walk he arrived in twenty minutes at a timber bungalow painted white, with a red-rusty tin roof. He thought it might have been bigger. But he couldn't be choosey, nor had he time to wait before a young woman appeared on the front verandah, as he approached with a friendly wave.

"Morning, ma'am. You must be Alice," he spoke cheerily. She looked at him, not sure she recognized him.

"I'm Paddy, or George, Arthur's brother, you 'member?"

Only vaguely, she thought, but nevertheless answered 'Yes', then went on: "He's out at work, down the dam. What you doing in these parts?"

"Looking for work, see me lil' brothers. William 'ere, too?"

"Working with Arty," she answered shortly.

"Oh aye. That's good to 'ear."

"They be home 'bout noon, for lunch. 'Spose ya better come in have a cuppa, then," she finally suggested much to Paddy's delight, because he thought she wasn't none too pleased to see him.

The conversation was a bit forced, the two of them having met only once before, briefly, after Arthur's Sydney wedding in 1914, if she could recall. Some vague recollections of Paddy being drunk then, or making a nuisance of himself, setting a bad example to his brother. Maybe that wasn't him? Maybe it was his father...? Perhaps she had heard of Paddy's troubles with his marriage and employment. It was too long ago... Three years? Four...?

She served him up a cup of tea and a biscuit, asking what he'd been doing, where was his wife, Emily, how was his last remaining kid, Emily also, all those petty things about family, travel, travails and plans, of which she was hardly interested as she went about the housework in the kitchen. He answered with equal disinterest in brief comments. It was like two strangers with only a tenuous connection.

To Alice's relief, and perhaps also Paddy's, he finished his tea then said he'd go out to the front verandah and have a smoke, and wait for Arthur and William. Luckily he didn't have to wait too long before he saw his two brothers riding up on one horse. They were of course surprised to see Paddy, and happy as well. Although they, too, had heard of their older brother's troubles with Emily and the Army, no doubt through Anthony Egan and their older sisters Mary, Grace and Teresa, they half expected all that to be behind Paddy, to have been left in Dubbo and Warren, and he was here now, in Bowral, seeking greener pastures.

William tied up the horse and gave Paddy a warm hug. Arthur was very much like Paddy, 6 foot tall, broad shoulders, and William, or Bill as he was called, also heading toward the same height and frame of his predecessors, although he was only 15.

Going into the kitchen Alice was relieved to see her husband and Bill come in, and she began serving up a wholesome lunch for all three men. They talked about the past times, and the present, and Arthur's future plans, while Bill lamented he had been too young to join up for WW1. Paddy joked he could join the next war.

"So where's yer wains, then?" he asked Arthur.

"One on the way, 'spect any day now," he nodded toward Alice, whom Paddy had clearly observed beforehand.

"Aye. Any more?"

"Aye. The youngest, he passed," Arthur whispered so as not to upset Alice. "The other two boys out back, sleepin' I figure."

"Aye. Let 'em but. Sorry t'ear 'bout the youngin."

"That why Bill came down, lend a hand."

"Aye, be a handful there but. How old they be now?"

"Arthur junior, he be 'bout four or maybe five, and John, near three. Grace, she be borned just last year, she be asleep in 'er cot."

Then they moved on to Paddy's plans, who answered that he was hoping to find work in the area.

"There plenty o' that hereabouts," Arthur told him. "With all the men orf to war and killed, can't find enough t' 'place 'em. Me and Billy helpin' build the dam wall down the way. I can ask if they want some more."

"Or yer can 'ead down Scrublands, Paddy," Bill interjected. "Sutt'n Forest, timber work."

"Aye. They needing a lot o' wood for the war effort, ya know. Or try the brick works," Arthur added.

"Aye, I do any o' that."

"So you be staying 'ere, I 'spect?" Billy asked with hope.

"Aye, if I can...for a short bit, anyways, if it be orright with yous," he replied with a cautious glance at Alice.

"Aye. Can't see why not. Ya can bunk in Billy's room."

"Thanks. Just till I get me own place, y'know," he said more to assure Alice than with any truth. "So Billy, ya working here?"

"Aye. No work up Dubbo, and don't wanna hang with the ol' man."

"Aye. But yer a bit far from town, ain't yer. Where does a man get a drink but?"

"Briars Inn, 'cross country from 'ere," Billy told him. " 'Bout two mile I reckon, on the Moss Vale Road."

"I tell yer what, Paddy," Arthur suggested, "we gotta get back to work, Glenquarry way. You start walking and I send Billy 'ere back on 'orse t' get ya, then yer can go t' Bowral, yer won't get lost that way. The 'orse knows 'is way back anyhows."

"Aye. That'd be great. We need some celebrating aye."

With lunch over, Paddy slung his swag into Billy's room and the men headed out. The two younger ones headed off on the horse toward the dam. Then Billy came back and met up with Paddy walking down the road. He mounted behind his brother and they trotted down to the dam where about five men were cutting, hauling and placing stones on a dam that was to supply Bowral with drinking water.

Arthur introduced him to all the workmen and the supervisor, and asked if the latter could take Paddy on for some work. He was told to come back the next day, he had to ask his boss, but seemed hopeful. After hanging about a little while, Paddy took the horse and plodded into town, which was now more livelier than his early morning leave-taking.

A main street of Bowral, circa 1920s.

It was close to 3pm when he got there, so thought he'd stop at the first pub and have a beer, and another... By 4pm he thought it best to head back, so he bought two flagons of rum, mounted the horse and headed it home. It was fortunate the animal knew where it was going, as Paddy could barely keep his eyes open.

Reaching the dam he found everyone had gone, so he directed the horse back to the house, finally catching up with Arthur and Bill walking up the mile-long drive to their house. There was no point now of getting Paddy off the animal, so they just walked alongside making sure Paddy didn't fall off until arriving at the front door. They hauled him inside and tossed him in Bill's bed.

Alice was both alarmed and disgusted, with Arthur saying he was just dog-tied, in some lame attempt to placate her.

"Be celebrating alone, then, Billy," Arthur declared, "just you and me."

They left Paddy to sleep it off, as they had their dinner and a nip or two of rum on the front verandah, Billy wondering if his eldest brother was always like this, and if he'd be fit for work the next day...

True to his form, Paddy was up and about by 6am the next morning, a little worse for wear, and ruddy in the face more from Alice's embarrassing stares. The other two boys joined him for breakfast with little conversation, then Arthur took Paddy down to the dam on horseback, and returned to pick up Billy. After the morning's work Billy rode up to the house to collect their lunches, after which they worked again till 4pm. The same process of the morning for getting home was followed. After dinner the men sat on the verandah and imbibed of the rum and tobacco, amidst small talk.

Almost 11 months of this routine went by, five days a week, to Christmas 1919, with the occasional ride into Bowral, usually on a Saturday, to get provisions and enjoy some time-out at the pub. The problem with this arrangement was the tediousness of transport with only one horse, meaning that someone had to shuttle back and forth, or stay at the house, which was commonly Alice or Billy, or both.

Paddy early on suggested they all contribute to a second-hand buggy, which would facilitate transport of people and goods. They all thought it a good idea and began looking for a suitable vehicle.

In the meantime, Paddy helped the household with various chores such as chopping wood and working the vegetable patches out back. But while he was glad to have a job and the money that gave him, and a place to live with amenable kin, he was getting restless. He missed the wandering life of adventure, and also now he had no family of his own, and he wasn't getting any younger. He was now 38, running close to 39 in October 1919.

By early 1919 Alice had once again been showing signs of pregnancy, and thoughts had turned to Billy staying in the house more to help out, but that would mean less household money. The Great War had surely ended, and indeed many of the troops—what was left of them—were returning home from Europe, which meant they would be wanting work and be given preference. There was also talk of that new germ, a bug, that was spreading, influenza they said it was, and people in Europe were dropping like flies.

A humorous ditty readily did the rounds, which, while making light of the pandemic, also drove home its seriousness:

I had a little birdy called Enza.
She flew outside,
I opened the window,
and in flew Enza.

But the worst was yet to come.

The three Egans and Alice meanwhile continued following a repetitive routine with barely a change. Arthur and Alice had had their latest, and thankfully last, baby, another boy in early 1920, and life and work continued-on much the same with the one new addition. But, when the Spanish flu had taken hold employment for the Egans was curtailed by restrictions on labour movement and the need to give preferential employment to the returning Diggers.

1919 had been for them perhaps the hardest year. While there was still some work to be had, it could be limited or intermittent. The Diggers that could work took over the jobs at the local brickworks, forcing Paddy and Arthur to work at whatever was available from time to time, most especially in Sutton Forest down south a few miles, doing lumbering and sawmilling.

Somehow they survived much of 1919, by which time the influenza was beginning to wane, and restrictions on the movement of people were relaxed a little.

The isolation of the Egans was a godsend, though, in one sense, but it also meant a very tedious, repetitive and boring existence. Paddy, after his earlier life of riding the rails and adventure, perhaps felt it most. He began to think there was no future in this life, *and* desired a female companion. The family having bought a sulky,

Paddy not infrequently took it into town and got drunk to blanket his misery, but then curled up on the seat and fell asleep on the way home.

Some months later, about early 1920, prospects had improved. Despite the return of WW1 servicemen, there was still a shortage of labour in all areas as the economy began to boom, unlike that in Germany. The flu epidemic had subsided, and with that so too did travel restrictions decline. The three Egan men and Alice resumed their routine of work, gardening, and more work, with occasional bouts of merriment. But for Paddy the lack of prospects and adventure, of travel, and of having a wife, continued to play on his mind. There seemed to be no fun in his life; he seemed to be missing out on the energizing social scene of the 'Roaring Twenties' of which they heard on the old valve-radio.

Also about this time, March 1920, rumour was about of the train line extending past Junee, which had long been a minor terminus. Paddy saw this as a chance to go back to his past endeavours, riding the rails, going places, meeting people, simply not tied down, but doing as he pleased. And so it was, at this instance, he raised with his brothers the idea of him trying his luck in this new adventure at Junee, based on a poster he saw at Bowral Post Office. He knew if things didn't work out he could probably come back to Arthur's home, so figured nothing chanced, nothing gained.

For the rest of March 1920, and with this plan in mind, he worked with his brothers, then set off for Junee with anticipation and excitement. He had been too housebound for almost 24 months. He had celebrated his 39th birthday last October, now he was running to 40. It was time to try new horizons and find a lady companion...

Eleven

Junee 1920 — 1926

A train ride of five-plus hours took Paddy from Bowral to Junee, stopping a short time at Goulburn, Yass and then Cootamundra. Junee wasn't as big as he expected, but a rather small pokey little place, surprisingly with four pubs, three of which were within cooee of the Station. It was now 8pm, and he was hungry, and thirsty for a beer.

He couldn't miss *Condon's Railway Hotel*, more commonly known as *Junee Hotel*, with a wrap-around verandah, solid brown-red brick and two stories high; every inch of colonial architecture. Any closer to the station and it would be on the tracks, he thought.

Junee Hotel circa 1924.

He strolled into the expansive downstairs bar and ordered a schooner of beer. Gulping down almost half of that he set the glass on the bar and took a look around. It was quiet, having only half a dozen patrons, none of whom paid him no heed. He turned to the bartender and asked:

"Any chance of getting some food 'ere? I been on t'train all day."

"Aye, maybe. Service is closed but you can ask the kitchen, out back," he thumbed. "There's a lass maybe whip yer up somfing. Clara her name."

"Aye. Thanks. And a room...?"

"Aye. Five bob, with brekky," the barman matter of factly told paddy, with what seemed a good deal of disinterest.

Paddy finished off his beer pretty quick then wandered through some corridors, following the smell of food. Like the Hotel, the kitchen was also large, and the door open. It was hot and steamy, with what looked like large tubs for washing, or maybe for cooking, bellowing steamy fumes upward, and two ladies sitting at a large wood table eating bread and cold meat.

"Even'in'," he cheerily greeted them from the door. "The barman said I might get a bite to eat. Been on t'train all day, from Bowral."

The women looked up, with little interest. Then the younger one spoke with carelessness: "We only got bread and salted ham. I can cook up a' egg quick if you want."

"Aye. That be fine, thanks."

" 'Ave a seat then," she responded.

"Thank ye," he answered, taking a seat opposite them, as the girl, who he thought must be about 23 or thereabouts, went to the stove and began frying two eggs.

"What yer doing down 'ere, then?" the other woman, shorter and plumper asked.

"Looking fer work. 'Eard the railways is lookin' for workers."

"That be right. Not too many men folk 'ere now, all 'cause the war and that bloody flu. Best ask t'station."

"Aye, will do, tomorrow, eh."

"Anyways, I'm Beryl," the short chubbier woman, who was maybe 30 years old, introduced herself. "This's Clara." She jerked her head toward the stove.

Clara turned a little to catch his eye. She was quite attractive, Paddy thought. Black hair, not long, wide-set green eyes, a longish straight nose, a curvy upper lip, and strong squared chin.

Clara Egan nee: Lampe, Keough. (Date unknown).

"Nice to meet ya," he answered, tipping his hat, then took it off and placed it on the table, only now realizing he should remove it. "I'm Patrick, or Paddy if yer like," he smiled.

"Oh a Patrick, eh," Clara declared. "My dad's name's Patrick."

"Oh aye. A fine name to go with a fine man, I dare say."

"And if he's name weren't Patrick...?" she quizzed with a raised eyebrow.

"Still be a fine man, I should think, if he raise a nice girl like you," he smiled.

"Yer staying 'ere, at the 'otel I mean," Beryl interrupted the flirtation.

"Aye. Unless yer know somewhere cheaper...?"

"There a room at Clara's, ain't there, girl?" she announced, looking at Clara as she now served the eggs, and cut some bread. "She stays at a boarding 'ouse in George Street, don't ya dearie."

"Yeah, not far. Five minute walk."

"Oh aye. That be good. I be lookin' a place for a while. What's the rent?"

"Dunno. Guess same what I pay, have t'ask. Chinese people. You don't care 'bout the Chinks, d'ya?"

"Nah, not me. I knowed all sorts. If the price is right...," he shrugged.

"Well... I finish up 'ere in twenty minutes, we can walk there."

"Aye. Good," he affirmed between mouthfuls of egg, ham and bread.

Clara went over to the wash tubs and pushed and pulled and heaved at some soaking sheets, then took them out back to hang on the line, while Beryl returned to shelling peas and tidying up.

He finished his food and stood, took his hat and said he'd grab another beer and wait for Clara.

"Nah, ya cannae do that," Beryl almost shouted. "Oh Lordy, the boss he don't want t'see yer walking out with Clara, what he might think, eh?"

"Oh. Yeah. Righto."

"And you got room 'ere, ain't yer?" she pressed.

"Sort of. Not firm. I asked 'em 'bout it, said five bob a night."

"They get pissed-off wif yer for cancellin' that!"

"Aye. I see. 'Ere's what I do. I just tell the barman a fella gave me a bed for the night, an ol' mate. Then I meet Clara outside, down the way a bit?"

"That be better."

"Righto. See ya later, ma'am. And thanks."

With that he sauntered back to the bar and ordered a beer, and two long necks for the rest of the evening. He was already thinking he might encourage Clara to have a drink...

The barman asked him if he wanted that room, but Paddy spun him a yarn about looking up an old friend nearby, so he was right for the night. The two take-aways seemed to substantiate his plan, as the bartender wouldn't be thinking Paddy would be buying beer for a woman.

It was almost thirty minutes later that Clara came out from the rear of the pub and started walking down Lorne Street, the main road. It was awfully quiet, as were most country towns at past 9pm. She caught up to him a hundred yards down and they walked together in silence.

Turning into George Street they entered the third house from its rear, where lights were still on in the kitchen. He could smell the Chinese food boiling and bubbling as he mounted the few back steps.

Clara went straight in and was warmly greeted by Mr. and Mrs. Tsai, he was told later. In stilted English she explained who Patrick was, and he wanted a room for a while. They motioned him to come in, eyed him over, seeing he was not some young ruffian, and showed him to a small, neat room with a single bed, a washbasin and some hooks on the walls.

They left him to get comfortable and unpack his megre swag. A few moments later he tapped on Clara's door of the adjacent room, and suggested she get a couple of glasses and they share a bottle of beer on the front verandah, if that was ok.

As they sat on the front steps she told him only one glass of beer for her. That was fine by him, as it left all the more for himself, and he felt he needed it after the long train trip. Although he was hoping to push Clara along a bit for some 'fun', the house setup at the moment didn't really inspire such a noisy activity. Nor did he know if Clara had a husband already, so after a swig or two and a reign of silence between the couple, he ventured to find out more about her.

"How long yer been livin' 'ere, then, Clara?" he began with an innocent question.

"I don't live here. Just stay here a few days when working at the pub."

"Ah, aye. So where's 'ome?"

"Coolamon. Ya know it?"

"Nah. Where that be?"

" 'Bout seven, eight miles west. On the west line."

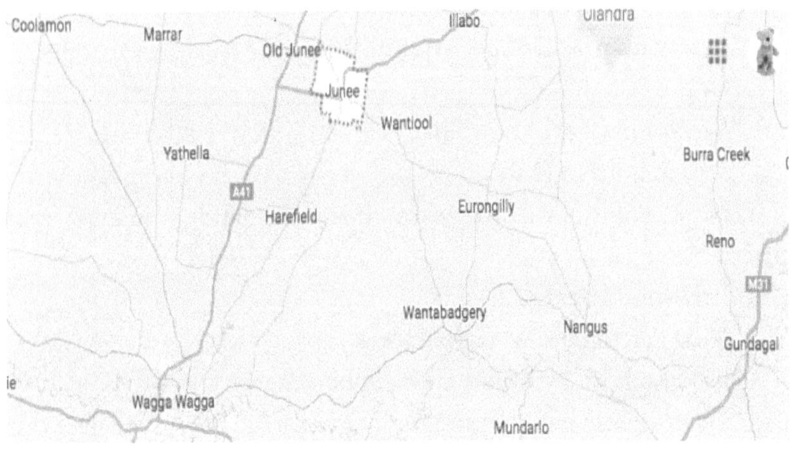

Map of NSW showing Coolamon, Junee, Wagga Wagga and Gundagai

"With yer folks?"

"Yup. Ma and Pa Keough. Everyone knows 'em."

"Keough, eh. You got kids?"

"One. Girl. Ruth. 'Bout two year old now, goin' on three."

"That be nice."

"You?" Clara asked.

"Nah. No kids. Not married, never."

"Oh? Why not? A man your age should have a woman, yer know."

"What yer mean *my* age? I be only thirty-six-on."

"So you never had a woman of yer own?" she looked at him skeptically.

"Aye, I did. A few years 'go, back in Dubbo."

"Dubbo!" she exclaimed. "Is that where yer from? I got a sister up that way."

"Oh have yer?"

"Yea, Nellie, she married back in nineteen-o-nine down 'ere, then moved up to a place called Warren."

"Aye, that's near Dubbo, orright. Who's the fella then?"

"Gee. George Gee."

"Aye, cannae say I know 'im."

"So you born in Dubbo?"

"Nope. Funny, I was born on a ship, in Fremantle. You know that place?"

Clara shook her head.

"Near Perth it be. Western Australia."

"I see. So how'd you end up in Dubbo then?"

"Don't rightly know, I just a wain. Me Da said he moved over this way to get work, building railways an' all that shite."

"I guess so." She seemed perplexed, having been almost nowhere in her life other than the local southwestern region, and not well schooled in geography.

"Where you born? 'Round here?" he pursued.

"Gundagai, fact is. Then me Ma and Pa moved down here."

"So yer got relos there, in Gundagai?"

"Yea, on me Pa's side, I think. Keoughs."

"This where you met yer husband, then, in Junee?"

"Yeah. But he died after one year, just after Ruth was born. Nineteen-nineteen."

"The flu?"

Clara nodded, feeling a little sad now.

"Sorry. It's been a buggar of a time, eh, wif the war and that bloody flu. We keeped to ourselves most o' the time, up in Bowral."

"We?"

"Me and me brothers."

"Oh. You get around, then..."

"Aye, yer could say that. Dubbo, Sydney, Bowral, now here."

"For how long?"

"Here? Cannae say. Depends... Depends on work and if I finds someone to settle with."

"So what happen to yer missus in Dubbo, then?"

"Oh, she found another feller, so... Better for me to leave, I reckon."

"But yer not marry her?"

"Nah. She be too young then. And her folks said wait. Then she run off wif some other feller," Paddy lied on the make, while spinning a sad-luck story that might spark Clara's sympathy.

"Ahh. I see. Well, I better get some sleep. Been working all day. Thanks for the beer."

Clara got up and went to her room, not giving much thought to anything but sleep.

Paddy finished off the one bottle, and also plum tired, went to his room, not finding it hard to doze off.

He was awoken at 7am by Clara tapping on his door then entering.

"I got ya 'cuppa. Sorry, but it's getting late. Going to work soon."

Paddy rolled over and moaned. "Ta." He sat up and took a sip of black tea. "Work?"

"Yea, laundry at the pub. If you're quick I show you breakfast in the kitchen."

Paddy swung out of bed, still fully dressed, and followed Clara to the kitchen to be met by Mr. and Mrs. Tsai smiling eternally. Clara gave him a bowl of soup with some kind of meat in it, and a bowl of plain rice. Several chopsticks sat in a glass on the table, but he had no idea how to use them. Reading his mind Clara handed over a spoon.

"You going down the yards then, today?"

"Sure am. See what's happenin'," he affirmed between gulping mouthfuls of the soup. "Guess I see ya tonight then, at the pub...?"

"Maybe... Prob'ly."

With that she left Paddy to his own devices. He had a wash, changed into his only other shirt, threw his swag over his shoulder, then said goodbye to the Chinese couple, trying to impress on them that he'd be back later...but not sure what that meant. To make sure they understood he gave them a ten shilling note, as a kind of surety.

He headed down to the rail yards. Being directed to the Supervisor's office he then got told he could work that day, right now, up at the turntable. He headed up there on the quick, and was first allocated to shoveling coal into the boiler to get a head of steam on the loco. That done he was told to jump a flat bed down the line where several other gangers were waiting, he'd be helping to lay new tracks and whatever out near Coolamon.

'Ah, Coolamon,' he contemplated. 'Be interesting to see what that place be like,' he smiled to himself, thinking of Clara.

She, on the other hand, was faced with a day of cleaning hotel rooms, stripping beds, then washing the sheets in big tubs. It was hard work, and the hot water and soap left her hands red, almost raw. But being mostly uneducated she had no alternative to unskilled, menial labour to support her daughter and help her parents and four remaining siblings at home.

At 4pm she left off other tasks and helped Beryl prepare food for the expected hotel guests, not that there were many these days, partly because other hotels provided stiff competition. So by 5.30 she was once again sitting with Beryl at the wood table in the out-back kitchen, de-podding peas, cutting beans, peeling potatoes, and so on, when Paddy almost staggered in with a beer in hand.

The two women looked up at the rather haggard man. "Yer look like the cat's dragg'd yer in," Beryl declared with a smirk.

"Aye. Thanks. Been working."

"That's good, Patrick... Paddy. Good t'know a man puts in a good day's work," Clara declared.

"Aye, would be good if I had some lunch but. *I'm bloody starving!*"

"Why's that?" Beryl insisted.

"Because I didn't knows I was gonna be working up the line all day, so didn't take nuffin wif me."

"Oh. And I bet that Chinese brekky went through yer like a siv!" Clara chuckled.

"Aye, that be right. So... What's me chances on getting some tucker?" he pleaded.

"Sit down then, you poor man," Clara feigned sympathy. "A shilling though. And you ain't paid me the bob for last night."

"Aye. I can pay yer." And with that he pulled two bob out of his pocket and thumped it on the table.

"Beef stew?" Clara queried as she got up to dish some food. "With potato and bread?"

"Aye. Grand. Potatoes... I *am* Irish, yer know."

"With a name like Paddy, I'd never'd guess," she teased.

Paddy hoed into the food, finishing half of it before taking another gulp of his schooner, then ate some more, as the two women watched on while cutting up vegetables.

Finishing off, almost licking the plate, Clara gave him another slice of bread as filling. "You working tomorrow?"

"Aye," he answered before finishing off his beer.

"Then you better come here before work, I make yer a sandwich fer yer lunch," Clara told him.

"Aye, that be grand. Another shilling but?"

"Sixpence," she laughed. Then she picked up the two shillings left on the table and put it in her apron pocket, which Paddy noted, but said naught.

"Aye. Was workin' out Coolamon t'day."

"Oh yeah? You like it?"

"Didn't see much of it, just the track."

"I'm going back there, tomorrow, home, see me bairn."

"Oh aye. Maybe I come with yer," he half asked, half declared.

"What for?" she quizzed with a furrowed brow.

Paddy shrugged his shoulders. "No reason. See the country side, new places, I guess."

"Ha! New places! Coolamon hardly new or worth seeing. Not even a *one*-horse town."

"Maybe a mule or two," Beryl quipped with a chuckle.

"Well, I ain't got nuffin else to do."

"Then you be right at home in Coolamon," Clara snidely observed.

"Then why you stay there? Don't seem like the place to bring up a kid."

"Yer can ask me Pa that. I half grow'd up there. Gundagai, then old Junee, then Junee proper, now Coolamon."

"Big landowners out there," Beryl explained. "McKinnons and McKenzies. Do horses and auctions, sheep and wheat, employ lots o' people."

"Yup. My Pa works fer 'em sometimes."

"Aye, I see. That why yous live there?"

"Sorta. Used to live in Junee, matter of fact. Ducker street, near the Chinks' place. You see, when Ruth was born, I weren't too well for a while, so me Ma looked after Ruth, official-like. A guardian they call it, because I was in hospital a bit and then after went to work in Narrandera. Needed the money, you know..."

"Aye. I been in that spot. But why yer in 'ospital?"

"Dunno really. They said weak blood, or kidney. Something like that. So Ma looked after Ruth. Then Pa was working for the McKinnons out that way, and rent too much in Junee, so we moved. Now they talking 'bout moving back 'ere, same 'ouse in Ducker Street."

"Geez. Cannae make up their minds!"

"Me Pa says he gotta go where there be work."

"Aye, that be true. So... you up to it?"

"Coolamon?" Clara shrugged. "Why not, if yer wanna waste yer time."

"Done but. We talk 'bout it back at the Chinks'. I gonna get a beer then head back."

"Wait for me. I be half hour. Down the street."

"Aye. I wait."

Paddy left the two women and returned to the bar where he bought another schooner, and another two long necks for the night. Then headed out to the street and waited for Clara to catch up with him.

Clara finished her cooking, cleaning, washing and tidying up and headed out to meet up with Paddy who, after more than 30 minutes, was getting anxious for a beer and relaxation. But in the end they sauntered into #3 George Street and greeted Mr. and Mrs. Tsai, who abruptly tried to return to him his ten shillings. Through Clara's experienced patience, Paddy informed them he would be staying awhile, and to keep the money as a deposit.

Then, having freshened up a bit with a face wash and change of shirt, he again sat out the front with a bottle of beer and two glasses. Clara joined him shortly.

"Aye, ya know where I can get o'bit o' laundry done?" he initiated.

"Here of course, ya duffa. They Chinese, ya know, always doing laundry. Give 'em whatever now and it be dry tomorrow."

"Oh. Aye. But... I only got two pair trousers, and I need both washed."

"You need a woman looking after ya, Mister Patrick. Go, get what you can, give 'em, and the comin' week you buy up some more clothing."

Paddy wasn't too savvy with all this, so he just followed what Clara directed. He went to his room, wrapped up some socks and long johns in his other trousers and shirt, and took it to the Tsais. Somehow through body language and jumbled lingo they got the idea. Then he returned to where he had left Clara on the front step.

"Geez, you knows a lot, don't yer," he declared.

"Ha! Growing up in the country ya gotta know."

"So you really goin' t'Coolamon tomorrow?"

"Sure am."

"By train?"

"Yup. Leaves 'ere five sharp."

"Mind if I tag along then?" he queried with a raised eyebrow.

"If you wanna waste yer time... But yer gotta be here by five."

"Aye. Cannae say I would be. But... But if I ain't I can meet up with yer at Coolamon Station. Howz that?"

"No skin off my nose."

"So I tell the Chinks I be back Sunday?"

"Yeah. I tell 'em. They know 'bout me. I gotta be back Monday early for work."

"Me too, I guess. So, what's yer Da do?" he asked to change topics, and dig a little deeper into the nature of Clara's family.

"Pa? This and that. Labour, the farms. Sometimes works for the McKinnons."

"An' yer ma?"

"Oh Ma! She runs the place. Has a shop, does this and that, everything, knows every one and what's goin' on. Regular gossip, she is," Clara laughed.

"So I better be careful eh?"

"*Real* careful. If she don't like yer there be no changing her mind. *And* some of her kin. The barking is worse than the bite, though."

"I keep that in min'. And yer last name Keough? Just in case I gotta ask 'bout yous there?"

"Ha! Only four streets, not hard to find. But yeah, me Ma and Pa are Keough. Mine's Lampe—with an E. Robert Oltman Lampe me hubby's name."

"Lampe?" Paddy looked puzzled. "Sounds foreign t'me."

"Is. My great grandfather, or maybe great great grandfather on my husband's side, born in Germany."

"Germany! Geez, that'd make you pop'lar just after the war."

"No one knows it. He born here, so his dad. I'd say that make 'em Australian. Anyways, my hubby fought in the war *against* the Germans. Figure that's where he got the bloody flu."

"Aye. Lot of it over there."

"And you? Irish?"

"Aye. Egan me last. Good ol' Irish name."

"Well, then, Mr. Egan, I be off to bed, then. Don't ferget pick up yer breakfast at the pub. I'll wake you at six. Night."

"Night," Paddy politely answered, but wishing it wasn't the end of their night together.

He liked Clara. She was not only good looking but also friendly and helpful, not like Emily, to whom he was still officially married. Emily had been too young, just wanted fun and things. Couldn't blame her, though, he thought, stuck with the bible-bashing Woodleys after having lost her parents, growing up with not much in the backwaters of Dubbo. And then him settling her down in Warren, more remote than the third-last black stump beyond Bourke. He finished off the first and second bottle of beer during his reminiscences, then went to bed.

Clara tapped on his door then immediately walked in at 6am, holding a cup of tea. She told him to get up and his breakfast was waiting in the kitchen. She'd see him at seven to pick up his lunch. Paddy liked relaxing at night and a lie in during the early morning, but now he was forced to follow Clara's commands and the demands of work on the railway.

By 9 o'clock he arrived at Coolamon with the rest of the rail gang, and set to work. The constant labour and chatting among the labourers made the time fly, so noon lunch came around quickly. Sitting with his mates he opened the canvas bag Clara had given him. There was more than a shilling's worth of sustenance in it: a thermos of tea he could heat up, four sandwiches of cheese and beef, a slice of apple pie, some biscuits, and even an orange.

'Bloody Nora!' he thought to himself. 'This woman's tryin' to fatten me up.' He wondered if she was just being nice, or it was her way of saying she liked him? After all, she *was* single and supporting herself with a kid, at least in part, and a new husband might be what she was after. And there weren't too many young blokes around after the war and epidemic.... 'Not usual to be single with a kid,' he pondered, 'people might think bad.'

The rail gang didn't finish laying new tracks out at Coolamon till after four-thirty; he would be hard pressed to get back to Junee by five even on the train that they had used, so he decided to stay in Coolamon and wait for Clara. He headed over to the town-proper, all four streets of it, and found the one and only single-level pub in the settlement, *The Royal Tavern*.

Buying a beer he sat out the front in the shade, from where he could see the station. He was almost done with his second beer when the 5.30pm train rolled in. He gulped the dregs and strolled the 300 feet to the station. He could see Clara crossing the tracks coming toward him.

"Oy!" he shouted and waved.

"Hello," she answered prettily. "I see yer made it."

"Aye." He told her how he thought it best to wait out here, he couldn't get back to Junee in time. "Pretty lil' town 'ere. With a pub but. Why you cannae work at that?"

"Oh, they don't want no one. Not enough work. C'mon. This way," she nodded forward.

"Oh aye. You wanna beer first but?"

"No thanks. I'm dying for a cuppa tea. My Ma go mad if she smell beer on me breath."

"Aye. I see. Better I have a smoke then."

Clara nodded. "Yes. She don't like drink too much. Bit of a bible-basher you know. Methodist."

"Oh shite. I'm Catholic but."

"Haha! So's she," Clara explained as they walked slowly up the dusty road. "Catholic-Methodist, C of E, whatever the day be, she be it."

"Crikey."

They turned right at the next corner then straight for fifty yards to Methul Street, which was sparse with weatherboard cottages. Clara's was on the corner, an unremarkable place with peeling paint and a mildly rusting tin roof. A dilapidated picket fence marked the boundary of the property. Clara led the way though where the gate used to be, up two steps and banged on the front door of faded brown, then marched straight in without waiting for an answer. Paddy held back on the narrow verandah. A very young child in cloth diapers warbled out, closely followed by a young woman, no doubt Clara's sister judging by her features.

There were all sorts of exciting squealing and squeaking and cooing, as Clara picked up her child, Ruth, Paddy assumed, with ensuing small-talk. She beckoned Paddy to come in to the darkened hallway, then led the way to a kitchen out back. The western evening sun was streaming in through large windows, revealing Mrs. Rachael Keough, no doubt: tall, as was Clara, with the same straight longish nose, similar wide-set eyes but not as endearing, and the same chin, but her mouth very different, drooping down at the corners. Her hair, too, was fair and braided, rather than black. Overall, she was perhaps fifty and rather stern-looking.

"Ma, this is Mr. Egan," Clara introduced him so as not to show any familiarity with the stranger. "He's down from Bowral, working the railway."

"Nice t'meet yer, ma'am. Call me Patrick, or Paddy." He smiled as he tipped his hat.

Rachael Keough looked up from her food preparations and stealingly eyed him then her daughter, who was still holding Ruth.

"Oh aye. My hubby's name Patrick."

Rachael and Patrick Keough. (Date unknown).

"What you doing in Bowral?" She wasn't quite sure at this moment what to say to Paddy, she needed to speak to Clara first, but right now was not the opportune moment.

"Riding out the Spanish flu, ma'am, working a few years, with me brothers."

"Aye. And the war I'd guess?"

"No ma'am, I did my turn in Africa back in nineteen-o, wounded a bit," he added and showed his right hand with some kind of injury.

"This is my baby, Ruth," Clara interceded to diffuse any awkwardness, "and my sis, Hannah, the youngest." She nodded toward the girl standing behind Paddy.

Paddy turned and tipped his hat, discerning a clear similarity to Clara.

"Where yer staying, then?" Rachael intruded abruptly.

Neither Paddy nor Clara knew if the mother meant where Paddy was staying in Junee *or* Coolamon, so Clara had to come to the rescue.

"He's staying at the Chink's boardin' 'ouse, Ma. Just arrived a few days ago." Paddy nodded and smiled. "Said he wanted to see the countryside out this way..."

"Aye, ma'am. A few days off work, look about a bit."

"Ha! Not much to look out here," Rachael affirmed with some bitterness.

"So, orright if Mr. Egan dosses on the lounge a night or two Ma?" Clara pleadingly asked.

Rachael couldn't say no, it was country and Irish hospitality to agree, and she couldn't see how he and Clara might get up to any hanky-panky given that Clara slept with Hannah and the baby. She looked at the pair with a penetrating gaze; there was no doubt what she might be thinking, but finally, after what seemed an interminable delay, said, "Aye. I 'spose you be wantin' tea?" she directed at Clara but also implied Paddy as included.

"Yes, Ma. Please."

Paddy would have given a barrel of whisky to put Ma Keough on his side, but he could see that was not going to be easy; and the only thing he could think of was buying a bottle of rum, but according to Clara, the mother didn't drink!

"C'mon Mr. Egan, I show yer out the back," Clara said to interrupt his thoughts. "Ya can get a nice view of the hills."

Clara led the way out to the back verandah, she still carrying Ruth and he his swag. Rachael nodded to Hannah to go with them; she was determined not to have any scandal in her house.

"Geez Clara," Paddy exclaimed in a whisper when they got outside and were leaning on a railing. "She keeps a tight rein but."

"Oh she's orright. She's just being me Ma. Wait till ya meet me aunts and granny," she laughed.

"Oh Lord!"

" 'Spect you be wantin' a drink by now?"

"Oh aye. A damn stiff one but!"

"Then best be straight up wif her. So long as ya don't get drunk and cause trouble, she won't stop yer." He eyed Clara wondering what she was getting at. "I mean, we can go t'pub and 'ave a wee drop. Maybe Pa'll come. Then you buy 'er a nip of Sherry, she likes that. Say's it warms the cockles, makes her sleep."

"Aye, I see. Medicinal eh?"

"Yup. C'mon, after tea." Clara turned back in and seated herself at the kitchen table, where all dining was done. There was no formal dining room in the small house, just a lounge room and three bedrooms to accommodate four or five siblings plus the parents.

Paddy pulled up a kitchen chair, and Hannah served out a mutton chop with mash, boiled carrots and gravy to each of them, then took little Ruth into her arms.

Paddy dug in, he was hungry and showed his appreciation of Rachael's cooking, as bland as it was, while Clara, Hannah and Rachael chatted about family or local events, as Paddy remained diligently quiet.

Ten minutes in to the meal Patrick Keough came banging in, stopping short at the door when he saw the visitor.

"Hi, Pa," Clara cheerily welcomed him. "This is Mr. Egan, Paddy, or Patrick like you, Pa. He be staying at the Chinks."

"Oh aye. Working Junee are ya?" the father enquired.

Paddy had immediately stood up and put out his a hand to shake, which Patrick reciprocated. "Aye, sir. Building the rail line out this way last few days."

"Where yer from, then?"

"I come down from Bowral, t'work, see the sights."

"Ha!" Rachael interrupted. "I told 'im no sights 'round 'ere."

"That be right. Just scrub an' sheep."

"And chooks," Clara added. "Lots o' chooks."

Rachael placed Mr. Keough's plate on the table, and he took a seat. Paddy could now have a moment to try to size-up the patriarch. He was a fair-sized man, dressed in drab khaki overalls and blue cotton shirt. His hair was black, so that's where Clara got her colour from, Paddy guessed. A short blackish-greying beard covered most of his face. He had deep eyes, close-set, that set him apart from the women's features.

'Looks like the women follow the mother's line, 'cept for the 'air', Paddy thought to himself.

Rachael poured three cups of hot tea, for which Paddy gave a polite thank you, and finished off his chop and veges.

"So how long ya be staying?" Patrick Keough interrupted his thoughts.

"Here? Just a day or so. I'm staying at the Chinks for the duration."

"And 'ow long the duration then?"

"I don't rightly know, sir," he replied, sensing this might be a hard family into which he could make welcome inroads. "So long there's work I be around, and if I can find a nice place t'stay. I was in Bowral for maybe five year," he lied so as to impress the audience with his stability, and to avoid further questions back beyond 1917 or thereabouts.

"Bowral, eh? 'Spect it be cold up there?" he observed more than queried.

"Aye, be that. Frosty in winter to be sure."

"Pa, Mr. Egan and me, we thought t'take a walk into town, show 'im 'round..."

"Aye. That take yers five minutes and all," Rachael chuckled as she clattered the dishes.

"Might stop at t'pub, 'ave a wee drink, maybe get yer a Sherry Ma?"

"Oh aye. That'd be nice," she commented with no obvious delight.

"Aye, we can do that. Friday night, nice air," Patrick affirmed.

"Yer like Sherry, Mr. Egan?" Rachael asked, showing the first sign as far as Paddy could discern of being mildly friendly.

"Aye ma'am. I don't mind a drop now an' 'gen."

Dinner finished, Paddy, Clara, Patrick Keough, and Hannah pushing a pram with Ruth asleep in it, took a stroll down the very quiet and largely deserted streets toward the only pub. Even a main street, Cowabbie St., was mostly silent.

Cowabbie Street, Coolamon.

Patrick led the way to the back area of the pub where ladies could be accommodated, and ordered two beers and two Sherries. Paddy was now getting a little worried about the cost of his amorous adventures toward Clara. He was thankful at least that Rachael hadn't joined them, not only because of her surly tongue but also because at the moment it was one less tongue he had to wet. But, if he was to make any impression on Clara, and ultimately her relatives, he had to spend. To this end he bought a small flask of Sherry for Rachael.

Since he had worked for almost two years in Bowral with few expenses other than beer, tobacco, and contributions to his lodgings, he had managed to save quite a few quid, and he still had a seemingly steady wage coming in at Junee, again with few outlays. He could now afford to enjoy life a little.

Over a few beers at the *Royal Tavern* Patrick Keough came out as an amiable man, hardworking and a disciplinarian, like his wife, but also willing to indulge in life's little pleasures. He and Paddy, with contributions from Clara, prattled on like old friends about work, farming, future developments, social changes, and all things other than religion and politics. The latter two were taken as given.

It was past 9 o'clock when they returned to the house, invigorated by the pleasantries of the evening and the alcohol, and Clara was especially pleased that Paddy had endeared himself toward much of the family.

They all promptly retired for the night, with Paddy having to bunk down on the floor with his swag, as the decrepit lounge was hardly large enough to accommodate two people sitting.

The next morning was an early one, as is common in the rural areas. Rachael had gone off early to attend to her business, what business, though, Paddy was unsure about, a shop so he thought from what Clara had said, and so left Clara to cook up some breakfast. Following that, Paddy and Clara took a walk, again with the toddler in the pram, around the town, and down to a creek. Rachael had indeed been right: there was little to see, and less to do, in this horseless town. This was the closest Paddy could get with Clara, just strolling, sitting, and talking, as a lady and a gentleman. He felt, and perhaps also Clara felt, that greater intimacy could be had back in Junee.

With those thoughts he suggested he had seen enough of Coolamon and should return to the Chinese boarding house that afternoon, giving the excuse that Clara could use her time better with her family, but with promises of meeting up in the 'big' town and perhaps seeking out some entertainment, such as the flicks.

With that arrangement agreed to, despite some consternation on the part of Rachael that Paddy would not be attending Sunday Church with them, he bade farewell to the Keough family and caught the 3 o'clock train back to Junee. This would give him almost a week when Clara came back to more closely court her, to whom he had clearly become attracted not just for her beauty but also for her domestic and familial qualities. She was 23, and he edging over 40, although he had told her he was 36. But it was not uncommon for young women to marry an older man with sensibility, rather than rash randy irresponsible ones, who were few and far between in any case since the war and pandemic.

He got back to Junee in due time, put his swag in his room, and went to the pub, the *Junee Hotel*, chatting with any locals or through-travellers there who would lend an ear. By 7pm he had had enough beer, he thought, and certainly enough boredom for one week. This prompted him to focus his musings on how he missed Clara's company, even though it had been only a few days since they had met. He began to realize that in some ways he had appreciated being married, even to Emily, despite all his adventures and wanderings, and he was not getting any younger, that it might be time to get tethered again, have a companion, someone who would look after him in the foreseeable future. His Da, he thought, expected his mother, Bridget, to be around a lot longer, so when she died in 1914 at a relatively prime age of 50, Da was pretty much left on his own. In some ways lonely. Paddy didn't want that. But here he was, on his own in an unknown town, and on a Saturday night to boot.

But of course the problem for him was Emily: he was still married to her, and a divorce would be expensive, even *if* Emily agreed. In any case, both Paddy and Emily were Catholics, and divorce was simply not-on, so he believed.

With these thoughts, he bought a few bottles of beer and went to the boarding house. Through misrecognized speech and body language he was able to indicate to Mrs. Tsai that he was hungry, and like any Chinese household, there was ready at hand warm soupy stew and rice.

With something in his stomach he sat on the front verandah, with two bottles of beer, barely cold, as his only companions, thinking about Clara, and how to court her. When he was young, with Emily, he was clumsy, naïve, and just bumbled along; but now with his age, and Clara being mature and experienced, he had to handle their relationship with a good show of responsibility and sincerity. But still the problem was he couldn't actually marry her. But even worse, he wouldn't be able to tell Clara *why* they couldn't marry. In the meantime, he had to keep as much of his past life to himself; he didn't want Clara's mother, who was as sharp as a tack, making enquiries, regardless of how long they might take.

Filled with tobacco, beer and misery he turned in at 8pm. The next day he would take a walk around town, find where things were... and wait for Clara.

Sunday went awfully slow for Paddy. He managed with the help of Mr. Tsai to wash his pants, then wandered aimlessly about the township. Everything was closed, except the Church, which he avoided. The streets were deserted. The pubs were closed till 4pm. In the afternoon he wandered down to the small river and sat on the bank, some way from a few families with kids strolling or playing. He used to do that kind of thing with his three kids, with what little creek there was in Warren. Most of the time the children of the village as they got older would just play together, make up activities, catch tadpoles, spiders or rabbits, or he would take them on the handcar to Nevertire to wait for a train to go by, or climb one of the few knolls in that flat desolate place. He was as bored there as were the kids and Emily; she wondered why they lived in the scrub, as she put it, but he had no misgivings at the time of going off working for days at a time, or just travelling, leaving her behind, expecting her to be there on his return, which was her duty and job, right? Every day was the same. 'Guess I can't blame her but, for wanting to go with George Sands, down to Taree and Newcastle,' he remonstrated to himself.

At 4 o'clock he was standing at the door of the *Junee Hotel*, the first to enter. He needed something to dull his senses. But Clara should be back at 5 or thereabouts, so he didn't want to overdo the grog and make out he was a drunken sod with no interest in life around him. He drank slowly, only two schooners, then realized she wouldn't come into the Saloon Bar, she didn't want people to gossip about his and her relationship, as innocent as it was.

It was 6 o'clock when he wandered out the back to the kitchen.

"Oh aye. Yer here, then?" he greeted Clara with apparent casualness, and gave a tout of his hat to Beryl, also present.

"Yup. 'Alf hour ago. Doing the sheets from the weekend," she explained while shoving some dirty sheets into the water tubs ready for overnight soaking.

"Aye. 'Spect so," he answered with some thought, rubbing his chin.

" 'Spect yer be wanting some tea? Or did yer eat at the Chinks'?"

"Aye. I mean, nah, I didn't eat there. Had their mush last night."

"Then c'mon," she directed, "earn ya dinner."

With that she clapped a load of fresh folded sheets and blankets into his arms and carrying a few pillows herself led the way to the back stairs.

They got to the first room; Clara took a bed sheet from him, left him still standing in the hall, and made the bed, then another top sheet and a blanket. It took her only 3 or 4 minutes, then they moved onto the next room, Paddy remaining quiet all the time, not really knowing what to say or do.

In the third room he gave her the last of the sheets and blankets and helped her lay and straighten them. The door was closed and as they both approached it simultaneously he could smell the sweet fragrant soap on her. He took a chance, putting his hand around her waist, hoping she would not push him away. He could feel her softness beneath the cotton dress, sensing she wasn't wearing a corset, thankfully.

"Oy! What's this?" she giggled, looking into his eyes, their bodies touching.

"Oh... Nuffin. Sorry... Just... I missed ya, that's all. Pretty lonesome today."

"Really? Yea, guess everything closed, not much to do 'ere on a Sunday."

"Aye. Not just that but. I miss'd just, you know, havin' someone to talk to, a pretty lady to look at."

"Oh yea. Who might that be?" she teased with a mild chuckle. "C'mon then, we better get you fed, before yer kiss me," she laughed.

"Aye. Wouldn't mind doing that but."

But he was too late. Clara had slipped past him and opened the door, giving him a smile as she led the way back down to the kitchen.

He looked a bit flustered and red-faced, which Beryl noticed but said naught, as Paddy took a seat and Clara served up some roast chicken and mash, with bread and gravy.

He ate the welcome food in silence, not wanting to add to his previous embarrassment, then asked, as he finished with a cup of tea, what time Clara was leaving.

"Soon.... Maybe fifteen. Meet ya outside and yer can walk me 'ome, if yer behave yerself," she laughed.

"Aye. I grab a quick beer first."

With that he paid his thanks, and a shilling, which Clara popped into her apron pocket, and sauntered back to the bar, where he ordered his usual schooner and two long necks.

Fifteen minutes later he went outside and saw Clara barely strolling slowly down the street. He hastened his step and caught up with her.

"Oh there you are!" she exclaimed with feigned surprise turning to see him approaching.

"Aye. Yer were too quick."

"So work tomorrow eh?" she raised as they began to stroll along side by side.

"Aye. Working man I am, regular like," he responded, trying to impress Clara with his steadfastness. "And yerself?"

"Same. Mostly laundry work."

"Aye. Not much of a future in that, I'd think."

"Nope. But what can a girl do, with a baby? Gotta keep some flesh on these bones."

"Aye. And nice flesh it be."

"Oh you cheeky bugger," she laughed. "I ain't no beauty queen, in case you missed it."

"Ha! Aye yer pretty enough. And yer seem to know what yer doin.'"

"Thank you. I know things, too. My Ma dragged me up right, I guess... Cook, sew, wash, stoke a fire..."

"Yer didn't finish school then?"

"Primary. Me Ma don't think a girl need educating, just be a wife and mother. And you?"

"Same. I not much one for schooling, better learnin' riding a 'orse and swagging. Anyhows, the Depression hit when I...," he began, about to say 'when he was 10 years old', which would mean that Clara could calculate his real age from 1880. "When I was a young bairn, so aye, schools closed, every kid looking for a scrap o' work."

"I see. Guess I missed the worst of it then. Eighteen-ninety-eight was my year."

"And a very good year that be, I dare say!"

"Of course!" she laughed, waving her hand in the air like His Majesty.

"Are yer off to Coolamon again this comin' Saturday, then?"

"I am, of course. It the only time I get to see me baby Ruth, and Ma of course."

"Oh."

"Why?"

"Oh, I just thinkin', maybe we could go t'movie palace, or sumfing...?"

"Ahh. *The Globe*, or in Narrandera. I lived there a bit with Robert. That where he buried, bless his soul," she sighed.

"Amen."

"But open only two days a week, I think."

"Have to check the time, then, and what's showing."

"If yer want. But what about work? Might have t'take day off?" she asked.

"Don't yous worry 'bout that. I see t'it. If Paddy wants, Paddy gets," he laughed as they turned the corner to enter the boarding house.

They paid their respects to Mr. and Mrs. Tsai, then followed a fast-established routine of having a wash followed by drinking on the steps of the front verandah. Paddy tried to push the idea of going to see a film, but although Clara was willing, she told him most films were old silent ones in black-and-white, and the movie palace was open only two days or nights a week.

Then he suggested they go for some kind of picnic down the river, but Clara pointed out the problem of their work schedule, and her having to go to Coolamon every weekend....

"So, yer can't skip a visit?" he almost pleaded, wanting just to have a date with her, to be together for more than an hour at the pub or at the boarding house.

"Nah. My Ma 'spects me, and when can I see my baby, eh?"

"Aye. I know that but. But can yer not come back Saturday night, so we can go for a stroll or sumfing?" Paddy was racking his brain to think what else they could do, that she might want to do, in this one-horse town of Junee.

"Oh, sounds like a date then," she giggled, and blushed.

"Call it what yer want, my dear. Just yer the only person I know 'ere, and I fond o' talking to yer."

"Just talking?"

"I cannae say. I like yer companionship, as the toffs say."

"Maybe. I gotta think. Ma'd get pretty cross with me if I didn't show up."

"Ok, so just tell 'er yer gotta work Sunday, some special do on...? Come back Saturday."

"I think about it, ok."

"How 'bout we go to Wagga? It not far."

"It's a big place, me Pa told me. My hubby, Robert, born there, too. But what's there? And how long? It's very far!" she exclaimed with a host of questions and concerns.

"Nah, not far. One 'our maybe, by train. Just find somefing 'citing to do, a movie or dance, nice place to eat..."

"We come back the same day?"

"If yer want. I tell yer what, next Sat'dee I go there, and 'ave a look about, report back t'yer?"

"Ha! Makes me sound like the boss."

"Aye. You *are* the boss, Clara," he declared as he put his free arm around her shoulder. He held it there while he took a slug of his beer, and she didn't seem to want to push him away.

"I gotta think about it, see what Ma says if I don't visit one day…"

Paddy didn't know what else he could say or do to persuade her; his past courting days were just natural and easy, and the girls—for they were girls—also were bored in their rural hick-towns and wanted to have fun, too, especially in the 1920s. But he wasn't a lad anymore, nor was she a girl. At 23 she would be looking for stability, respectability and building something together, with a partner. He would like to take her to Sydney, experience the city life, but that would mean leaving her daughter for a week or more, and her job, as well as he losing a week's pay and spending quite a few quid. For the moment he was stuck with mundaneness and distance from anywhere that could break the spell of solitude.

Clara finally went to sleep, telling Paddy to finish off his beer and pick up his lunch at the pub before going to work the next day, Monday. Work. Work, work, work, that's all he did, and nothing much to show for it.

And that's what he—and she—did: work. He picked up his lunch from Clara at the pub, paid a shilling which she put in her apron pocket, and then went to work. He asked his mates about things to do in Junee and Wagga, some shrugged, others suggested a few places and things in Wagga. He learnt that a train left 8am sharp next Saturday, and a return trip at 5pm, so he would make the journey, pay to have a good time for himself, then report back to Clara on Sunday.

So for the next week he worked, met up with Clara each evening, washed his clothes, and drank, just as she worked also: mopping floors, changing linen, cooking meals, and not much more that was fun in any sense.

On Saturday Clara of course visited her family in Coolamon, and Paddy put into action his plan of visiting Wagga Wagga—although everyone called it just Wagga. The train trip of almost 90 minutes was more than the hour he expected, although he didn't worry except insofar that if Clara came with him, she might be impatient; it would detract from the time they could spend together actually *doing* something more meaningful.

Paddy spritely walked about the bustling town, asking cabbies—long before Cook's tours reached Australia—questions about what there might be good to do with a young lady on his arm, places to see, restaurants of some repute but not extravagant, and even some low-key hotels or boarding houses. Overall he liked the feel of the town, its energy, activity, variety, its bustling of people going about their business and even the traffic. This was a place he could see himself living in, a far cry from Bowral and most especially Narromine and Warren; and it would give Clara a vibrant lifestyle.

He noted down in a small notebook that he had acquired some of these things such as the Botanic Gardens; she would like that, he thought, pretty, natural, quiet. And one or two Cathedrals which might appeal to her religious bent. Then there were novel attractions such as the cheese factory, a delicacy he and she perhaps had not tasted; then something exciting such as the horse racing and a forthcoming folk festival, much like a circus he thought; and finally, a quiet time together, so she could reflect on his sacrifices for her: boating on the Murrumbidgee. He stopped at various pubs throughout his ambling, and so enjoying himself by 5 o'clock he had plumb forgot his return train.

'Aye, then nothing to do but, just enjoy the night life of this sprightly town', he thought. He had another beer, then, sensibly, realized he had to eat, or would end up drunk and useless.

A fella he met at the last pub, and quickly became mates with, suggested they eat at a cheap but wholesome café he knew, so Paddy couldn't turn down that offer. Over tea of toasted tomato sandwiches and fish this feller, Henry by name, suggested they spend a few bob on satisfying themselves with some women. It was only £2—more than a week's wage. He had no shame. He was not committed to Clara, *yet*, and it had been a long time since he had had a woman. But the next morning after dossing in a cheap boarding house, it did indeed make him realize how he missed all the trappings that went with being married. He missed that with Emily.

Feeling less rich money-wise at least, Paddy jumped a freight train back to Junee at 10am. It would give him time to spruce himself up and look sober before Clara arrived back in town about 5 or 6 o'clock.

But now his mind-set had changed somewhat, to be more determined. Clara was a nice, friendly and respectable young woman, and attractive, a woman who offered everything he could want, and that he had forsaken for almost 5 years. He had fallen in love, not just with Clara, but with the idea of what Clara could mean to him. She could offer companionship, regular meals, housework, respectability, and intimacy...not necessarily in that order. All the things that still counted in the 1920s.

While the rest of the world, apart from Germany perhaps, was kicking up its collective heels having survived the war to end all wars and an influenza pandemic, in rural NSW the traditional values of hard work, land ownership, family, love, kinship, offspring and survival if not progress held sway. Things were a'changing, but also old ways of thinking and doing still remained the same. Both he and Clara grew up on the values of the late 19th century, in rural places that were close, where kinship was important, and people survived physically and morally with a partner, working together.

Emily was supposed to provide that, but perhaps she had been too young, as was he! And perhaps ironically Paddy's gallivanting did not endear commitment. Now he had to get his life back on the moral rails, and Clara might be the one to help him achieve that.

As usual Paddy waited in the evening at the bar of the *Junee Hotel*; at 6pm he slipped out to the back kitchen.

"Hello," Clara cheerily greeted. "How'd it go?"

"Great. Aye, good. Lots to tell yer," he smiled. But he said no more in front of Beryl.

Clara served him up with his dinner, now a frequent engagement, and she slipped the one shilling again into her apron pocket. He finished up, downed a cup of tea amidst small talk, then returned to the bar for one last drink, again buying two bottles of beer to take back to his lodgings. As was now routine, he waited for Clara outside, soon enough walking together back to the Tsai household.

Joining him on the front steps for a beer she pushed for a full description of his trip to Wagga.

"Aye, it was grand. Lots of shops, even 'arcade. And a botany garden, yer can walk frough for naught and see all dem flowers. Y'd like that, I be sure."

"Nice. What else?"

"Oh there be markets, big. Yer can buy anything, fish, vege, meat, chickens... A few big churches too, just in case yer need to pray," he chuckled.

"And why might I wanna do that?" she looked at him with a cockeyed frown.

"Dunno. Just thought... Anyways, they big. *Real* big. And there be horse racing, maybe we can win a pretty penny or two."

"Sure. Why not, but I don't know nuffin 'bout betting and racing. What else?"

"Aye, there be a cheese factory. You ever tasted good cheese? There be one in Bowral when I there."

Clara shook head.

"And a zoo, and some kinda carnival, and nice caff's. And people everywhere, autos too, and buses. It be a big place, Clara, with lots to do."

"Oh aye," she sighed wishfully. "Seems better than this dump. But we can't afford live there I bet."

"Maybe. Maybe they pay a good wage there. Get a 'ouse. Live on the outer a bit. Cheap rent. Get a bicycle," he dreamed out loud.

"Huh? You want me to live with ya?" Clara belatedly realized. "We not even married yet."

"Aye. I just thinkin' ahead. Anyways, yer don't have to be married to live together. Modern times, yer know."

Clara looked at Paddy skeptically. Even though she was ten years younger than him, her morals, her Ma's morals, were well in advance.

"My Ma and Pa would go crazy if they hear yer speaking like that, Mr. Egan!"

"Lotsa folk do," he whined. "All depend on intention. If they *intend* to get married, then nuffin stopping 'em shackin' up together."

"Oh fine, and then what? What happens if they don't get married after all?"

"But you wanna get married, don't yer? I mean, again?"

"Dunno. Maybe. If the right fella come along."

"Fine then. But what say yer we spend a day in Wagga?"

"I gotta think on it, ask me Ma. Anyway, I got no money to spare."

"I can help yer out there. I got a job and no 'spenses like you, like, no kid. I just pay me board 'ere and food, a few beers, tobaccy. I'm a simple man but."

"I think about it. Going to bed. See ya tomorrow."

And with that she heaved herself up and left Paddy to think over his desires and strategies.

Was it too early to tell her he loved her, he pondered? Did he in fact love her? Did she love him, or even like him? Or would she just laugh in his face? He couldn't work her out, but just thought she *should* want what he wanted, and what every young woman wanted and needed.

For the remainder of the week Clara and Paddy followed their established routines, meeting in the evening, walking home together, sharing beers and conversations, going to their separate rooms. She was as glad of the evening company as was he, and also began to yearn for a better, livelier life. But she didn't know what to think of Paddy Egan: he was a nice enough bloke, she thought, polite, clearly interested in her, enough to meet her family leastways, seemed to have work, the kind no worse than that of her Pa, and did seem to like his drink although to date he had never been drunk or quarrelsome.

He was of course older than her by 13 years, if 36 was his age, but that was no big deal: her former husband, Robert Lampe, was also older than her by almost 14 years. And her sister, Nellie, had married at age 17 George Gee in Narrandera when *he* was 45, making an age difference of 28 years!

Despite what Clara knew of Paddy, it was what *he* had told her and her own observations; she really didn't know his *family* background, having come from Dubbo. With Robert, however, and also Nellie's husband, they were raised by large families in the Narrandera and Wagga areas, with whom the Keoughs would have mingled, and about whom Rachael and Patrick Keough would have enquired, for sure.

Indeed, Clara's mother had said very little to Clara about Paddy after his brief visit to Coolamon, but seemed rather surly toward him—but then, Rachael was pretty much surly toward everyone, so it was difficult to know her mother's true attitude and thoughts.

But, suspecting Paddy might be interested in Clara, Rachael wrote to her other daughter, Nellie, who was then living in Warren. She mentioned Clara and her 'friend', Paddy, and enquired if Nellie knew anything of his family, the Egans. She replied quite quickly, saying that there used be an Egan family in Narromine but had never met them personally, and she did know that several years past an Emily Egan in Warren had a baby girl soon after her own arrival in the township in 1909, but that woman had moved to Cobar. She went on to say she heard a story that Emily later married a Mr. Sands and moved to the coast of NSW. So all this was rather vague, but did suggest that if Emily was somehow connected with Paddy Egan, she wasn't *married* to him, for how else could Emily, according to Nellie, marry Mr. Sands? Ergo, Paddy was not married—well, at least not to Emily. But Rachael kept this information to herself.

But for now, what was Clara to do? She liked the idea of getting out and having some fun. She had married Robert at age 19, just when she was beginning to blossom, and soon after became pregnant with Ruth, to which she didn't object, but the added burden of having to raise a child as a widow had robbed her of all opportunities youth might have offered. She was now of necessity living back home with her parents and some siblings, working at a mundane job to support her child and contribute to the household income, stuck between two small towns, Junee mediocre at best.

She knew Paddy fancied her, and although she hoped he wanted what she wanted, she was also experienced enough to know men wanted to fulfill a common desire among men. But was he willing to commit to a permanent relationship to satisfy that desire? And was she willing enough to test it? It's not that she had her virginity to lose, of course, but the economic and social scandal that could ensue if she got pregnant, again, and this time with Paddy and he did a bunk.

Perhaps an element of her youth, or her wayward spirit, got the better of her, so in the end she thought she could trust Paddy, initially, have some fun, and try to ensure that she did not get pregnant, for she well knew that if he was to shout her a day out in Wagga, maybe even a day and a night, then she would have to come across. It could be worse, she figured: some young horny buck with several girls on his sleeve, who would most likely take *no* responsibility without being at the barrel end of a shotgun.

So, after about two weeks of thinking and procrastinating, and more evening conversations, she told Paddy of her decision to go to Wagga with him. She told her mother, as Paddy had suggested, that she had to help out at the *Junee Hotel* for some vague special function the next Saturday, all day and evening, and might be able to get to Coolamon only on the Sunday for a short time. She added to this story when she told Paddy that he would have to help bump up her wages for that week, for surely her mother would ask about the extra day's pay...

A week later, early Saturday, they caught the Junee train into Wagga. Paddy didn't know what to bring with him, so he brought his swag, his whole kit and caboodle. Clara had a small brown suitcase with sufficient change of clothing for two days, and had made some sandwiches the night before. She was quite excited, as was Paddy for the same reason of doing something unboring.

The next problem Paddy faced was indeed their luggage; it was hardly fitting to troop about the 'city' lumbering suitcases and swags, so he suggested they check them in at the cloakroom of the Station, or check into a cheap boarding house and leave their things there. Clara didn't muck around, saying she may want to 'freshen up' during the day, so they should find a boarding house. This took Paddy by pleasant surprise.

That done, they first took a stroll through the Botanic Gardens, then the zoo adjacent. It was well past noon by the time they splurged on a cab out to the horserace track. Paddy asked around and observed, then decided he'd follow some guy's advice and put a quid on a horse, rejoicing when he got £5 in winnings. By this time, having only nibbled on Clara's pre-packed sandwiches, they were pretty hungry, so caught a bus back into town and found a seafood restaurant that for them seemed a bit plush.

A few hours at the pub followed, with Clara keeping a tab on Paddy's consumption, as she had only a Sherry or two.

Clara was used to waking up early, and she did the next morning, slipping out of the bed quietly so as not to wake Paddy. She went downstairs and scrounged a cuppa from the landlady, then another for Paddy which she took up to him.

She didn't want to say anything about last night, and Paddy thought it best to keep quiet, let her initiate any issue. But she just told him to hurry up and get dressed, breakfast was waiting for them downstairs and they had a train to catch.

At 10.30 Paddy alighted at Junee, taking his swag and Clara's suitcase to the Tsai boarding house, leaving Clara with just a handbag, inside of which was a new toy for Ruth.

While Paddy had a lie down and later changed clothes to go to the pub at 4pm, Clara continued on to Coolamon, where her mother was none too pleased with her not coming home on the Saturday. But Clara quickly placated her by handing over some of her wages and an extra ten-bob, part of the horseracing winnings.

But Rachael was not completely appeased. "Where's yer man friend, then? He ain't been out to visit a long time," she added with some mild sneering.

"Sleeping, I guess. Not seen 'im since Fridee arvo."

"Oh aye. Then he not wooing yer but?"

"No Ma. We just friends. Eats at the pub sometimes, we just chat in the kitchen at the 'ouse, that's all. Why you asking Ma?"

"No reason. He single ain't he?" Rachael unexpectedly asked.

"Yea. From what he tells me."

" 'Ow old he then?"

"I dunno Ma, I think be 'bout thirty-something."

"So what yer think o' him?"

"He's ok Ma. Polite. Works steady. Needs some new clothes but. Why Ma?"

"No reason. Just thinking if you be considerin' 'im...? Yer know, been a while since Robert passed, a young woman gotta have a man look after her."

"I know Ma. But some fellers don't wanna get straddled with another man's kid."

"Ain't your fault. If he loves yer he 'cept the kid."

"Fine Ma, I'll ask him," she teased her mother.

Rachael fell to a few moments of silence apart from her bustling about the kitchen.

"What *you* think of 'im then, Ma?" Clara finally asked, boldly breaking the silence with the question that had been on her mind awhile.

"Ha! I only clapped eyes on 'im once, don't know much but what he told when he be 'ere."

Clara was at a bit of a loss as to why her mother was suddenly asking all these questions, most especially the day after she had made love to Paddy and had lied to her mother about her work. It was as if Rachael had a spy in Wagga, or could just smell something fishy.

"So... Ma... What would you think if he wanted to marry me?"

"Not my place. Yer old enough to know. If he decent and hardworking, treat yer right..."

"And not a piss-pot, right?" she queried her mother with a stare.

"Aye. Don't mind a man 'ave a drink sometimes with his mates, but there be a limit."

The inquisition petered out as Clara attended to Ruth who was wailing and wanted some attention. Then at 4pm she had an early tea and strolled down to the station to catch the 5 o'clock train back to Junee, turning over in her mind what her mother had been getting at, and what in fact might be next with Paddy from here on in.

Clara met up with Paddy at the Tsai house for their usual evening drinks, sitting close to him, telling him about Rachael asking questions, which worried Paddy a little, but he said nowt. He would see how things played out. But she also added that her parents were moving back to Ducker Street in Junee the next week or so, and Clara would go live with them so as to save money on rent at Tsai's. This worried Paddy.

"Oh aye," he sighed. "So we cannae sit an' 'ave a wee drink at night then?"

"Not as bad as that," she assured him. "We can still do that, and you can visit. And I be in town on Saturday and Sunday, so we can go for a walk or whatever..."

"Aye. That be nice. Still... Not the same, having yer all t'meself."

"Oh do you now?"

"You know what I mean. When yer livin' wif them, yer not be wif me."

"Oh wow. Sounds like someone's fallin' in love," she chuckled. "I'll be just 'round the corner, Mr. Paddy."

Meantime, he and Clara returned the next day—and for the rest of the working week—to the routine drudge of work. By the Saturday the Keoughs were indeed on the move. They had borrowed a horse-drawn wagon to drag all their furniture and personal belongings into Junee, with the women of the family carrying what they could on a train trip in. This included Clara, who had gone out to help. Paddy waited in Ducker Street to help unload, which did not go unacknowledged. But this change in residence, the packing and unpacking, left Clara too busy for two days to attend to any needs of Paddy.

It was only on the following Monday evening that she walked home with him to the boarding house, and had a farewell drink and chat. He helped carry her meagre belongings the few hundred yards to Ducker Street, and kissed her goodnight, amidst promises to walk home with him again tomorrow, and every night if he wanted. She said she would make excuses to visit him at the Tsai house on evenings when she could. So, instead of the steady, almost predictable arrangement they had had for a few weeks, the relationship had now become somewhat furtive and disjointed.

For the next few weeks she would pop out to visit Paddy at the boarding house after Ruth had been put to bed, telling her parents she was checking on Paddy, to see if he needed anything, or paying some kind of courtesy visit to the Tsai family. Paddy now always kept a flask of Sherry for her, so as to avoid the smell of beer on her breath, which undoubtedly Rachael would detect. On other occasions, but not too often, she would invite Paddy home for a short visit, for a cuppa, and then walk him back to the boarding house. By one means or another they would be with each other to the satisfaction of Clara, at least, although not always sufficient for Paddy.

This arrangement continued for a few weeks, perhaps six weeks after the trip to Wagga, until Clara noted that she had missed her menstrual period. It was now early September, Spring of 1920. Another month went by, and again Clara failed to have her period. There could only be one explanation, and she had to tell Paddy and work out a plan before her mother would recognize the signs of motherhood.

It was a Saturday evening when they took a walk down by the river; it was not an easy task to break the news, she had no idea how he might take it, how he might act subsequently.

At first Paddy was stunned, speechless. Typically as a male, and from ignorance of these womanly matters, he questioned her certainty.

"Are you sure?" he of course asked, rather than give overly excited congratulations.

"Of course I'm sure. What else could it be? I'm not sick ya know!"

"But it's mine?"

"Who else? What are you suggesting!?" She understandably grew angry, realizing the inference he was making.

"I don't know... I mean... Yer might have a boyfriend, or somefing...," he shrugged in defence.

"Well I don't! And it seems you ain't me boyfriend either!"

"Don't get mad. I just askin'," he sheepishly whined.

"You really have no idea, d'ya, what you just said!"

"I dunno, I mean, well..."

"No! I don't have a bloody boyfriend!" Clara began to sob.

"I'm yer boyfriend, then, Clara. A man's gotta take responsibility. So it mine, I guess..."

"Of course it yours, I don't go sleeping 'round yer know!"

"Aye, ok ok. So what we do?"

"We have the baby of course. And we have to marry."

This suggestion spooked Paddy no end. He was *willing* to marry Clara, but he *couldn't*. He was still married to bloody Emily! And he couldn't tell her *that*. So how was he to get out of this spot?

"Aye. But, maybe we need think a bit first, like, see if it a dud...."

"It ain't no dud, Mr. Egan."

"Aye, I know, I just saying, maybe we have the kid first, see it alright... Beside, gotta save money for a wedding, rent a 'ouse, and 'ospital bills and all..."

This was, fortunately for Paddy, enough to placate Clara, it seemed to her that he was saying he *would* marry her, but just needed time to figure things out. For a moment he thought he *could* marry her, maybe no one would find out he was still married to Emily, but *if* they did... Well, he thought that'd be a hanging offence.

Clara cut short his thoughts: "So you *do* wanna marry me?"

"Aye. I marry you. Been wanting to marry yer for a long time. Just we gotta plan this yer know. Like I said, things to plan," he vaguely remonstrated.

The conversation went on like this for awhile longer, Paddy now saying all the right things, although continuously suggesting they need wait and plan, but in the meantime they could set up house together; Clara liked the latter idea, it seeming to suggest he was serious about being with her, looking after her, that he wasn't going to do a bunk.

"When it due?" he casually asked.

"About June, I think. 'Bout seven, eight months."

"Aye, then we got time find a 'ouse. 'Spect yer have to stop work sometime."

Over the ensuing weeks Paddy and Clara regularly met in the evenings and took a stroll through the gardens by the river in Hobbin Park of Junee. After a while they began looking for a small house to rent, and found one in George Street, just a stone-throw from her mum's place. When Clara announced this to her family it confirmed what Rachael had long suspected about the pregnancy. But she said nothing derogatory, being of the same mind as Clara that, since Paddy had remained in town the last few months and he and Clara were organizing to live together, then he was serious.

But Rachael was less convinced that Paddy would actually marry Clara, concerned the child would be born out of wedlock, technically illegitimate. When she pushed Clara and Paddy about this state of affairs, Paddy again remonstrated that now, even more, they could not get married because of the 'additional' expenses of paying rent, buying furniture and 'baby things', and that Clara would be giving up work shortly, thus having to rely on just Paddy's wage. In the end, they all had to accept what was less than satisfactory, and settle down into a rather mundane routine of daily domestic life in a one-horse rural town.

On June 20 1921 Clara's second child was born at the Keough home in Ducker Street, where Rachael and a midwife and Clara's sister could attend to the needs. The baby was a boy, Walter, or Wally as he came to be known, and he and Clara were both healthy.

The birth registration showed Wally to be 'illegitimate', and his surname as Lampe. Rachael had insisted on this, saying that by keeping the name of her first husband, Robert Lampe, people in the future might simply assume he was also the father, or in the least that Clara did not have two husbands. Clara was agreeable to this naming, also adding that until Paddy married her, she was still a Lampe and could not legitimately give Wally the name of Egan. Paddy had no say in this, but was nevertheless agreeable in any case, as it excluded his name from any official documents and hence possible scrutiny as to his whereabouts or marital status.

Four the next 5 years, almost, Paddy and Clara settled into marital 'bliss', raising both Ruth and Wally, with Clara working only when she could get piecemeal work, and that only when either Rachael, Hanna or Paddy could babysit. Even though Paddy had consistent work, money was always short: four mouths to feed, rent to pay, outgrown clothes to replace, and a tendency for Paddy to spend too much on tobacco and liquor. The latter increased as he became more and more bored with the mundane life of Junee, and not helped by the often back-breaking work of a labourer on the railways. He could tolerate that at age 41, but now he was nearing 45, and after work more frequently spent longer times at the pub, to ease not only the physical pain but also the emotional stress of all too familiar domestic life and boredom. It wasn't a case so much of domestic violence as domestic avoidance. Oh he still loved Clara and cherished what she did for him and their family, but he was restless and frustrated, frustrated that he couldn't break free of the blandness of their lives. He often recalled the good time in Wagga when he was courting Clara, but even a repeat of that was now out of reach.

During these five years there were of course the usual celebrations that disrupted the mundaneness of their lives—Christmas, baptisms, weddings, funerals, public holidays, most of which included visits from the Keough relatives: the Smarts in Coolamon, the Croke clan in Goulburn, Keoughs from Gundagai, and so on. There were no Egans in attendance other than Paddy himself because, as he said, he had no relatives in the region, and indeed no siblings at all—although Clara did recall him once saying he had brothers in Bowral. Of course people wondered about this: a single man, born on a ship on the other side of the country, with no obvious local connections, who said his parents were dead, not even siblings in far away places—very unusual, so many thought, not to have a brother or sister or two, given that it was customary for NSW rural folk to have large families. Robert Lampe, for example, had as many as 13 sibs; the local McKinnon family was very large, Patrick Keough had *quite* a few siblings, and even Rachael had at least 6 children. Paddy often distracted any queries about this by regaling listeners with extravagant tales of his gallantry in Africa during the 2nd Boar War, making the point that he was so keen and loyal that he had lied about his age to join up in 1900, at age 16, making him 4 years younger than he actually was.

And such holidays as they had were often embellished further under the influence of the free liquor on these occasions, so not only were some seeds of doubt sown amongst his kin-by-marriage, but also the view that Paddy was a bit of an opportunistic drunkard. Despite these flaws, he did maintain a reasonably steady work ethic, treating Clara right at home and never wandering from marital loyalty to her.

Clara had long before warned him that if he thought Rachael was hard-nosed, then she presented more as a pussy-cat compared to some of the Smart's older women, one in particular commonly call Granny Smart, who had a biting tongue like that of a viper. She took no liking at all to Paddy, for which he could not fathom any reason, and at a later date was to provide a stinging comment on Paddy's character and care for his family.

But all this did not stop Clara's and Paddy's household from growing. In 1924 she again became pregnant, delivering another boy, Jack, on May 31, 1925. As with Wally some 4 years earlier, Rachael insisted he be given Lampe as a surname, and Clara again agreed, putting pressure on Paddy to marry her if he wanted his children to carry his heritage.

Then came some good news, quite unexpected.

A letter arrived from his father, although Paddy didn't say who it was from, because he had always maintained that Anthony Egan was dead. It had been forwarded by Arthur Egan, Paddy's brother, in Bowral, so didn't reach Junee until late January, 1926. Anthony had written barely a note, saying that Paddy's legitimate wife, Emily Oakley, had died in Newcastle on November 18, 1925. Anthony included a newspaper clipping of the inquest, adding that Mrs. Woodley had come to visit him to give the news, not knowing where Paddy was.

Paddy put the papers securely in his pocket and went to the pub.

He was quietly happy, indeed very happy, not at Emily's death per se, but by the realization that now he could marry Clara. He read the letter and newspaper clip over and over again, which noted that Emily was 40 years old when she passed, living with her 'husband' George Sands and had 5 children by him. Apparently she was epileptic and had suffered a fit and thus a fall down the steps of their house, fatally injuring her head. It was odd, he thought, in reading the newspaper report, that George Sands was almost reluctant to acknowledge Emily as his *wife*; then he realized: of course they weren't married; just as Paddy couldn't remarry without a divorce, so too was Emily stuck in a de facto relationship.

After a few beers he realized he had to stay as sober as he could, or he might blurt out the news to Clara while in a stupor. He also realized now that if he officially married Clara, then maybe her kin might be more inclined to treat him, and his kids, more kindly. He went home after four schooners to break the news.

"Aye, Clara, I got some news fer yer," he slurred.

"Oh yeah. What might that be? You win on the 'orses? Is that what that letter 'bout?" she steadfastly quizzed him, standing with arms folded against her chest.

"Aye. Sorta. Anyways, we gonna get married."

"Ah aye. And when that be? When the cows come 'ome?" she rebuked him in disbelief.

"Nay, this year, darling, this year. You set t'date. Talk yer ma. I leave t'yer. But, simple, mind. Nuffin too fancy."

"You're drunk Paddy. What brought all this on?"

"Just... Just don't look a giff 'orse in de mouf. Yer wanna get married or no?"

"Ok. But I believe it tomorrow when you say it sober."

The next day Paddy confirmed his proposal, and Clara had a word with her Ma, who soon enough came to their house to interrogate Paddy. It took a bit of convincing, but finally the two women, and eventually the rest of the clan, came to accept he was serious, and began to make plans. A few weeks later Paddy was even more convincing when he took Clara to the local pawnshop and suggested she buy a wedding ring. It was all a bit unorthodox and cheap, but better than nothing, and keeping in mind that Paddy insisted on a simple occasion.

Twelve

Junee 1926 — 1932

Clara chose August 28, 1926, primarily to give the couple time to plan and save for the auspicious event. And so it came to pass at St. Luke's Church of England, Junee, at which Paddy informed the Officiate that he was born in 1888 and hence was 38 rather than being 46 years old, that he was born on a ship 'somewhere off Albany, WA', that his father Anthony Egan was deceased and his mother, Bridget Egan nee: Ryan, was alive, when in fact his mother had died in 1914 and his father was still alive in Dubbo. For some reason Paddy didn't want his heritage and past to catch up with him.

There was a respectable reception at the Keough's home, which provided more space and better logistics for cooking, catering and kept the children out of the way. Several of the Keough clan as well as the Smarts attended, among whom some wondered why there were no kin of Paddy's present; surely he had had time to notify them...?

What honeymoon there was took place in a local hotel, at least giving Clara, and to a lesser extent Paddy, a break from domestic duties and childcare of now three children stretching from 7 years old to barely one—Ruth, Wally and Jack.

Subsequently, life returned to normal as much as it could, at least until late 1929 when dark economic clouds beckoned formidable change and poverty. But unaware of that pending doom, Clara once again, by accident rather than by design, gave birth to two girls, twins, on June 4, 1928. One of the babies was still-born, the surviving girl was named Lillian May Egan. Finally, Clara had bestowed her new husband's name on the child.

By this time, also, before the official onset of the Great Depression and the sudden Stock Exchange crash of October 1929, the economic and labour situation had been declining, particularly in rural areas of Australia in that wheat and wool prices had dropped, and other commodities experienced overseas competition. Unemployment was on a rapid rise. So both Rachael Keough and Paddy Egan with their respective families moved from Junee to Old Junee, where rents were cheaper. This was hardly surprising, given that Old Junee was far less than even a two-donkey town, as Beryl would say, consisting of all of 5 streets and a railway station on the Western line 5 miles west of Junee. It had never been much, originally being a stagecoach stop between Temora, Wagga and Cootamundra, eventually becoming a spot on the branch line to Hay, having at various times a small shop, a butcher and even a pub. To a limited extent it serviced the surrounding sheep farmers, and particularly egg farming.

Paddy continued with his work on the railways, at times intermittent, as much as he could, and any other casual work he could get, while Clara was encouraged to breed chooks for eggs. But for all their efforts, matters took a turn for the worst in 1930, just when unemployment was soaring, to reach a peak of 32% by 1932.

And Paddy was among them. There were draconian cutbacks by government in capital works and State employment; and industries were less than taking up the slack, they also were letting staff go. Unable to work, unable to pay rent, Paddy succumbed to pennilessness, barely scraping by on the 'susso'—the 'succulence' that government and charities provided to the beggars. As a result Paddy's family had to move back to Junee, not to a weather-proof house, but to a self-built makeshift lean-to of old timber and tin, and a weather-worn canvas tent. He joined hundreds of other likewise families in what became known as *The Triangle*, a vacant block of land wedged in between Junction Street, Main Street and Castle Street to the north of the town and respective parallel rail lines, right behind the *Junee Hotel* where he had first set eyes on his beloved wife, Clara. A road on one side, a rail line running through the middle, and across that a miserly creek that supplied water. At least here, Paddy thought, he was closer to any work opportunities that *might* arise.

We're on the susso now,
We can't afford a cow,
We live in a tent,
We pay no rent,
We're on the susso now.
(Nat Museum of Aust.)

While the kids in *The Triangle* may have playfully danced to such a ditty, there was yet worse to come.

Already laden with 4 children, Clara again became pregnant, delivering on July 25 1930 a second daughter, Marjorie Egan (or Marj as she came to be called). It was either this pregnancy, or all the combined pregnancies, or perhaps just the hard life endured, that caused Clara to become somewhat chronically ill. This of course left Paddy to undertake much of the day to day care of ostensibly his 5 children, detracting from his ability to even look for work. Luckily, Rachael was able to take on much of the burden of baby Marj's early days.

But, just as one might think things could get no worse, Clara's sister, Nellie Gee, in Warren also took ill. Rachael was now of the belief that many of the women in her line of the family carried some flaw—well before genetics were understood—since she was soon to learn that yet another daughter, Dorrie Smith (who had been married to Lawrence Smith locally, but deceased in 1928) would soon die in 1931 in Wagga. She was barely 31 years of age.

But for now, in October 1930 Nellie Gee's husband telegraphed Rachael that her eldest and perhaps most favoured daughter was very ill, and so Rachael and Patrick set off in a car belonging to a wealthy relative, to Warren. Unfortunately, by the time they had reached Parkes some 200 miles away, after more than 6 hours on bad and muddy roads, news reached them that Nellie, at age 38, had already died, and because the roads were now impassable after recent heavy rains, they returned to Junee.

At the same time Clara had been admitted to Junee hospital, and said to be in a poor condition. Despite Paddy's best efforts and great concern, as were Rachael and Patrick also, Clara (Keough/Lampe) Egan passed away in Junee Hospital on January 22, 1931, at age 33. Clara was buried in Junee Cemetery, the whole family together unable to provide a headstone in such harsh economic times.

This loss was devastating. Rachael took charge of matters, as Paddy had no stamina and no local contacts. She suggested that Marj stay with herself, as she was barely 6 months old, but later at age 2 she would be sent to one of the Keough's relatives by the name of Smart, in Gundagai. The two boys and Ruth went with Rachael and Patrick, who had recently moved also due to their dire economic straights to Goulburn where they shared accommodation with relatives, while Lillian, who was now two-and-a-half years old, would stay with Paddy.

Rachael's thinking on this dispersion was that Ruth, Wally and Jack were of the true Lampe name, in one sense the kids of Clara's original marriage, and although Marj was an Egan, she was simply too young to be given over to relatives or left with Paddy. This left Lillian, an Egan, to be the sole responsibility of Paddy Egan. But it also reflected the underlying attitude of the Keoughs toward Paddy as an outsider, as largely an unskilled, irresponsible drunkard and opportunist, who had never quite fitted in and gave their daughter, Clara, no hope for betterment.

Quietly, the Keoughs blamed Paddy for Clara's death, by having so many children—ironic given that so many rural families had so many children—and by eventually having to live in a makeshift dwelling in *The Triangle*, although this, too, was no fault of his. These factors, and the idea that he was a non-Church goer and somewhat of a drunkard led Granny Smart, one of the Keough relatives, to declare in private that 'everyone would have been better off if Paddy Egan had stayed in Africa.'

In an emotional stupor Paddy tried to manage as best he could, living at *The Triangle*, where everyone tried as much as possible to help others, which was at best minimal. Although Paddy got the '*susso*' from time to time, it was never enough, and he continued to look for even a half day of work in Junee, as well as jumping the infrequent trains to Old Junee, Coolamon and a little beyond to ask for work or handouts. He couldn't take Lillian with him, and couldn't leave her too long at *The Triangle*, although some kind folks there would try to take care of her.

But soon winter would be approaching, and his makeshift dwelling would be too cold to be habitable. So, in autumn he began swagging, taking Lillian with him, jumping freight trains out to Cootamundra, Wagga, Narrandera, and even Goulburn, living and sharing in the swaggy camps that had sprung up, with a real shiralee.

As winter neared ever more close, and the temperatures began to drop, along with snow from time to time, he headed for Gundagai. That was where Clara had been born, and he might be able to pull some heart strings there—after all, Lillian *was* Clara's kid, a direct descendant. He told Lillian they would ask 'aunt Mary' to give them shelter and food in exchange for whatever work he could do in return. They had a big property, and fit, experienced young men were still scarce; many of the lads who had survived the War and flu epidemic were only now just nearing fifteen years of age.

Aunt Mary, so Lillian called her, was the formidable matriarch of the homestead, but felt sorry for her poor 'niece', and hardly worth complaining about having to feed such a skinny kid. As for Paddy, well Mary had heard stories, no doubt, and was skeptical of his authenticity, but she couldn't turn him down and keep Lillian. She put Paddy to work to earn just his keep: chopping wood, clearing land, tending animals, running errands on horseback, getting supplies from the town, and driving the family in a buggy to Church every Sunday. Paddy couldn't complain, he needed the roof over his and Lillian's heads. The only downside, he thought, was the lack of cash income, so getting a drink was always a problem.

But worse than this, Mary and her kin folk looked upon Paddy with disdain, and were not short in making snide comments behind his back which he nevertheless heard about indirectly. Like Rachael Keough, Mary and her ilk, without knowing the full story, similarly thought Paddy was responsible for Clara's sickness and death, overlooking the fact that 3 of the Keough sisters had all died within 6 months of one another in different parts of the State; and while they had no direct evidence, they were also suspicious of Paddy's sobriety.

For his own sake, but more especially for Lillian's, he bit his tongue, swallowed his pride, and plodded on with his sod lot, until the warmer weather in early 1932 enabled him to move on...

Thirteen

Perth 2021

"So mum, you told us a bit about living in Gundagai," Mark and Elizabeth again addressed their mother. "What can you tell us about living in Junee, especially a place they called *The Triangle*?"

"Oh I remember that. It was just cold... Or hot, depending on the weather. I think we went there in the summer, it was so hot and dry. Dad couldn't afford to rent a house anymore, because he didn't have work, like many families."

"And it was just an open area, near the Station?"

"A bit further. But had the tracks running through it, I *know*.... Because we had to step over them all the time. And you how big they are for a four year old! And they got hot in the summer sun. Could fry an egg on 'em."

"If you had an egg to fry, I dare say."

"Ah yes. Food, always short. Dad used to get the dole tickets once a fortnight, I think, but barely enough to buy food. And he would often sell 'em for grog."

"I suppose he figured if he sold them for that then other people would chip in for your food?"

"And they did! I didn't eat much at that age. Dad would tell me go over to another tent, you could see the smoke and smell something, go over when they're cooking, and they take pity on me. They all knew dad was on the drink again."

"I guess many of them were. What else could they do? Must have been frustrating, and boring."

"For him, boring. But us kids we banded together and made games."

"So, it was all tents? No running water, or electricity, or loo?"

"Most were tents, some lean-to's, made up of old timber and tin. There were a couple of old houses on the fringes, and a creek we got water from, and further down went to the loo and had a bath."

"How long were you there?"

"Oh... I don't know, not long I think. When autumn started dad said it was going to be too cold to stay, so he packed up his swag and we went travelling."

"Where to? And how?"

"Well, we walked a lot. Sometimes we jumped on a train. I don't know where we went, maybe Wagga, or Goulburn. My grandma Keough had relatives there. I remember staying at a house there a short while, maybe a few days, but I don't think they liked dad, so we left. I do remember going to Cootamundra, though. But all the places were the same to me, old quiet towns, camping by a river, there were what they called swaggie camps, lots of men mostly, and a few families."

"Do you know where you stayed at Goulburn?"

"The Smarts I think."

"Isn't that where your brothers were? Jack and Wally?"

"Yes, but not at that house. I didn't know it then. And I never saw them."

"Didn't your dad know? Or tell you?"

"I don't know if he knew. Grandma Keough never told him anything, so I only found out later, much later, from Marj. The last I saw of any of them was going off with Granny Keough somewhere, everyone saying they'd be back, sooner or later."

"How did you feel about that, then, ma?"

"Well that's a silly question! I used to live with them for nearly three years, and then suddenly everything was uprooted. I was just told this and that, lied to basically, but I didn't understand, and just accepted it. I didn't even fully understand that my mother had died, they just said she was in hospital and has to stay there awhile... Lies. All lies!"

"Yea, I guess so."

"The worst of it was they never told me where they had gone, so I couldn't even write to them. And they didn't know where I was! The Keoughs and Smarts didn't want any of my siblings to have anything to do with my dad, *their* dad!"

"Maybe they lost track of where he was? After all, he was moving about quite a bit."

"Maybe, but they *did* know he ended up in Bowral, because Marj wrote to him."

"Yes. So, how *did* she find out? That must have been about nineteen-forty-six, when he married Adele Moore?"

"I don't know what year, but if it was nineteen-forty-six then Marj would have been sixteen, and I was eighteen, and living in Manly."

"Maybe the Smarts had relented a bit, maybe she kept asking questions, and they thought she was old enough to know...?"

Fourteen

Bowral 1932 — 1952

The red rattler suburban train from Parramatta rambled into Central and stopped with a jolt. Paddy moved across the concourse to locate the Country Trains. An old steamer to Bowral was sitting at Platform 7 and scheduled to depart at noon, an hour hence. He bought a one-way ticket for 3/6, returned to the train and took a seat. *Deja vu.*

He would soon be on his way to Bowral once again, not having been back since, when was it...? 1919? 1920? "Bloody hell! Twelve...? Thirteen years...?" he muttered to himself.

He hoped Lillian would be alright, that the three hail Marys would do right by her. It was all for the best. He couldn't drag a 4 year old kid around with him while looking for work; he didn't know what to expect in Bowral, if his brothers were even still there, and would welcome him. He couldn't take Lillian with him, and load her on to them, things were bad enough already. No, she be better off with the Holy Marys, the Bankes, leastways for awhile. 'Till this blasted Depression were over. He'd write her as soon as he got settled in Bowral.

He settled into a seat to await departure. He couldn't snooze, he had too many things on his mind. He picked up an old copy of *The Telegraph* newspaper that someone had left on another seat and began to flip through it half-heartedly.

It was past three o'clock when the train pulled into Bowral. He gathered his scarce belongings and looked out the window. Once again he could smell the fresh green hills of the southern tablelands, instead of the cowdung-laced dry brown paddocks of Junee.

He stepped out onto the small platform into the warm sunshine and looked about. Nothing had changed since 1917 or thereabouts. It was still awfully quiet.

He half expected Lillian to be standing behind him, clasping his leg, but, turning around and looking down, he felt strangely odd that she was not there. "Poor little mite," he mumbled, then thought, 'Nah, she'll be alright.' But it did feel strange that now, once again, he could do as he pleased, no longer having a shiralee.

But this time there was no old-man Station Master. 'Maybe cut back on workers 'cause of the Depression', he thought. 'Or he retired, p'haps, or even dead... Been fourteen years, after all... Never mind, I knows me way.'

He strolled across the tracks and the road beyond to the *Royal Bowral* pub, where had stayed a night, back in 1917. It was deadly quiet inside, only one other patron sitting at a corner table. He bought a schooner of beer, then turning to the bartender stupidly asked:

"Busy?"

"Ha! Yer gotta be kidding, mate," the burley publican scoffed good naturedly. "No body got no money. This nineteen-*thirty*-two, mate, not twenty-two."

"Aye, that be sure. I was here a few year ago, got a lift with one of the travellin' sales-men down to Greentrees. They still coming through here?" he thought to ask, since so much had changed, economically. He was right.

"Not on yer nelly, mate. Told yer, no money, no body buyin' stuff."

"Aye. D'ya knows how I can get t'Greentrees, but. Down by the dam?"

"Why you be goin' there, then?"

"Me brudders, they live 'n work there. Arthur Egan."

"Oh aye. Egan. He be there, but not the younger one. Arty hangin' on by a thread, I 'ears. Best yer walk, mate, maybe hitch a ride anyone passin' by. But gettin' on dark nows, better orf in the morn. Can give yer a room fer two bob, and two bob fer tea," the bartender suggested in a solicitous way.

"Aye. Been a long day. But four bob a bit pricey. Can yer do me for three bob all up?"

"Aye," the bartender affirmed, thinking he would make a few more bob from beer sales judging by the way Paddy was gulping down his schooner. "Another?" he asked, eyeing Paddy and the glass.

"Aye. Then some tea but."

Paddy was given another schooner, and the barman left to get his wife outback to cook up some fish and mash. Paddy strolled about the saloon, looking out the window onto the deserted street, wondering what the bartender had meant when referring to his brothers. Well, he'd find out for sure the next day.

He finished his second schooner and then sat at a table as the barman brought in his tea, with an additional slice of bread and butter. He ate in silence, with just random thoughts swilling about of Clara and his loss, about Lillian and the three Marys, and now Arthur and William.

He ordered his third, and last, schooner, and idled away the time. It was a lonely existence. He hadn't expected Bowral to be so desolate compared to the last time he was there—but that was 14-odd years ago, he kept reminding himself. What a life. He was 52 now, almost. Seemed to have gone full circle: Dubbo, Sydney, Bowral, Junee, Gundagai, Dubbo again, with all the little towns in between, then Parramatta, now back to Bowral. Junee was perhaps the best of his round trip, with Clara for near-on ten years, despite his in-laws, but he also liked Bowral, he had his brothers there, and the green, wet countryside suited him.

With nothing else to do he took to his allotted room, asking the barman to wake him at 7am.

Like clockwork Paddy was awoken with no courtesy at 7am sharp. He shambled downstairs, and to the kitchen out back. He had a strange feeling of *deja vu*, but alas it was not to be. Clara was not there, nor even Beryl. But the cook, the barman's wife he suspected, a solid country woman with ruddy cheeks and flaming orange hair in curls covering a large round head, Scottish he thought, looked him over and without a word poured him a cup of tea with fresh milk. *There* was something to be said for living in the Highlands. He sipped at the hot brew.

"Will ya be wanting breakfast?" the woman almost demanded to know.

"Aye. Thank ye."

"Eggs and corn beef, with toast. A shilling it be."

"Aye. A shilling then."

He dug into his pocket and found a shilling, and placed it on the table. In less than a minute she had the food on a plate in front of him, and topped up his tea. He ate his breakfast, which he knew he would need, in silence, neither he nor the redhead it seemed wanting to be sociable. It all the more deepened his feeling of having lost what had been dear to him in Junee.

Courteously he thanked the woman, retrieved his belongings from his room and headed out the door, stopping to buy a flask of rum which he knew he would surely need at nightfall, and thanked the barman as he passed on. The morning air was nippy, but invigorating. He began to walk. Nothing on the road passed him for the next two miles, then his luck changed a little for the better. A rather old jalopy, something from the early '20s or before, he figured, came down and stopped as Paddy put up is arm in some form of a hailing position.

An older man, perhaps well into his 60s was driving, and invited Paddy to jump in when he learnt they were both heading down toward the very dam that he had long ago helped build. They arrived without much talk in about 10 minutes, and Paddy with thanks jumped out. He knew the roadway up to Arthur's house, another half mile or so; he was now keen to walk it, hoping it would lead to good times, as in the past.

It was now past 9am, so he half expected Arthur and William to be gone to work, or about to leave for work, as though nothing had changed in 14 years. But as he approached there was nothing: no horse, no dog, no chickens, no kids, it was terribly desolate and unkempt. But he could see smoke whiffing out of the kitchen chimney. He sighed relief.

Clambering the few steps to the front door he tapped loudly, not too loudly he hoped. It was a good minute before the door was swung open, and a young girl, perhaps 12 or 13 peered out with a frown of curiosity.

"Morning, miss. Is yer pa or ma home?"

She didn't reply but mostly closed the door and yelled into the house for her Ma. Paddy could hear a bit of kerfuffle inside, until Arthur's wife, Alice, boldly flung open the door and peered at him, the young girl standing close behind, gawking around Alice's shoulder.

"Morning Alice," Paddy greeted cheerily, although also a little sheepishly. "Paddy. Paddy Egan if you recall?"

She continued to gape at him, speechless, trying to take in what must have appeared to her as an apparition.

"Oh my Lord! After all this time.... S'pose you better come in, then, get some tea. In the kitchen." She led the way, leaving the young girl to close the door and follow suit. "Arty still in bed," she told him over her shoulder.

"Aye. And William?"

"Not 'ere. Sydney. In the army."

William (Bill) Egan, circa 1940-1942

Now Paddy was left dumbstruck. "And the wains? They about but?"

Alice nodded toward her daughter, Grace. "She was born just before you arrived, r'member? In school, only there ain't no school no more, can't pay the teachers, can't afford send her. No 'orse to get 'er there."

"Aye. Oh my Lord, she be...?"

"Fourteen thereabouts now. And the boys, one off working, the oldest, the other two doing what they can 'bout 'ere."

"And Arty? You say he in bed? He sick?"

"Aye. 'Ere yer tea. Sorry, no sugar," Alice announced, handing him a mug of tea with milk, one of the few things they could get in Bowral, it seemed. "Cannae afford luxury. Cannae even pay the rent. Thinkin' sellin' up."

"Why that?"

"Arthur not working...much. Had a fall some time ago, not been himself ever since. The boys bring in a bit, William sends what he can, me and Grace take in some laundry work... What we grow we cannae sell, no one not got no money."

"Bloody shite! I was 'oping I could stay 'ere abit...?"

"Aye. Could do with some man labour, but gotta pull yer weight."

"Aye. I do that, Alice, no fear on that 'count. I no spring chicken I know, but got experience, that counts."

"Well, Arthur be pleased to see yer least wise. Yer bunk with the boys. C'mon, we say hello to Arty."

Paddy followed Alice into the main bedroom at the front of the house, Grace continuing to follow closely, Paddy not sure if this was for security or out of curiosity. Arthur was sitting up in bed, not looking too sick, but nevertheless pale and with a blank stare. He had lost a bit of weight, Paddy noted.

"Hi ya going mate!?" Paddy greeted cheerily, taking a spot on the end of the bed. "What's all this, then? Alice say yer had a fall?"

Arthur stared at him, then Alice, with a questioning look.

"It's Paddy, yer brudder, Arty. Yer 'member him darnt yer? Paddy Egan," she told him, because it became apparent very quickly that Arthur didn't recognize his brother.

Alice turned to Paddy: "He has 'is good days, an' bad. Sometimes he's as fit as a fiddle, others, well, you can see, like a veg, don't 'member anyfing."

"Aye. So what the doc say?"

"Cannae afford doctor, took 'im t' Berrima 'ospital when it 'appen, say he had a fall, banged 'is 'ead, knocked his brains 'bout. Just give it time, they say. Been six month now."

"Aye. I try have a quiet word with 'im, see if we can get a spark," he smiled hopefully.

Alice left him to it with Grace still standing by the doorway. Paddy started off telling Arthur what he'd been doing the last 'couple' of years, without mentioning Clara's death which he thought might frighten Arthur. He was hoping some memory or curiosity might spark a question or nod, but Arthur just gazed as though stunned into oblivion. Then Grace fetched a mug of water and Arthur readily took it from her but with a vey shaky left hand.

"He cannae move his other hand," she told Paddy who had given her a quizzical look.

"Oh aye? Then I try agin, a bit later."

He left father and daughter to ask Alice what needed be done. Invariably she told him to cut wood when he got time, and have a look about, see what needs attending and what he could do. This he did, finding not much around the house or yard, or in the shed. There was no buggy, no horse, just the garden tools that had grown old and withered.

He returned to the kitchen where Alice offered him an early lunch: eggs yet again, from the few chickens they still had, cheese, and homemade bread with butter. It seemed in this this part of the country dairy food at least was not in short supply. Not a morsel of meat. Things looked pretty grim.

Alice suggested he get down to the *Shrublands* tomorrow, early, see if he can't find a bit of work. But he'd have to walk, or hitch a ride if he could. Meantime she took Arthur his lunch, vegetable soup and a boiled egg, while Grace tidied up and went out the back to continue with some washing. He watched her awhile, while he had a smoke, thinking, 'It must be hard for a young lass stuck out here, no friends, no suitors, bored, the same shite day in and day out. Maybe by the time she's 16 or 18 this fecking Depression be gone.'

Paddy went and chopped some wood and made kindling. Then took another look around the property, at the pitiful vege garden, the fallen fences, the paddocks without sheep or cattle.... There was a fair bit of work to be done here, he thought. But no point if there was no food to keep up his strength, and there would be no food without money. And without a horse it would be difficult to get around to look for work... He returned to the kitchen.

"Arty's asleep," Alice told him, when he sat down. "Have a cuppa." She poured him a mug of tea. It would take him awhile to get used to it without even a smidgen of sugar.

They discussed what needed to be done about the house if he had no work. Alice said her boys could help with the vege garden, but they didn't know anything about fixing fences, or getting some sheep in to eat the grass. Then she told him if he had no luck in the *Shrublands* he could try down in Moss Vale, the Lansdowns had a big property there and only a widow, Rose by name, and her aunt, managed it. Both were getting on a bit, Rose being in her fifties, she thought.

"Aye. Well, there be nowt to do here t'day. I'll just start a bit on the veges. Grace can show me what's been planted. Need to get a horse but, so can git around and use the manure."

For much of the afternoon Paddy divided his time between sorting out the vege garden and chopping wood, and straightened a few fence posts. At 5 o'clock Alice's boys, John and Les, 16 and 12 years old each, arrived home. Each had a few pennies from working a few hours at a wood mill near town.

They didn't really recognize Paddy, only the older one recalled him with some clarity. But they were nevertheless welcoming and friendly. They all sat down in the kitchen to await tea, which wasn't much. The boys had brought home a few beef sausages in addition to, almost in lieu of, any real wages, so Alice added them to the vege soup and bread and butter. Grace was happy they were home, someone she could talk to.

It was still warm weather so Paddy took a perch on the back verandah, inviting the boys to sit with him and tell any tales they had of growing up. John was old enough to share a drink of the rum Paddy had bought that morning, and he even gave Les a nip. He told them they would be helping on their free days—and learn about fencing and gardening—while he picked their local knowledge for any work he could do or where he might get a horse.

There was not enough liquor to last much more than an hour, so all but Paddy hit their respective fleapits at about seven. Paddy lingered another five minutes, glad for a moment of quiet to reflect over the dregs of his hip-flask of rum.

He had missed Bowral, although he hadn't realized it until now. Even though he had loved Clara and enjoyed being with her and the kids in Junee, it was in Bowral that he felt he *belonged*. He should have brought her here, he thought, but he never thought of it. Life in Junee had become just one hectic moment to the next. But here, in Bowral, he had family, *his* family, he was not an outsider, even though Alice had shown initial disdain for him back in '17.

At that time he had two brothers, and work, a house he could call a home of sorts, even though it was not his, so long as he pulled his weight and behaved himself. He didn't have in-laws and their kin looking down on him, sneering, talking behind his back, and at times even to his face. He wondered if that was how Alice had felt then, as an in-law, back in '17?

But now, Alice seemed to have matured, had rallied to the aid of her husband, *her* family. She even seemed glad to have Paddy help out, not just physically, but in a way as a mentor to her boys, and someone with whom she could talk about Arthur. Unlike himself in Junee, Alice had become family.

Alice was up at the crack, 5am, stoking the fire, boiling the kettle, scrapping together some scrambled eggs and the left-over veges and meat—bubble-n-squeak. As soon as breakfast was done, Paddy was on the road at 6am, heading to the *Shrublands*, and maybe Moss Vale nearby. The boys went north toward Bowral, hoping to get another few hours at the wood mill.

For once in a long while he had a bit of luck. A passing truck driver gave him a ride to a big property, the driver saying the large estate he was delivering to needed someone to help clear obnoxious scrub, lantana and prickly-pear and the such. Paddy was hired on the spot and put in six hours with two other blokes, earning himself ten-bob. At two o'clock he was let go, the foreman saying it was too hot, but he should come back the next day as early as possible.

A mile away was the Lansdown property, so he set off for that. He didn't know what to expect other than what he had already been told: a widow in her fifties, an aunt in her sixties maybe. Nothing about menfolk or children.

He strolled up the long sandy drive and knocked on the front door. A rather frail, small woman with silver hair opened the door, and looked at him suspiciously.

"Afta-noon, ma'am," he introduced, taking off his hat in courtesy and presenting a wide friendly smile. "Me name's Patrick, ma'am,

Patrick Egan. I was told, ma'am, that you might be requiring some work done 'round here…"

"Egan?! The Egans up on the hill, near Bowral?" the lady cut him short.

"Aye, ma'am. That be us. Greentrees property."

"Ah. And I suppose you lookin' for a handout then?" she continued to eye him with suspicion and contempt.

"No ma'am, I'm lookin' to do some work that might be needing. I work for me keep, ma'am," he replied, still keeping a cheery smile.

At that moment he could hear another voice, a woman's, calling from within as to who was at the door, but before the old lady could answer the other female, quite attractive for her age so he thought, appeared.

Again Paddy went through the friendly gestures of salutation and explanation, only to again be brought up sharp.

"You know this is hard times, *Mister* Egan. It's true we need some things fixing 'round the property, but can't afford it. We had a band of vagabonds coming 'round here… Just the other day."

"I ain't no vagabond, ma'am, ladies," he addressed them both. "Me brother's Arthur Egan up at Greentrees. I just moved up 'ere from Junee after losing me wife…"

"Oh. I'm sorry to hear that," the younger woman commiserated as the older lady gave a sign of the Cross.

"So I come from good family, that be sure, willing to work for whatever you can provide, ma'am."

"Mmm. You better come 'round the back, then. We can discuss it. I'll make some tea."

"Thank you ma'am. Tea would be nice, thank ye."

The two ladies retreated into the house, closing the door and bolting it behind them, as Paddy headed around the quite large stone house, looking up and around, thinking it must have six bedrooms at least.

Reaching the back verandah he stood about, refraining from smoking, taking in as much as possible the features of the house and property. The younger woman came out and took a seat.

"So you're the brother of Arthur and Alice, then?"

"Yes ma'am."

"Nice couple. Work hard. How is Arthur? I heard he'd taken ill."

"Aye ma'am, laid up in bed, not quite 'imself. But he'll be orright."

"Then let's get to business. We have had many layabouts come through, but not trustworthy, you know. Just *any* old vagabond just passing by. So what are your plans, Mr. Egan?"

Paddy went on to explain how he had heard about his brother's misfortune, and given that his own wife had passed away, he would come to Bowral to help out, so he was looking for work, any work, not just 'passing through'.

"We can not afford much, Mr. Egan. Since the depression we have had to sell off what he could and make do with what we have, a little bit of income to see us through."

"Well, ma'am, I cannae work fer nothin', I sure you understand, but you can pay me in chow, or whatever you can afford. I be happy to take a sheep for our land, or a horse if yer can spare. I see yer got four o' 'em."

"Oh yes, four, and costly to feed. And no one to care for them. I'm run off my feet as it is. And my aunt, aunt Gilda, can't do much. And a buggy to fix. Can you fix a buggy, Mr. Egan? Makes it hard to get into town without transport."

"I sure can ma'am. Fixed 'em before. Handy man, am I, ma'am. And a 'orse ma'am would be grand. We can discuss the price and I do the work for that."

"Mmm. Let me think about it. Here's your tea," she interrupted as Gilda brought out a small tray with three cups.

"Well, ma'am, the way I see it, I ain't just passing through, but reliable and honest. You know where I live."

"We need to feed the horses too, and posts fixed, and wood chopping, and the sheep rounding up... Can you do all that Mr. Egan?"

"Aye ma'am. And to get started I bring down me nephew, a young lad, but honest and hardworking."

"Oh, but we can't afford two wages, Mr. Egan."

"No bother there ma'am, two for the price of one. Whatever yer see fit."

"So you want a horse?" she pointedly asked.

"Aye ma'am. To get from here to there and about. If yer can lend me a horse..."

"*Lend?* That's an idea. I can *lend* you a horse, Mr. Egan, and you can work to pay him off. But you have to feed him, take care of him..."

"Done ma'am. It's a deal. I can start t'morrow mornin', ma'am, first thing. Seven o'clock?"

"Very well then, we can try that for a time, see how things go. But please, stop calling me ma'am. My name's Rose."

"Yes ma'am, I mean Rose. And call me Paddy," he grinned.

"Come then, meet the horses. We'd like you to fix the buggy first thing, so my aunt and I can get about."

"Consider it done, Rose. You got no menfolk 'ere can lend a hand then?"

"Alas no, Mr. Egan. I am a widow, and all my children are grown and scattered to the four winds. Why? Why do you ask?"

"Oh, no reason, ma'am...Rose. Just a bit odd for two women be living on a place so big with no 'elp."

"My sons did, before, and we had a handyman, but he moved on... So, choose the horse, Mr. Egan. They all old and gentle," she directed as they reached the barn.

Paddy looked over the horses, giving each caressing words and tender touches, careful not to spook them. He imagined they would all be glad to get out once in a while to roam, rather than being cooped up in the stable and dusty paddock.

"I'll take this fella then."

"Noddy. His name's Noddy. You have a place to keep him?"

"Sure do. We had a 'orse before, got a barn, green grass paddock, and growing vege, so he can have a carrot as a treat. You like that boy?"

Noddy neighed, making believe he had understood, as Paddy stroked his neck.

"So what about you Mr. Egan? You have family?" Rose asked to make some conversation.

"Nah, not really. Two boys, that be all, belong to me wife. Her first husban' dead from the flu, back in 'eighteen. None me own but," he lied.

"I see."

"And yer husban', ma'am, he also passed?"

"Yes. Quite some time ago. In Queensland."

"Queensland!? That be far off."

"Yes, it is. We married here, then moved up north, big spread. He passed away, after maybe fourteen years, kids grown up, so I moved back here. This place used to belong to my father. The Lansdowns. Now my aunt takes care of it."

"Aye. Well, then, we get this place ship-shape, bring in a few shillings with the sheep and all that...."

Paddy took Noddy out of the stable and mounted him, without a saddle, then walked him down to the front. He seemed placid and happy. Rose opened the front gate for them to pass through, saying she expected them back tomorrow morning.

Paddy and Noddy ambled up Robertson Road for a bit, letting the horse get a feel of his rider, and stretching his legs. When they reached the road junction they turned north, back to *Greentrees*. Paddy gave Noddy a pep talk. "C'mon boy, let's see if you cannae do a trot for a mile or two, eh." And with that he spurred the horse forward by whipping the reins gently and giving him a mild kick in the sides. Noddy took off at a trot, glad to be out in the open fields.

They arrived back at *Greentrees* in about 15 minutes. Paddy wasn't expecting the grand welcome he got. Grace saw them first and alerted everyone, then came running out, followed by the two boys who were already home from work, and then Alice, who heard the ruckus. They all crowded around at a respectable distance from the sight of Paddy sitting high and smiling atop Noddy.

"Oh Lordy Lordy, Paddy Egan! Don't tell me ya stoled that 'orse?"

"Ha! No Alice. He be on loan, for a time, and we can pay 'im off. I tell yer all 'bout it."

The children slowly came forward and caressed and talked to the animal.

"What's his name, Uncle?" Grace wanted to know.

"Noddy." Paddy felt very proud for bringing home a little bit of happiness, as well as a final sense of belonging when Grace called him 'Uncle'.

"I'm gonna get Arthur," Alice declared. "This should perk 'im up!"

Alice rushed into the house as Paddy dismounted, then opened his swag and pulled out two hip-flasks of rum. "We be celebrating today, boys. Don't tell yer Ma, ok."

"Where yer get that Uncle Patrick?" Les asked, wide eyed.

"Shhh. They be in the barn with the 'orses...." He smiled.

"Horses?!" Grace cried. "You mean, there be more than one horse?"

"Aye, Four! And a buggy."

"Can I have one, Uncle?" Grace pleaded. "Then I can get to school."

"Not on yer nelly, sis, I need a horse to find work," John asserted.

"Well calm down you lot, we talk 'bout it t'night. Meantime, we got our work cut out fer you lot t'morra."

At that moment Arthur came out, putting some of his weight on Alice. John rushed to help them join the small throng. Arthur put up his left hand to pat Noddy and spoke to him. Then turning to Paddy he said:

"Well boy, you be 'ere one day and yer come 'ome wif a 'orse. Where you get this fella?"

Alice was beside herself; Arthur was talking, and talking normally, showing some interest in something, and getting a bit of exercise. But she, and Paddy, noted that Arthur still didn't recognize who Paddy was.

The kids were sent off with Noddy to a green paddock to allow him to feed on long grass, while being enthusiastically brushed. Paddy meantime helped Alice get Arthur up to a seat on the front verandah, catching the last warm rays of sun.

"Tea ready soon, gents," she told them. "Rabbit stew. Then you tell us all about this 'orse."

Tea finished, Paddy retired to the front verandah, closely trailed by the two boys. He poured himself a rum, and one for John, and again a small nip for Les. Then he told them to help their Da out to join them. Soon Alice, Grace and Arthur also were seated wherever they could lay their haunches, so Paddy could begin the story of his day.

When he had finished without interruption, the children sat gawking, amazed at how much things had taken a turn for the better in just one day.

"So 'ere's the plan t'marra," he decreed. "John, I take yer down that place that's cleaning out the scrub, instead of me. Les, yer start walking, I come back on the 'orse collect yer. If yer finish early, John, yer come down t'Lansdown place. Me and Les gonna fix that buggy there, let out the 'orses t'graze, 'erd in t'sheep, and start the fencing."

"What about me, Uncle?" Grace entreated. "I can herd and muster, too."

"Aye, lassie yer can at that. But let's take it a bit slow at first, eh. I don't wanna frighten the ladies. I talk to t' Lansdowns, see if they be willing to lend us another 'orse, or maybe there be some women-like work inside t' 'ouse they need doing.... Not rush it, yer 'ear. One step at a time. But I sure they 'preciate a bit o' female company, feel safer, yer know what I mean?"

With this plan set they retired to bed, and awoke early, 5.30am, before the chooks were up. Dropping John off at Paddy's former workplace with a guarantee the boy could do the job, he rode back and picked up Les who had walked about a mile closer. Then they headed down to Rose's house, took Noddy inside to be with his fellows, and then all four out to a paddock which they quickly made escape proof. Paddy took Les out to where the sheep had been grazing overnight and showed him how to herd then into another paddock and secure it with whatever he could scrounge. Then Les met up with Paddy back at the stable, where Paddy had wheeled out the buggy and was busy with woodwork and axles.

Rose came out at 9am with mugs of tea and some buttered scones.

"It'll be done by tonight," Paddy assured her. "Then we start on the fencing, make sure it's rabbit proof, so to speak," he chuckled.

"That's good. Then we can get into town tomorrow, maybe sell a sheep."

"Sell? You only got half a dozen, Rose, you need breed 'em up, double yer take. Nobody know how long this depression last."

"We need the money, Mr. Egan," Rose firmly informed him.

"Aye. I could suggest I take a few off yer hands, on loan that be, breed a few more, but lambing season over. Better sell a horse that ain't doin' nuffin. Yer only need one 'orse to pull this 'ere buggy."

"Sell the horse!? For meat, you mean?" Rose was quite stricken by the notion.

"Nah. I mean for work, plowing, travelling. There's a fella up the road a bit, clearin' 'is land he is, maybe he buy it, or yer rent it out. Let me ask 'im. See what I can do."

"That would be better."

"Me niece, she needs a 'orse so t'get t'school, but nah, she cannae 'ford it. No body got no money, 'cept the rich folks."

"Well, that's *not* us, I can assure you. We have *some* savings, but even that's running out."

Paddy rubbed his chin in thought. "I gotta think on it, ma'am. Problem is, even if yer got somefing to sell, no folks got the money to buy it. Seems just gotta raise yer own food and rent stuff out."

"Yes. It seems so. But growing food is slow and back breaking. I'm too old for that. And now it's too late, winter in three months..."

"Ah, yea, but there some crops yer can plant already, be ready in two month, cabbage and cauli."

"Yes Mr. Egan, all very fine. But what do we eat while we're waiting for it to grow? And when it *is* ready, what do we eat? Cauliflower soup every day?"

"Haha. Well, then I reckon we make a deal, and maybe even expand later on... I got a garden in tow right now, potatoes, carrots, peas... We grow some cabbage and parsnips and cauli 'ere, and do a' s'change. Shoot some rabbits. Me niece, Grace, she can come down next few days, along with Les 'ere, we get a garden going, and git some more chooks... Give yer meat *and* eggs... *And* fertilizer. Build a proper chook pen keep the fox out. Maybe even a pig or two, they breed pretty quick."

"And what's in it for you, Mr. Egan? Almost sounds like you're moving in already."

"Nah, not moving in, just expanding to be able t' *ex*-change, and the work I do pays off the 'orse. Me niece, Grace, willing do that, and maybe she can 'elp in the 'ouse a bit, if anything need doin'?"

"I will think about it. Maybe the end of the week. In the meantime, we need that buggy fixed, and if you and your kin can start on a vege garden, we should at least try it. Tomorrow?"

"Aye. Get this buggy rollin' and we start on the fence, keep the 'orses and sheep in."

"Then I'll leave you to it. There's some oats in the shed for the horses if yer set fit to feed them."

"Aye. No problem."

"Oh, and your niece, she can do some washing?"

"Aye ma'am. She fourteen, and been doin' washin' our place near on a few years."

"Good. Then send her down. We'll talk later."

Rose returned to the house.

Les helped Paddy with the buggy until lunch time. The axle needed greasing and the wheels properly and securely fitted, a few bits of wooden frame reinforced, and some leather bits replaced. Les only needed to help with the wheeling, then Paddy took him off to the nearest fencing in need of repair and showed what need be done.

They stopped at 1pm for the cold lunch Alice and Grace had prepared: chicken, bread-an'-butter, and cheese. Rose came out and found them, saying there was hot tea on the verandah. All this time Paddy was mulling over how he could make this situation work to his, and his newfound family's, advantage, to the mutual advantage of Rose and her aunt.

So far, and quickly at that, he had managed to borrow a horse to get him and his nephews and niece around, and a bit of possible work for them, but he couldn't see how any of this was going to put food on *their* table. The blunt fact was that no one other than the toffs had any money—for buying or for wages. Even Rose and her aunt were struggling. They could sell some of their land, of course, but again no one had the money for it, or if they did, what would they use it for?—growing crops that no one could afford...? It was a vicious circle. So, he began to slowly realize, the only 'currency' was bartering, exchange, and the only thing he could exchange at the moment was his labour. If he could convince Rose to grow vegetables, then at least for the coming winter they could ride out the storm. But meat was a real problem, and they needed meat for protein and strength. There were plenty of dairy cows around; it might be possible to swap a horse for a cow or two, get the milk daily and sell that, and in winter slaughter a cow... Or, he thought, Rose and her aunt might have something valuable in the house, a painting, jewelry, furniture....? Could he find a market for them in Sydney? If he could just get a few quid to kick-start things and break the cycle of poverty....

By mid afternoon John had finished his work of clearing land and joined his uncle and brother at the Lansdown property. Paddy quickly put him to work helping Les with the fencing. He knew he couldn't ask Rose to pay three wages, but he figured if they got a few essential jobs done then he would be in the good, Rose would trust him, and there would be more to do in exchange for... Well, for *something*.

At 4pm they called it quits. They had achieved a good deal. The buggy was fixed, and Rose almost commanded that one of the lads drive her and her aunt into town the next day. As a bonus, although little they could afford it, she gave Paddy five shillings, saying maybe they could buy some beef or pork.

Paddy and the two boys left for home, hitching one of the other horses to the buggy, with Paddy saying he wanted to road test it, and one of the lads on Noddy. Grace was keen to see them arrive, and impatient to hear any news. Paddy told her she could come the next day, see what eventuates, assured that Alice could cope with Arthur, who seemed a bit more enlivened. Once again he came out to view the ruckus and declared something to the effect that one day Paddy comes home with a horse and the next day he's got two horses *and* a buggy!

He showed them the five bob he had been paid, and how they would buy up 'big' tomorrow on beef or lamb. Over dinner that night he again laid out the plans for the next few days. Grace would do some work inside the Lansdown house with a view of getting in the ladies' good-books, and maybe that leading to Rose lending her a horse, or use of the buggy maybe. Grace had to snoop a bit around the house, see if there was anything worthwhile for the Lansdowns to pawn or sell.

"Ya not gonna steal it from 'em are yer, Paddy!?" Alice reprimanded.

"Nah, 'course not. See if there be anything they don't need they can sell, pay us some real wages, build up their mutton stock, and so on. Long term, that's how we gotta think."

"You can write Uncle Bill," Grace suggested. "He be in Sydney, maybe get a better price up there?"

"Good idea lass. Can yer do that t'nite, lass, post it tomorrow. The ladies goin' t'town t'morra, can post it then."

"Aye, and while yer at it yer better write yer aunts, Teresa and yer namesake, aunt Grace, tell 'em Paddy's 'ere and about yer Pa and William," Alice ordered.

"Geez ma, it be like writing a book!"

Paddy went on to detail how they all had to pitch in with growing veges and stocking up on chooks and sheep and pigs, a grand farm he declared.

The next morning, as was becoming customary, almost the whole Egan clan set out for the Lansdown property: Paddy and

Grace on the buggy, he teaching her how to drive it, John and Les riding Noddy. The kids hadn't had so much fun for as far back as they could remember.

Paddy put the two boys to work finishing off the fencing and moving the chook pen into the barn and making it more secure against foxes. Grace and Paddy set to cleaning up and extending an old vege patch. He would look about the region for seeds of any broccoli, Brussels sprouts, English peas, spinach, turnips, cabbage, cauliflower, and carrots. They also slung together old canvas and hessian bags for nighttime use, to keep the frost off.

In the midst of all this the two ladies came out the back to inspect the progress and provide a pot of tea. It was now past 9am and Rose and her aunt were rather dressed up to go into town. But first they directed Grace on how to do a pile of washing in the outside troughs.

Paddy and the two ladies squeezed into the single bench seat of the buggy and set off for Moss Vale. Paddy mentioned on the way his idea of Rose selling or pawning anything of value they no longer needed. She mentioned that she possessed her husband's ring, a pocket watch, cufflinks, a cigarette case, a shaving case.... She had forgotten about these, surprised she hadn't thought about them as saleable. She said her husband had died about 12 or 14 years ago, so she had no need for the items, nor much attachment to them. Besides, these were very hard times, and everyone had to make sacrifices. Paddy told them that Grace would make a small description of each one and send the list to Bill, his brother in Sydney, to see what he might be able to do about selling them, thinking they would get a better price in the City. Rose seemed very practical, and willing to go along with this plan. All she had needed in the last few years was a guiding hand and new ideas.

Rose drew out a short list of her needs in the house: a sack of flour for bread and pie pastry, some meat, vegetables, especially potatoes, sugar, tinned food, maybe a fish... And paddy suggested getting a few more chooks, and any vege seeds or cut-offs they could use for the garden. In the end they all had a fruitful day, returning by 4pm with most of the provisions required—and Paddy a bottle of rum, to boot.

The boys had finished off the fencing; there were still a few chores yet to do over the coming days. Grace had done much of the washing. The ladies asked her to return the next day to help with some housework, and she wrote out a brief description of the ladies' items they wished to sell. She would communicate these to Bill in the next mail. Six chickens and a rooster were added to the coop, and Paddy had acquired a tin of corned beef.

The Egans once again drove back to their own house, Grace once again driving the buggy so as to practice, for as Rose indicated, Grace or one of the lads might be required in future to take the ladies out. In the meantime they were surprised to find that Arthur and Alice, inspired by Paddy's plans, had put some more effort into their own vege garden; it seemed that Arthur was on the mend, socially and cognitively at least, for otherwise his right arm was rather paralyzed.

So, over the next week they all continued with these various activities, with John doing some paid work for the other toff property, pulling out obnoxious weeds again, and occasionally Les working at the wood mill, thus bringing in some cash with which to buy meat.

About two weeks later the family received a letter from Bill, saying he would ask around Sydney about selling the items of the Lansdowns, and might pay a visit. That was indeed followed up by Bill coming down on leave for a few days, and bringing some much needed tin food, compliments of the Army. It was a great time for all; finally it seemed that matters had taken a turn for the better.

Winter came on, they hunkered down to survive the cold of the highlands; work was done to secure the vegetables and animals from the frost; and exchanges, both socially and in terms of foodstuffs, took place between the Egans and the Lansdowns. Bill had taken Rose's items back to Sydney, and having sold them sent down a significant amount of money to help tide over the Lansdown ladies.

Spring came, and with it the warmer weather and lambs and chicks. Christmas soon loomed, and although no one expected anything grand in December, they celebrated being together and in doing relatively well, with another visit by Bill to add to the festive mood. Rose gave Noddy to Paddy in appreciation of all the work he had done, and allowed Grace to use the buggy as much as she needed, although she couldn't go to school yet because it was still closed. She and Paddy were frequent visitors to the Lansdown household, just to check on things and help out, and Arthur got better and better each week passing. A few letters arrived from Arthur's and Paddy's sisters, mostly Teresa, with little news of any significance about themselves or about Da in Dubbo.

Passing into **1933** life was plodding along, with more work coming their way.

Then tragedy struck. In February Rose's aunt suddenly passed away of natural causes. She would have been seventy or more, for sure, by Paddy's reckoning. Of necessity a cheap funeral and burial was organized, with only one child of Rose able to attend at such short notice.

Then in June, Arthur took up a job, having regained his strength, but after five days suddenly fell ill and was admitted to Berrima hospital again, where he remained for 3 months. It was suspected that he had a stroke or similar, or heart attack. His hospital confinement upended many things, not least adding frequent visits by family to his bedside. Then in August the unthinkable occurred: Arthur passed away at the young age of 43. Again, another cheap funeral was had, and he was buried in Bowral Cemetery. It was too costly to send telegrams to notify relatives in time, so the ceremony was local with few in attendance because of travel costs.

Life marched on, and the Depression was beginning to wane. Alice of course was distraught at the loss of Arthur, but she mustered resilience; she still had children to attend to. They, and Paddy, carried on with work and farming, and attending also to the needs of Rose who, now living alone, welcomed visitors, of which Paddy was a frequent one.

Again they straggled through another year, with nothing much new; it was the same-old-same-old of work, farming, resting, and petty entertainment. For Paddy it was reminiscent of his earlier days back in 1919. Although he loved the Bowral region, the highlands, he was nevertheless listless once again, as well as similarly without a female companion. These were the very same reasons he had embarked on a journey to Junee in 1920, but now he was getting old, quite old, at age 53.

1934 came around with little change in life, other than that more paid work was now available, and hence more money, some of which Paddy could too readily spend on grog.

Then came another blow, although it wasn't one that Paddy took much to heart. In mid year he learned from his sister, Teresa, that Anthony Egan, the patriarch of the clan, had passed away at age 79 from a heart attack in Dubbo. The death notice reported in the Narromine papers mentioned Anthony being survived by two sons, Paddy himself, and William, both in Bowral, and three daughters who were married, living elsewhere in NSW.

1935 arrived in its due time. Grace had grown into a marriageable woman; Les, now aged 15, was becoming a man, and John at 19 a full adult. The eldest son, Arthur Jnr, had not been seen in all this time, but had written over the years. He was successfully working up the north coast of NSW, and now about to marry at age 21. There were rumblings of problems in Europe, although not yet of war; still, Alice worried that her sons and also Bill could be called upon if war ever did break out. As distant colonialists of Great Britain, the Egans, like most Australians, particularly in the rural regions, didn't pay much heed to news of faraway places that were not of direct concern. But little did they know, of course, that in just 4 years lives and livelihoods would be shattered.

In the next few years the two lads at home drifted into Sydney to find work in manufacturing, that was increasingly developing if not yet fully gearing up for war production. Grace finished high school, met a chap who showed promise as a partner, and took a job in the regional city of Goulburn. This left Alice and Paddy. Eventually she moved up north to live with her eldest son, Arthur Jnr., while Paddy was enticed to move into Rose's large, almost empty house. *Greentrees* was mostly abandoned, except that Paddy maintained it as best he could in case any of the Egans wished to return to Bowral.

When war was declared in September 1939 Paddy was glad he was too old—at a few months shy of age 59—to join up, but he worried about the young lads he had known. He didn't keep in regular contact with them, other than Bill, who, already married and living in the south-western suburb of Campsie in Sydney, enlisted in the war in 1940 at the rather older age of 38.

By **1941** Rose was almost 63, two years older than Paddy, and not of good health. They decided to marry to socially legitimate at least their co-residence. But the marriage lasted barely a year: toward the end of 1941 Rose suffered a sudden heart attack; she died quickly at home.

It seemed that Paddy was cursed. First he had married Emily who ran off with another feller and died in 1925, then he married Clara Keough in Junee in 1926, who died barely 4 years later, and now, in his greying years, he had married Rose....

Some of Rose's close relatives were informed by telegram, as she had earlier instructed, and came down from Queensland to attend the funeral. Unlike most folks in the Bowral-Moss Vale area, Rose had chosen to be buried at Rookwood Cemetery in Sydney.

Paddy was now alone once again, and having to look after himself. Perhaps his only solace was steady work at a local timber yard, and drink. He had had no contact with any of his children from previous marriages, not Wally, Jack nor Ruth, and not even his Egan kids, Lillian and Marj.

What's more, Rose had left him almost nothing in her Will; she had not expected to die so soon, nor so quickly, so everything other than a few trinkets went to her children. *They* had no use of the house and land and set about selling it. For a few months after Rose's death Paddy stayed in the house, alone, until matters were settled. The house and the land, the vegetable garden he had developed and tendered, and the horses he had cared for and loved, the fences and chicken coop he had mended more than once, all the work he had done, were taken from him, but not his memories. Eventually Paddy had to move, to a place called locally as the *Shack*. It was near the timber yard owned and operated by a Mr. Lamb.

So Paddy worked to keep body and soul together, and to buy enough drink to forget his patchwork past and miserable present. Just as in Junee there was not much in Bowral to entertain him, to give him hope. He loved the lush green hills of Bowral, for sure, but green hills were not enough to keep a man company.

Bowral pub was his favourite watering hole, not only because it was the closest, but also because it was where he had started out in Bowral. Occasionally he might go to Mittagong for a change, to the "*Top Pub*" as locals called it. He was not sure why he visited *that* pub, perhaps he was hoping that a change in setting might bring change in his life. And oddly enough, it was again *deja vue*.

By 1942 Bill, his youngest brother, had returned from the war, discharged early because of some injury. Not knowing of all the events of the past ten years, other than of Arthur's unexpected death, he came with his wife to *Greentrees*, thinking he could pick up from where he had left off. But by this time all he found was the old house and the land leased to and occupied by another family.

It was a small community, so it was not difficult to find Paddy, and catch up with the stale news over some beers at the pub in Mittagong. He wasn't sure what he was going to do, but thought he would find a house, somewhere local, and wage work. Paddy was not part of his plan, now that Bill had a wife, and a kid on the way, and *Greentrees* had been taken from their lives.

Paddy's sojourns to Mittagong's pub became more frequent as he developed a familiarity with a barmaid there, Adele Winifred Moore. Originally from Sydney—Surrey Hills to be precise, a rather run down working-class area of terrace-house tenements—she was now a widow, as many women were. As with Clara some 20 years previously, he took a bit of a liking to her, and, as the then new parlance would have it, started 'dating' her. Neither were looking for romance as such, nor marriage, but just companionship as two lonely people.

Adele had moved to Mittagong with her now deceased husband, surviving after his death on his measly war-widow pension, supplemented by working part time at the pub, where she also rented a room. She wasn't initially interested in marriage so soon after her husband's passing, so she and Paddy simply enjoyed their free time together. But, perhaps as some form of closure on the war and the past, by 1946 they decided to marry. Paddy was now nearing 67, and getting too old to work and look after himself alone. Moreover, he had been injured in a recent car accident, and had to give up work, and thereby become a pensioner. After such an active, physical life, of being so independent, this turn of events was unfortunate in the sunset of his life. He began to see himself as rather emulating his father's last years of existence, although Paddy did not have LingLing.

And so, he married Adele Moore in Surrey Hills; that was where any of her family still lived, so it was convenient for them to attend the wedding. It was no skin of Paddy's nose, he didn't have any 'known' children or relatives, other than Bill, and was happy to go along with what Adele wanted. Returning to Moss Vale they moved after a year or two into a small house called *Eggleston*.

About a year into the marriage Paddy was surprised to receive a short letter from his youngest daughter, Marjorie Egan. However, she had addressed the letter to *Greentrees* in Bowral, and by chance the new residents there had passed it on to Bill, who gave it eventually to Paddy. Even so, Paddy was at a loss to know how Marj knew his whereabouts at all in the Highlands...

Marj was about 16 years old by then, and mentioned she was living with the Smart family in Goulburn, as he knew. She would be finishing school soon. He replied very briefly, merely stating Marj would be welcome to visit him and her step-mother, Adele, and he wished her good luck with her exams. He wasn't much of a writer...

As for Lillian, he had never written to her, nor ever gone back for her as he had promised. Unbeknown to him Lillian was reasonably well cared for, at least in terms of food, clothes, education. Discipline was not harsh but stringent with the Bankes sisters, but she did need to meet with frequent religious requirements.

As she grew older she learnt housework skills, attended a local Catholic school, and was often reminded that when she was old enough she would take the vows of a Nun. She also learned to play the piano, although not very well, tolerated school insofar it allowed her to be away from the watchful eyes of the three sisters, and made some friends, many of whom no doubt were in the same religious situation as her.

Of course he wasn't to know, but in 1936 Mercedes Bankes, the eldest of the Bankes sisters, had died suddenly, just when Lillian was eight. This left the front bedroom vacant for Madeline, the second-most senior, to move in, and for Lillian to now share a bedroom with Elaine, as well as escaping the less diligent discipline from the remaining two sisters.

But this whole arrangement lasted only another year or so, until in 1938, when Lillian was ten; she and the two remaining sisters moved across the entire city to Manly. Walter Bayliss, who had fully retired, accompanied them, or perhaps initiated the venture. They occupied two adjoining houses at 44-46 Fairlight Street, a ten minute walk from the Manly Pier and Corso. There the ladies and Walter ran a *"Select Guest House"*, of which there were already many in the Manly area. But this particular set of dwellings was owned by none other than Flora McKinnon, sister-in-law to Hilda McKinnon in Narromine, the former having inherited the premises from her mother Mary McKinnon in 1930. But Flora never lived there or directly operated the house, preferring to move to Junee until well into the 1950s. Indeed, when Flora passed away in 1962 she bequeathed the estate to one Ethyl Tempest-Mogg, originally from Adelaide. It was a rather odd bequest, for there seems to be no social or kinship connection between the McKinnons and Ethyl, although it seems the latter did live in Manly for a while. Indeed, she (had) spent some 25 years in Oxford, and had helped establish Warnborough College in Britain and elsewhere. Very odd indeed.

In the meantime, however, Lillian was overjoyed with being at the seaside, the very place that Hilda had told her and Paddy about several years earlier, in 1932. Only it wasn't Paddy, her father, who took her to Manly. And, as she matured, Lillian was able to traverse the more exciting streets and shops than those which existed in her cloistered life of Iron Street, Parramatta. Indeed, she was enrolled in St. Mary's Catholic School in Whistler Street, Manly, which required almost a 30 minute walk down to the Corso and along Whistler Street. Of course though, it was not a life of luxury and indulgence, as she had to attend early morning Mass at another nearby Church most days, as well as fetch the daily milk, and undertake additional chores in the *Elite Guest House*.

However, as WWII progressed, the boarding house was less and less elite; the ladies were now required by law to take as many boarders as possible, some of whom, to the sisters' lament if not horror, were not even Caucasian.

Notwithstanding this, and the various restrictions brought about by the war, Lillian for the first time had begun to enjoy her life and new experiences. Indeed, when she turned 18 in mid 1946 she was easily able to get a job at the Tax Office in Sydney. Needless to say, on the one hand, the two Bankes sisters were glad of the additional income to their household in the interim, still expecting Lillian to join a Nunnery at age 20, and on the other hand, Lillian felt free to be away from the household from very early morning till evening, to travel by ferry across the harbour with a friend, to explore Sydney town during her lunch break, and to have a little bit of money for herself. Add to that she developed her typing and telephony skills, which stood her in good stead for her next job on the administrative staff of Manly Hospital at the beginning of 1947. It was much closer to 'home', up on the Eastern Hill of Manly, which she accessed by the old Curtis 135 bus for half a penny, on the up-hill journey. But always smart, she walked down the hill after work rather than catch the bus, and thus was able to pocket herself the fare, amounting to a princely sum of two-and-a-half pence a week!

It was at the Manly Hospital that she became acquainted with Joe, a British ex-army corporal also working at the hospital. However, he also had a wife, Pearl, who was a patient there. Nevertheless, Pearl was soon transferred to Randwick hospital, no doubt to be closer to her own relatives in that area, and not long after died of TB.

Joe had for a time taken a shine to Lillian, and similarly vice-versa. But just as important, Lillian perceived the prospective marriage that Joe proposed as a way to escape the religious clutches of the Bankes sisters and pending Nunnery.

Elaine and Madeline were horrified with this turn of events, and even more mortified when Lillian asked if she could bring Joe home to meet them. It was a resounding NO! If they could have had their way they would have locked Lillian in a room, but instead Lillian eloped, and married Joe.

So, in 1949 their first and only daughter, Elizabeth, was born. All of Lillian's hopes and dreams seemed to be coming true. Within another year their first son of four, Ian, was born in 1950, followed in 1951 by another, Gordon, and another in 1953, and yet another in 1955. The Egan family tree was growing, if not in name.

In the meantime the two Bankes sisters returned to Iron Street in Parramatta, and Walter Bayliss, now quite old and unwell, went to a nursing home in Granville, near Parramatta, passing away in 1952. Madeleine died a year later, in 1953.

Fifteen

Perth 2021

Following a routine established over several weeks, Mark once again arrived at the house of Elizabeth and Lillian. There were still a lot of gaps in their mother's story, but at least now it was reasonably coherent, and linear. It was time, he thought, to get his mum to reflect on some things, to tell more of her own story and feelings, rather than just facts.

As usual Elizabeth opened the front door and she and he headed for the kitchen to make the invariable cup of tea. Their mother soon joined them at the kitchen table—a place that was familiar for the working class, ever since Paddy's father, Mark reckoned; it was the place for a family to sit and discuss things.

"So mum, what was it like living in Parramatta, at Iron Street, how did the three sisters treat you?" he began, once they were all settled.

"At first it was ok, maybe because I was so young, and new. A novelty to them, also, maybe. And it was all new to me, too, of course. But I wasn't allowed to touch anything. Well, there wasn't much to touch, they led a very spartan life. We all got up at the crack o' dawn, mumbled some prayers—I wasn't even allowed to go to the loo until they were done. Then we had a cuppa tea and piece of toast. Elaine the youngest always made it. It was like a pecking order from the oldest sister down. Then we used to tidy up, make the beds, and I had to take the ladies' potties out to the loo. But I was never allowed into Mercedes' room without her being there, she even locked it when she left it! It was as neat as a pin, with all kinds of religious pictures on the walls, and statues, and she had a writing desk and bookcase, and a rug on the floor. But not much else.... Except, paintings. Ones *she* had painted, just stacked up in a corner, maybe twenty or so. She never showed them to her sisters, she thought they wouldn't appreciate them, and she didn't like criticism. But she did show some to *me*."

"Oh, why's that?"

"She was different from the other two. She thought of herself as cultured, educated, even as an accomplished artist! But she never put her works up for display, well, maybe she did before I came. I think she showed me because I couldn't criticize, and maybe to inspire me."

"So who was the nicest of the three?"

"Oh that was Dollie, Mercedes, the oldest. Sometimes she could look very stern, but more rather cold, stone faced. She controlled things in the house with a simple word or look. She took as God-given her place as *the* authority. And... She knew that Maddie and Elaine hated one another. I don't know why. But Dollie took advantage of that, you know, divide and rule, play one off the other. Sometimes she would be sweet to one of them, then another day to the other. But to me, she was almost always sweet and calm, and if she was angry she would just give you a look, maybe a word or two, and walk away."

"What did she look like? We don't have any photos of the three sisters. Only Roger when he was young."

"She was completely different to her sisters: self-disciplined, tall, slim, snow white hair, blue eyes that were gentle and kind, soft voiced, she was a dreamer, and tried to instill in me a love of art, music, and books and reading. That was my salvation. They had a piano in the dining room, so she would teach me."

"And the other two?"

"Shorter, a bit plump, and sharp features, with black hair, and loud and biting. Almost could have been witches. They had no interest in art and books and music, and Dollie didn't try to encourage them. So they resented me learning the piano and reading and trying to do paintings, they thought Dollie was foolish trying to teach me. They thought the more practical things of life, like domestic duties, were more important, and when they got cross with me Dollie stood between me and the other two, often turning aside their wrath with me, she mothered me, healing my hurts and tears."

"Sounds like those two were bored, and boring, and maybe lamented not having any men interested in them?"

"I don't know about men, but they certainly weren't attractive, but then, they *were* in their forties when I arrived."

"So generally you were happy with the ladies?"

"I wouldn't say happy, it was tolerable, so long as Dollie was there, and I avoided Elaine and didn't upset Maddie. But Elaine was the worst. Maybe she resented me, because she had always been the youngest."

"So Mercedes was your favourite....?"

"Oh no, I wouldn't say *favourite*. She was more like a mother or nice aunt to me, supportive, but stern. It was Maddie—Madeline—I liked best, she was more like a sister, she was always willing to play with me. We used to go picking fruit together, in the orchard out back. You'd never get the other two doing that!"

"And they all wore black?" Mark wanted to confirm.

"Yes. All the time, nothing else but black, or black and a little bit of white. Even I had to wear black, except at the house doing work and when I went to school; the uniform was dark navy blue but," Lillian chortled.

"So school...? Did you like it there?"

"It was ok, at least I was learning to read and write, and there was a library so I could look at books, but could never take them home. The nuns ran the place, so every day we had hours of preaching and reading the Bible. Then Wednesdays we attended the Chapel."

"And Church on Sundays, with the three sisters?"

"*Every* Sunday, rain or shine, and special days, Saints days, Christmas... Easter was the worse—four bloody days of it! The best part was the singing. Hymns of course."

"What was it like at the house, then?"

"Lonely. I didn't have any brothers or sisters to play with, and only allowed play-time for one hour a day, or do things with Dollie when she was in the mood. Elaine resented that. Dollie would come and get me to keep her company, to read or paint or play piano, so the other two sisters were left to do the housework, or do nothing. But most of the time I was shown how to do this, do that, washing up, laundry, sweep... As I got older I was given more and more to do on my own. They said they were teaching me domestic skills."

"But they wanted you to be a nun, so why would you need learn those domestic chores?"

"I don't know, Mark, I was a child. They gave me clothes and fed me while I was waiting for dad to come back. They kept on saying we're in a Depression..."

"As if you would know what that meant at age four or five!"

"They said things were hard outside, people with no work or homes to live in, so I should count myself lucky. They would point out the bums hanging about the streets or coming to the Church charity shop, saying I was lucky not to be one of them."

"Ha! So much for Christian charity. And no doubt inferring that if you went with your dad you *would* be one of them!"

"Yeah, but he was my dad, you know, I should've been with him regardless."

"When did you begin to understand he wasn't coming back?" Mark tried to delicately ask.

"Oh I don't know. So long ago. Time meant nothing when I was that age. I always expected him to come back any day, then, maybe after two years, I began to give up hope, and the sisters kept on saying things were hard outside, maybe he didn't have the money yet to come back."

"Yet! Ha! I suspect he never had much money at any time. And he didn't write?"

"No. Or maybe he did and the sisters never told me. You see, his swag was there, where he had left it, so I always thought he'd come back. But the worst of it was when I was older, I realized he would never come back. I didn't know what happened to him, could've been dead for all I know. Then later, when Marj found me, she said he had been living in Bowral. It was so close, but he never tried to contact me."

"And he never wrote?"

"No. Maybe he did, and the sisters never gave me the letters..."

"Or maybe he thought better let sleeping dogs lie? I mean, if he wrote or visited it would just bring back memories and hope?"

"I don't know, Mark. He didn't write to *any* of us. I don't think he was much of a writer. He only replied to Marj when she wrote to him first."

"Yeah. Guess we'll never know," Elizabeth observed. "Seems he was easy to let things go, when you think about it... He let Emily go, then moved on rather quickly after Clara died, left Dubbo easily enough, and Bowral, all that left behind, and remarried after Lansdown died, too. No indication he attended any funerals—his mother's, his father's..."

"Yes yes. But he wasn't a *bad* man. Him and me got on alright," Lillian defensively asserted.

"So what was good? Or the best part of living there, in Parramatta?" Mark changed tack.

"The orchard out back. It felt like the countryside, Junee. I felt free to run, laugh, pick fruit, especially if it was just me and Maddie, she was the fun one of the three. But I had no friends except at school. And I wondered all this time what had happened to Jack and Wally, and Marj and Ruth..."

"Yeah, must have been dreary."

"Sometimes, on a public holiday mostly, after prayers of course, I would go with them to the shops in Parramatta, not for nice things like clothes or treats, but for shopping, groceries. But they never bought anything else, anything nice....," Lillian lamented. "You know I had an aunt and uncle living in Parramatta? But I didn't know it then, not till much later. Who knows, I could well have passed them in the street!"

"Yes, mum. We found that out. Your aunt Grace, who had married George Herring. They lived in Granville, almost the next suburb over. She died in nineteen-fifty-six. But also, I think Paddy didn't know it either. And you don't know if you might have been better off with them. Could have been worse."

"At least they were blood, and might have known where my dad was."

'Yes, Grace *did* know, in fact', Mark momentarily paused in thought. Both of Paddy's sisters, Grace Herring and Teresa Green, knew he was in Bowral because various obits in the 1930s to '50s mentioned the fact.

"I know, mum. Just... Fate I guess. But think, if you didn't live with the three Bankes women, you wouldn't have gone to Fairlight, and so you wouldn't have met our dad..." Mark smiled.

"Well, that's another story. Going there, to Manly, changed my whole life."

"For the better I hope. But," Mark hastily added, "what else can you say about living with the three sisters?"

"Oh, I don't know. They had a piano, so I liked learning that," she repeated as though it was the thing that saved her sanity, or at least gave her delight. "But of course churchy music only."

"And Walter Bayliss? What can you say about him?"

"Not much really. He was scary at first, short, fat, loud, old, but he was alright when I got to know him. Kinda like a grandfather, and if I was in trouble he would try to side with me. I figure he must have been a good judge of character, always formal with the sisters, but stepped in if Elaine or Maddie was mad at me."

"Did things change when Dollie died? Nineteen-thirty-six, I think it was, so you would have been eight, and been at Parramatta about four years."

"Oh yes. I was really sad, but the other two wouldn't let me cry about it. Maddie moved into Dollie's room and changed everything. She threw out Dollie's paintings, but I think Mr. Bayliss saved them, maybe stored them somewhere or took them to the Charity shop to sell. I never saw them again. So, no more piano playing or reading, it was just housework and school."

"And then about two years later you all moved to Fairlight?"

"Oh yes, thank God! It transformed my life in so many ways. Even though I had more work to do, I also had more freedom, and it was much nicer in Manly."

"How did that come about? The move?"

"I don't know, really. I just heard that Mr. Bayliss had bought that place in Manly and spent three-hundred pounds fixing it up, and it was run as a boarding house."

"I see..." Mark scratched his head, as though trying to stimulate some neurons. "We know the sisters, only two now, and Bayliss and you were there, but we can't figure out how they knew about the place, or maybe they were offered the opportunity to run it as a boarding house. And, what did they do with the Iron Street property?"

"No idea. But I know when Roger died one or two of the sisters went to Narromine for his funeral, I think. Maybe they met that woman...the one running the boarding house there, and she told them..."

"Hilda McKinnon. Yes, possible. That was nineteen-thirty-three, about a year after you and Paddy left Narromine and went to Parra."

"Maybe."

"But I can't figure out why Hilda would mention it to the sisters. I mean, it's not exactly the hot topic of the day, and she *did* have a run-in with Flora McKinnon a few years earlier. So all I can think of is that Flora wasn't actually in Manly, she had gone back to Junee, and the Fairlight place was leased. Maybe Flora had asked Hilda to lease it, but she already had her own business in Narromine. And maybe the Bankes sisters if they went to the funeral were staying at Hilda's rather than Roger's house—because that would have been crowded at the time, with a widow, three kids and the Bankes' father—and so just in the general conversation of things it cropped up?"

"That's a lot of maybe's. But I would agree the three Bankes sisters would want their own place to stay, they didn't like crowds and noise, so staying at Roger's house would be horrifying for them."

"Indeed, I could imagine. And doubly so if Bayliss was with them for the funeral. Maybe Hilda told *him* about the Fairlight place? But that was nineteen-thirty-three, you didn't move to Fairlight until about nineteen-thirty-eight, five years later, when you were about ten years old."

Lillian gave a sigh, of both tiredness and exasperation.

"Wish I could remember, but I was so young then. All I know is that Elaine went back to Parramatta when Maddie died, and Bayliss too, I think."

"Yes, Maddie died in nineteen-fifty-three at age sixty-nine, so getting on a bit. Bayliss died in nineteen-fifty-two at age eighty-seven, and in Parramatta, a nursing home there. So I suspect he got too old to deal with the Fairlight house, returned to Parra' and maybe Maddie followed suit soon after. That left Elaine on her own and she was no longer a spring-chicken by nineteen-forty-six:

she was fifty-seven, running to sixty by nineteen-fifty, eh. So maybe not able to carry on, on her own…"

"But she also went back to Parramatta. I'm not sure when…," Lillian added. "But I did go and see her at some time."

"Oh well, not so important. Just curious now who took over till nineteen-sixty-two when Flora McKinnon died and gave the place to Ethyl Mogg. Do those names ring any bells, mum?"

"Nope. Not a jingle."

"Well, very strange indeed, all that. It seems Flora never married, so for some odd reason bequeathed the place to Ethyl Tempest-Mogg—her full name, nee: Tempest-Hay, originally from Adelaide, but her folks lived in Manly. That was in 1962 when she got the place, and she died in 1969. So how the heck did Flora know her, why give this valuable property, presumably a boarding house still, to Mogg? The only thing I can think of is that Flora held Ethyl in some kind of womanly esteem, worthy of beneficence, because Ethyl helped establish Warnborough College in the UK. But that is a long shot! Mogg/Tempest-Hay was from Adelaide, lived in Manly, sure, but Flora meanwhile was living in Junee! At least most of the time. She did come back to Manly at some time, living in the *Carlton Private Hotel*, in Victoria Parade."

"No idea," his mum insisted.

"Oh well… We'll keep searching… But, one last question: we came across some evidence that Walter Bayliss was married, maybe even twice—not sure about that. Pretty sure he was married to Georgina Gunning in nineteen-thirteen, lived in Wagga, she died in nineteen-forty-three in Bulli, down near Wollongong—have to check that. So, we're wondering, where was *she* when Walter B. was at Parra? And, most importantly how the feck did he get to know about the Fairlight place?"

"So, what's the question, Mark?" Elizabeth sought to clarify.

"Was Bayliss always at Parra, mum?"

Lillian looked at him with irreverence. "Of course! He moved with us to Fairlight. That's all I know. He was always with the sisters, until..., I don't know when, he went back to Parramatta. Maybe when Maddie died..."

"I need look at electoral rolls, or the census," Elizabeth explained. "That should tell us. But as for knowing about Fairlight Street, maybe Bayliss went to Roger's funeral in Narromine, met McKinnon there, maybe because he stayed at her boarding house, and she mentioned it to him."

"Possible. Would make sense," Mark agreed. "Bayliss was a friend of Roger, we *assume*. Would certainly have known him, or *of* him, living with the three sisters. Besides, not the proper thing to do in the thirties for a woman to go traipsing alone across the countryside to a funeral, so maybe Walter accompanied one of the sisters, or all of them..."

"I don't think they needed an escort, Mark," his mother suggested. " they were pretty formidable."

"Mmm. Maybe so. But I was thinking not for reasons of security or safety, but chastity, as a chaperone, kinda. It probably wasn't right for a woman, *any* woman, to travel alone in the thirties."

On that note, without a great deal of more detailed information, but rather mostly ideas and innuendos, Mark once again left his mother and sister. No doubt he would return again another day.

Sixteen

Finale 1952

In 1952, on May 4, Paddy Egan passed away from stomach cancer at age 73, at Berrima Hospital. This of course was unbeknown to Lillian.

His sister, Teresa Green, died but a year later, in 1953, and for her obit it was noted she was survived by only one brother, William, now living in Campsie, not so far from Parramatta, and a sister, Grace (Herring) living, ironically, in Granville, also very close to Parramatta. She died not long after, in 1956.

Paddy Egan was buried in an unmarked grave in Bowral Cemetery.

And so ended Paddy's story with that of his eldest daughter, Lillian, having set out together from Gundagai all those years ago, in 1932. Lillian had matured from a 4 year old wain to a 24 year old woman, as attractive as her mother Clara, with her own family. She had traversed half the State with her father—Junee, Gundagai, Cootamundra, Dubbo, Narromine, Warren, Parramatta—to end up in the idyllic setting of Manly, by the sea. And in her final days lived in Perth, ironically the very place that Paddy had *claimed*—very dubiously—to have been born, on a ship.

Wally Lampe (top left) Jack Lampe (lower left).
Marj Egan (top right), Ruth Lampe (lower right),
Lillian Egan (centre)

Paddy *never* did come back to get Lillian, as he had *promised*, and poignantly he had been living so close in Bowral for those last 20 years, which was within easy travelling distance of Lillian in Sydney. But Paddy never contacted her, and *she* had no way of knowing how to find him, nor for that matter her other siblings—Ruth, Wally, Jack, and Marj. It was only in the late 1950s that Marj initiated a search and reconnected all the siblings, and the whole story begun to unfold.

END

EPILOGUE

This historical-fiction narrative began when my sister and I were tracing our ancestors. We had *some* information, both documentary and anecdotal, and informal documents such as letters. Some were from our mother, Lillian Egan, while she was alive, although not always lucid or accurate.

We know for sure her mother and father, and her sibling (Marj) and possibly half sibs (Ruth, Wally, Jack). But before 1926 the trail was totally cold. We cannot be sure that Wally and Jack are or are not Paddy's children, but it would be reasonable to assume that Paddy did not simply turn up in 1926 and have a whirlwind romance with Clara and immediately marry her; he would have needed to court her, often a long, slow process especially under the watchful eyes of the Keoughs; and if Wally was born in 1921, that would mean the father (Paddy?) would have been in town 9 months earlier, in 1920; or are we to assume that Clara had another lover or other lovers? Doubtful, given the need to consider her social reputation in a close, Christian moral community. And one could easily envisage the Keoughs' and Smarts' disapprobation of Paddy getting Clara pregnant out of wedlock and he unwilling—largely because he was unable—to marry her until 1926.

And then after 1932 the trail becomes more narrative and speculation. We picked up the trail of Lillian's father, Paddy, essentially, and ironically, when he died in 1952 in Bowral. Working backwards we found that he had been married to Lansdown before his last wife (Moore, 1946-52) in the Bowral area, and of course in 1926 to Clara Keough in Junee before that. We then had our mum's story of being left by Paddy at the house of the 3 Bankes sisters in Parramatta, in about 1932.

Thus Paddy's narrative, our grandfather, had many and quite large gaps: where was he before 1926, and in fact how old was he when he married in that year. (However, even if we work backward from his age at and date of death (73 in 1952), we have no surety that he was 73 then; that is what *he* had told his then wife, Adele Moore. Indeed, what *did* he tell Adele? He didn't seem to have or produce a valid birth certificate. Adele informs the Coroner that Paddy was born in Ireland! Did he tell her this, or she simply assume it? Nevertheless, the age of 73 does correspond with a birth year of 1879-80).

How the feck did he even meet Clara? And what happened to him and Lillian in1931 to sometime in 1932? We have it on reasonable authority, our mum's recall, that she, at least, went to Gundagai and/or Goulburn for a while, then Paddy took her to Parramatta via either Sydney or Narromine. But this is the memory of a 4 year old, told over the next 60-plus years, no doubt with variations and embellishments.

While we are confident Lillian was raised by the Bankes sisters from 1932 to about 1949, then questions arise as to how that came about? How did Paddy avail himself of their guardianship?

By chance, largely, we also encountered a George A Egan and his clan in originally Molong and the Bathurst/Orange region, and then Dubbo and Narromine and Warren, beginning in 1855 when Anthony Egan, George's father, was born. George was born in 1880; his parents were Anthony Egan and Ann Bridget Ryan; ultimately, we found that Paddy's details matched these dates and parents. Could George and Paddy be one and the same person? Putting together some of this information it would be reasonable—*some* may say speculative—to suggest a narrative of these "two" men as one, which could account for the gaps in the historical narrative of both.

For example, why is that Paddy had no siblings, whereas George had 13, as was common? How is it that Paddy arrives on the scene in 1926, and possibly a few years before that, out of nowhere, without any documentation, just when George disappears from the narrative in 1917?

Now most genealogists, or ordinary folk tracing their ancestry, might agree one needs *proof* of relationships; that *evidence* might be suggestive, and strongly so, but it is nevertheless not *proof*. And many genealogists, as the self-acclaimed experts, declare one needs 3 pieces of proof. But who is to say categorically, without question, that one needs 3 pieces of proof, and what might happen if that "proof" itself is wrong (or contradicts other proofs)? And indeed, who is to say what kind of proof?

Even so, assuming one has all the proof in the world, drawing linear and vertical lines on a kinship chart might all be well and good, but hardly puts flesh on ancient bones. Lines on a chart do not tell a story but are themselves subject to sometimes speculative narrative and interpretation.

It is only through language, though literature, that things come to life. Literature endows things and people with smell, shape, meaning, form, thoughts, and feelings. Indeed, life is created because someone describes it, because someone put pen to paper and wrote, "Once upon a time...."

In these terms, books, narratives, are magic. They make silent facts and connections visible. They transform their readers, metamorphose them, open doors into other people's heads, bodies, lives, even when they've been dead for many years. Readers explore someone else's mind, dream someone else's dreams, walk in different bodies, feel what strangers felt in their misery, desperation, passion, joys, and travel through different lands and times. Stories turn people into travelers through time and situations, relationships and alternative possibilities.

Such stories are testaments to family and social history, as the story-teller lived it; and every story matters, not simply stories of the great, the famous, the rich, or the evil, or stories of trauma and upheavals such as we witness about POWs or holocaust survivors. While these are certainly worthy of narration, the fact is that *every* story tells a story of how ordinary people lived in whatever circumstance, revealing in their own way the human social condition.

So what if Paddy is (was) George A Egan? And of course vice-versa; the one and the same? How could we give a reasonable life to that one narrative, one that makes it possible, even perhaps probable?

Paddy's story attempts to do just that, and in so doing draws on some remarkable similarities between the "two" characters, as well as tensions in their different accounts.

Issue #1.

1. There are no records at all of Paddy/Patrick (George?) Egan prior to 1926.

2. The first information encountered is a marriage certificate to Clara Violet Keough in Junee in which *he* provides the information of his age (38, born in 1888) and that his parents were of the same name, Ann Bridget Ryan and Anthony Egan (deceased) as George A Egan. In fact, Ryan was deceased in 1914 and Anthony was still alive (d. 1934).

3. There is a reliable death record in Bowral of him dying in May 1952 at age 73 = born in 1880.

4. His daughter, Marj, writes to Paddy in Bowral in 1941-46.

5. There are 2 reliable marriage certificates of Paddy marrying in the Bowral area in 1941 and 1946.

6. So we can put Paddy in Junee and Bowral between 1926 and 1952, but where was he for 46 years prior?

7. There are significant records/accounts of George A. Egan (GA) until mid 1917: Birth registration (declared by his mother in 1908 in Narromine), railway work 1906-12, marriage to Emily Oakley in1903, and supposed military/war records of 1899 and

1917. He declares his age as 37 years (b. 1880) in 1917. This makes him about age 72-73 in 1952, the same age when Paddy died.

8. His birth shows October 1880 and his parents as Ann Bridget Ryan and Anthony Egan in the Molong/Bathurst area, and subsequently living in Dubbo and Narromine.

9. No records after 1917 exist; there are no death or burial records, no marriage record after that with Emily in 1903 (and he does not remain with her after 1915). No divorce record? Emily dies 1925.

10. GA's two sisters, Grace (Herring) and Teresa Green, mention their brother, George, living in Bowral in 1934 when their father, Anthony, dies in Dubbo, and that he is not there when Teresa dies in 1953. A brother, Arthur, lived in Bowral until he died in 1933.

11. There is no official record of GA after 1917, only incidental records of him living in Bowral in 1934 and prior to 1953.

Are we to assume, then, that there were *two* George/Paddy Egans, with the same parents' names, of the same age, living at the same time in the then small town of Bowral?

Issue #2.

1. Lillian Egan, Paddy's daughter, refers to him has having an "injury" to one of his (right) hands, possible a damaged/missing thumb or having two thumbs.

2. George A Egan is recorded in a newspaper report in Dubbo of having damaged his hand in a shooting accident, and his military medical record also indicates some hand damage.

3. Lillian also mentions in a letter or note about her and Paddy going to Narromine in about 1932 (to visit relatives?). It is never mentioned that Paddy had any relatives at all. Why would he go to *Narromine*—of all places, and in the midst of the Depression? And to visit relatives he supposedly did not have!?

4. George A Egan has several relatives in the Dubbo-Narromine area.

So, we now have two Egans of the same age with the same damaged hand, one having a lot of relatives in the Dubbo/Narromine region, and the other, Paddy, with no known relatives, visiting for no known reason that very region. And, moreover, Paddy possibly meeting with Roger Bankes and/or Hilda McKinnon with, respectively, connections with the Bankes sisters and Manly, where Lillian ends up.

Issue #3.

1. Signatures by Paddy and George A Egan on 2-3 documents closely resemble one another.

Issue #4.

1. An "aunt" of Paddy's makes reference to Paddy having been in Africa (ie. he should have stayed there). The is no indication Paddy had been in Africa, but GA had been.

2. Paddy has no known siblings—very unusual for the times. GA has 13.

Précis

1. Gundagai — Cootamundra 1932

Paddy's and Lillian's journey from Gundagai to Cootamundra then by train to Dubbo.

2. Perth 2021

Mark and his sister, Elizabeth, question their mother, Lillian, about travelling across NSW, especially to Gundagai and Cootamundra, and meeting relatives.

3. Dubbo 1932

Paddy/George meets with his Dad, Anthony Egan, and catches up on various news. He makes plans to go to Narromine/Warren and talk to Roger Bankes, etc.

4. Narromine — Warren 1932

Paddy and Lillian go to Narromine, meet Hilda McKinnon* and Roger Bankes, then George Gee in Warren. Paddy arranges with Roger to take Lilly to the Bankes sisters in Parramatta. He and Lilly leave Narromine/Dubbo by train for Parramatta.

* It's not clear that they did meet Hilda McKinnon (as indeed there was another Mrs. H. McKinnon of a rather large McKinnon clan in Narromine, and who *did* run a boarding house). Hilda married Alan Hugh McKinnon in 1927 in Balmain; he died a year later, in 1928. His mother, Mary McKinnon, ran a boarding house at 44-46 Fairlight Street, Manly, Sydney; she died in 1924. The house may have been inherited by both Hugh and his sister, Flora, and Hugh ran it for a few years with Hilda, until perhaps 1930, in which year Hilda and Flora had a legal dispute over money that Hugh owed to Flora. Records subsequently show Hilda as a widow living in Sydney Road in 1934, and dying in Sydney in 1937 at age 33-34. Meanwhile, Flora lived in Junee from about 1930 to 1960. By 1962 she had returned to Manly, where she died that year.

So the question remains: how did Paddy and Lillian—or at least Lillian and the Bankes sisters—come to know of the Manly house, and before that how did Paddy know of the Bankes' house in Parramatta?

5. Perth 2021

Mark and Elizabeth discuss with Lillian a few issues about her stay in Narromine/Dubbo and going to Parramatta in 1932, and any connection with the Bankes family.

6. Dubbo 1880 — 1917

Paddy sleeps on the train and 'dreams' about his past/upbringing in Dubbo etc. He recalls signing up for the Boar War in Africa, returning in 1902, and marrying Emily Oakley in 1903. George Sands meets Emily. Paddy enlists for WW1, but is discharged shortly after in 1917. He disappears from known records.

7. Parramatta: Arrival 1932

Paddy and Lillian are on the train to Parramatta. They go to Iron Street, meet Walter Bayliss and the three Bankes sisters.

8. Perth 2021

Lillian talks to Mark and Elizabeth and reflects with confusion about events going to Parramatta.

9. Parramatta: Departure 1932

Paddy stays a few days in Parramatta, then leaves Lilly. He goes to Bowral, reflecting on the journey where it all began: Sydney, Bowral, Junee, Gundagai... Full circle. Leaving Emily and the Army he had gone to Bowral and lived with his brothers, Arthur and Bill, then had gone to Junee where he met and married Clara Keough/Lampe in 1926. He raised a family until Clara died in 1931.

10. Bowral 1917 — 1920

On the train in 1932 to Bowral after leaving Lilly, he reflects on the past from 1915-17 to about 1920 when he decides to go to Junee.

11. Junee 1920 — 1926

Paddy arrives in Junee 1920, meets Clara, lives in a boarding house, gets job on the railway, visits Coolamon and meets the Keoughs. Clara gets pregnant, Paddy agrees to marry her but he can't. News that Emily has died arrives early 1926. Paddy marries Clara.

12. Junee 1926 — 1932

Life goes on but the Great Depression looms, Paddy loses work, moves to Old Junee, then to The Triangle in Junee, Marj is born in 1930, Nellie dies 1930, January 1931 Clara dies, Keough clan takes Marj, the 3 others move to Goulburn with the Keoughs or Smarts, Lilly stays with Paddy to the end of 1931 then they go to Gundagai.

13. Perth 2021

Comments from Lillian about her sibs, her mum dying and living in The Triangle.

14. Bowral 1932 — 1952

Paddy had been reflecting about his past of 1915-17 to 1931; back now to 1932 having dropped off Lilly at Parramatta, he goes to Bowral again. Bill is in the army, Arthur sickly, (he dies in 1933), Paddy swags around Bowral. He builds up the farm, marries Lansdown (1941), then Moore (1946).

15. Perth 2021

Lillian talks about being at Parramatta and Manly.

16. Finale 1952

Paddy dies in 1952, and Lillian has married and is busy raising 4 kids; she reunites with her sibs.

Other books by Warrior Publishers

warriorpublishers@outlook.com

warriorpublishers.yolasite.com

1. The Habitus of Fertility: A Tale of Two Families.
Paul Mathews.
ePub ISBN: 978 13 7075 5837
smashwords.com/books/view/775568

Ever since 1968 when Lynch wrote the Church and religion had no effect on Filipino fertility the topic has been taboo and ignored. This book challenges that legacy, suggesting there is a fertility differential between Catholics and Protestants. Part 1 narrates the lives of 2 families showing how a fertility disposition is acquired and operationalized. This is greatly expanded in a 2018 novel (A Tale of Two Families). Parts 2 and 3 show how an idea/disposition can be operationalized, and across generations.

2. I Can Never See My Self.
Sanitee T'Chong.

Mark, a retired, divorced professor, looking for a young female travel companion, falls in love with one of his research subjects, Annalyn, and sets out to educate her and help her poor family in the rural Philippines. But her education changes her to reject Mark's love and exploit him. Despite helping other similar girls, he is left with no girlfriend. Finally, he embarks on helping yet another girl. Through these engagements he realizes that these girls cannot see themselves as perhaps others do, nor the possibility of a better life; and the only way they can move forward to that is with outside help, of sorts. But in order to benefit from such patronage they need to see themselves as something other... As Mark travels the country with different girls their adventures depict and remark on various aspects of Philippine culture, society and life. Mark's search for love shows that desire is sad, sometimes cruel, and girls beguiling.

Amazon paperback 978 15 2205 9813
Amazon: ISBN-13: 978-1093912999
smashwords.com/books/view/738824
ISBN: 9781370673988

3. Male Prostitution: Two Monographs.
Paul Mathews.

smashwords.com/books/view/662166

The 1st paper describes salient aspects of male prostitution of Manila in the 1980s and '90s, its reasons, how boys reconcile their activities with church and morality and how they construct their sexual identity. The 2nd paper critiques Being A Prostitute. Certain categories of male prostitutes have been excluded in studies, to suggest that male prostitution derives from a recurrent economic determinism, contrary to a broader structural approach.

4. Are They Serious? The Discourses of Family Planning, Bio-Citizenship and Nationalism in the Philippines.
Paul Mathews.

smashwords.com/books/view/681248
ISBN: 9781370152902

Explores the discourses of bio-medicine (Family Planning), nationalism and citizenship in the Philippines. The nationalist narrative is constructed in terms of neo-Malthusianism with the objectives and consequences of maintaining high population growth. The over-riding question is: why would the State implement a FPP for the lower classes when it was thought by policy makers that the former were incapable if being uplifted?

5. Education and EFL in Taiwan: Policy and Practice.
Paul Mathews.

978 13 7046 4418
smashwords.com/books/view/718304

Focuses on systemic problems and issues of EFL teaching in Taiwan. Goal posts shift, nothing changes: rote learning, exams, hierarchic structures, culturally-based vis-à-vis earned respect, cheating, plagiarism, credentialism, profiteering, linguistic incompetence and political infighting persist. After 9yrs of EFL many college graduates are not competent in English.

6. Samantha Guimoi and The Trinity of Terror (A narrative of power).

Sanitee T'Chong.

smashwords.com/books/view/444048

978 064 65 71478

amazon.com.au/Samantha-Guimoi-Trinity-Terror-Sanitee

A 17 year old ABC student ensnares a litany of men in her life to further her own selfish ends.

Beware the Ides of March ! 17 year old ABC student, Samantha Guimoi, ensnares the men in her life to further her own selfish ends. Mark was but one of a litany of men—and not the last—with whom Sam flirted, seduced, and fucked, to achieve her goals.

Samantha had the power of erotic capital, but the moral and administrative power of bitch brigades and feminine discourses were blind to its capacity. In their myopic view of the world that they fabricated, they inverted power relationships, claiming all women, especially young, nubile Asian student girleens, were victims, Asian victims, of tacit male power.

This is a tale about a monster.....but who is the monster ?

Mark's relationship with Samantha at the University of No Ideas exposes the dark secrets of the ivory-tower. His relationship with Sam is as much about sex as it is about feminism, student-teacher relationships, and the silly laws and moral discourses that govern the Academy. It is also about the media, moral terror, cyber terrorism, sexuality, fat people...amongst other fat things.

Amazon:

7. Naked in a Nipa Hut: I'm a Cybersex Gurl and I wanna tell you my story.
Paul Mathews.

smashwords.com/books/view/579749

ISBN: 9781310141461

A sequel to: Asian Cam Models. Presents case studies of ACMs, in their own words; and outlines the structure of the sex industry in the Philippines.

8. Asian Cam Models: Digital Virtual Virgin Prostitutes?
Paul Mathews.

smashwords.com/books/view/447769

ISBN: e-book: 9781310001314

Explores the cybersex industry in the Philippines. Pioneers research in economics, labour relations, sexuality, globalization, digital technology. Identifies piecework relations of a new global industry.

9. MY RIDDLE BOOK. 170 all-time riddles and jokes.
Jhenna Umali.

smashwords.com/books/view/456860

ISBN: 9781311113498

10. TRAVELLERS IN TAIWAN Reflections of Formosa.
Shi-Hui Lee and Paul Mathews.

smashwords.com/books/view/458374

ISBN: 97813 113 49897 (English);

97813 111 22759 (Chinese).

What do foreigners think of Taiwan? How long do they stay? What do they do? Are Taiwanese friendly and smart? Should Taiwan join China? Find out what these strange "white monkeys" get up to in this Formosa...

11. The Can: Benny and The Gems.
Bruce Roberts and Paul Mathews

smashwords.com/books/view/598910

ISBN: 978 13 1103 8692

Set in the 1970s when petrol was leaded and cell-fones weren't even a dream, The Can was written while Ben was in jail. It tells the story of how he came to be there, following a series of crazy, hippy events on the NSW Nimbin-vego north coast. Ideal for teens, those who never read, or remedial reading.

12. DAZE OF OUR LIVES.
Bruce M. Roberts and Paul Mathews
smashwords.com/books/view/619690
ISBN: 9781311726292

Ben Coady is the epitome of a free-living hippy. He has a knack for getting into all sorts of strife and usually comes out of it by the skin of his smoke-stained teeth. A sequel to The Can.

13. Complementary Therapeutics. A Selected Annotated Bibliography.
Paul Mathews and Heidi Boon.
ISBN: 9781311871466
smashwords.com/books/view/602281

As a chronology, it traces a change in beliefs and attitudes, where the body, health, nature and society have come to mean different things and imply different consequences for the individual and society.

14. Directory of Filipinists in Australia and Bibliography.
Paul Mathews and A Fisher.
ISBN: 978 13 1076 6961
smashwords.com/books/view/621655

Lists the names, qualifications and interests of Filipinists who have made contributions to Philippine studies in Australia.

15. Collected Poems...and Philosophical Essays.
Paul Mathews.
smashwords.com/books/view/623150
ISBN: 9781310395543 Free

15 poems and 5 essays on controversial issues: Images of Public Servitude, Land Rights for Gay Whales, Lost in (Third) Space [How I Lost My Ethnic Identity].

16. Princes of Beauty: Boy Prostitution in Sydney.
Paul Mathews.

ISBN: 9781311368256

smashwords.com/books/view/639594

Male sex-workers are motivated to achieve; they cannot be considered in purely psychological or sexual terms. Boys choose to be prostitutes vis-a-vis classical stereotypes. It questions male prostitutes and their clients as gay, dirty and unmotivated. A sociological study with case histories and a review of features, causes and literature.

17. THE THINGS WE DO FOR MONEY. . . ! Everything you always wanted to know about taxis but the driver wouldn't tell you . . .

Paul Mathews.

ISBN: 9781370551415

smashwords.com/books/view/658100

An insight into taxi driving and crazy passengers. The stories will keep you amazed and laughing, and the pictures of historical value.

18. A Tale of Two Families.

Paul Mathews.

ePub ISBN: 9780463250174

Amazon paperback ISBN-10: 1980979049; -13: 978-1980979043

smashwords.com/books/view/822236

amazon.com/Tale-Families-Paul-William-Mathews/dp/1980979049/

Here I narrate with insight and drama the lives of two families, one Protestant, the other Roman Catholic, in the rural Philippines. I narrates how the Garcia family, Catholics, headed by Juan, live out their lives. Up the street is Wenico and Lennie Valdez, Protestants. The story depicts, also, how they live their lives. Other characters impinge upon both the Garcia and Valdez households, bringing twists and turns, and highlighting certain characteristics of not only the two families but also of everyday life in the Philippines.

Both the Garcia and Valdez families are about equal in socio-economic status, and largely in terms of education, also. But there are differences, as will become evident. Perhaps the main difference is their religion, and it is worth exploring how and why this affects how each family, and each individual, lives out their lives according to the underlying perception of the world, grounded in their religious orientation. In particular, Mark, an anthropologist in the narrative, is particularly interested in why Catholics vis-à-vis Protestants have more children: it's not a matter of "if" but, for him, why.

The other characters and events highlight differences between the two families, and between Protestants and Catholics, between rich and poor, exploiters and exploited, powerful and powerless, men and women, and so on. But what is fundamental to their similarities and differences? How do they actually come about?

19. Mabait: A Foothold in Life.

Paul W. Mathews

smashwords.com/books/view/927160

amazon.com/dp/1090642709?ref_=pe_3052080_397514860

E-Pub ISBN: 978-0-4634-5800-6

Amazon paperback ISBN-13: 978-1-0906-4270-7

The lives of Cielo, a sex-worker, and Angie, a bureaucrat, briefly but antagonistically intersect in Manila. Several years later Angie seeks the help of Cielo, but neither are aware now of who the other is. They both come to realize that each has barely a foothold in life and that they both want the same things: family, love, respect, dignity. In their respective struggles to attain these, each girl recognizes the other as fundamentally mabait (good at heart).

20. Bankrolling Poverty.
Paul W. Mathews.
ISBN: 13- 9798224782260
smashwords.com/books/view/15273512024
Read more about Cielo and her life here, how she was always mabait and rose above where she had been initially planted.

Cielo, a poor, exploited Filipina who works hard just to survive, is entrapped in Rodrigo Tiago's cycle of puppetry—until she realizes a means of retribution, freedom and justice. Using her beguiling performative skills learnt from the streets of Manila, Cielo manipulates Tiago's troll-like accountant to bring down the house of Tiago. A final quirk of nature purges her from the Spirit of poverty.

21. The Magical Shahua and fifty shades of fur....
Paul Mathews
smashwords.com/books/view/949920
amazon.com/dp/1082326445
ISBN: 9781082326448
ISBN-10: 1082326445
Shahua is a very magical cat, who can cross time and space, bringing luck and good fortune to those hoomins who deserve it. In Taiwan Mark and Kitty save Shahua from certain death. She/he magically brings good fortune to Kitty and her family of cats. Twenty years later Mark meets Ping, "the cat lady" in Australia. He helps her feed the cats, and coming to know her they fall in love. But Ping thinks she is ugly because of her deformity. Mark helps with Ping's life and together they discover a prophecy from Shahua. Following instructions, they discover Ping's father has left her a large inheritance. Now she is able to fulfill her dream of having a safe-house for abandoned cats, to fix her hands, and marry her 'prince'. But in this journey Mark and Ping also meet with a 'fairy'. Is

she also an incarnation of Shahua? While the narrative tells of Mark meeting Ping and their good fortunes, it also draws parallels with a story that Mark reads to Ping about his experience with Shahua in Taiwan. It is the same story across time and space, of how we cast out those who are disabled, strange, or simply different, much to our regret. It is purely magical.

22. Someone Like Me....Of Difference and Anguish. Sanitee T'Chong.

smashwords.com/books/view/960737

ISBN: 9780463235584 Free

This long book (450pp) is about bullying. James' basic thesis is that his early life is representative of many young people growing up; it is a period of growth in which they encounter many trials, tribulations and small triumphs, in a society that is unable or unwilling to acknowledge these tribulations, and especially the sexuality of young people and the bullying they experience, and its effects. James was different, and he dared to be different. As a result, he was teased, bullied, marginalized, labeled strange, and experienced a lot of anguish. Thus, his life was often about finding someone like him, to avoid loneliness and friendlessness, to be understood.

James wrote this narrative diary to tell his story, without clear intent. And when one looks at it, it does seem to be all about him. But when you begin to look at what he experienced, suffered, it is in fact more about the society in which he lived; and although it is set in the 1950s to '70s, many of the conditions, thinking, social attitudes and so forth continue to exist as they were, as some legacy of bygone days. Time has marched forward, but attitudes and behaviours have not.

James' story, the story of his life, then, is not about him, but the effect that myopic social views have of individuals, not least of which is bullying in some form or other, to the effect, at the extreme, of suicide or murder. And if it is suicide as a result of bullying then it is murder....social murder.

Nonfiction, Biography, Autobiographies and Memoirs, Sex and Relationships, Men's sexuality, teens, psychology, bullying

23. Lost in Transition. A Narrative of Bullying.
Sanitee T'Chong

smashwords.com/books/view/1096465
ISBN: 9781005048808 Free

Everyone would like to say they had a good, happy childhood, a nice home, with plenty of food, a loving family, supportive siblings, a friendly neighbourhood, friends, and who enjoyed school, and did well in their studies.

But that can't be said for Langley Badcock, or Lang for short—or gangly Langley as he often thought of himself. No, he was one of those kids we see in American movies who can't get a prom date, or in fact any date. But the Melbourne region, Australia, doesn't even have proms like the Yanks do; oh, more recently High Schools have adopted a facsimile now, a Graduation Night, mostly formal, maybe some dancing. But when Langley Badcock was growing up, finishing High School in the early 1970s, there was barely such a thing. Just as well, he often thought when he saw those stoopid B-grade feel-good American teen movies, for he would never have been able to get a prom date. I mean, he was so ugly, as skinny as a blade of grass, scrawny, unkempt, and "known" to be a poof, that no girl would ever even look at him once, let alone twice. Besides, he went to an all-boys school, so where the hell would he come in contact with girls? Hire one for a prom?—now there's a business for an entrepreneur! Ask his sister if one of her ugly friends would pretend to be his date? And even if he could get a girl, he would loath to attend any school or public function for fear of being ridiculed, teased, bullied, and especially in front of a girl of all people!

No.... Better to skip social occasions altogether. He was destined to be just one of those boys who never fitted in, would never fit in.

FREE ISBN: 9781005048808

24. A Murder of Sorts.

Sanitee T'Chong

E-Pub ISBN: 9781005674182

smashwords.com/books/view/1175886

In 1970 London, Constance Foster takes care of identical twin girls, Melody and Melanie Markle, forsaken at birth by their mother. Given a new lease of life from the pitiful orphanage they had known for 12 years, the twins travel to Venice with Connie and her friend, 'aunt' Amanda. There they stumble upon a cold case of alleged murder, for which Eddy Downton is about to be hung. Can they save him from the gallows at the eleventh hour, and expose a nefarious kidnapping scheme at the same time? Will the twins be reunited with their long-absent mother? A charming, traditional and intricate British mystery. No damsels swooning at the feet of narcissistic macho-men, but ample drama and romance, antics and laughter, a touch of cuteness, and twists and turns at every step from London to Venice. Follow the footsteps of this feel-good drama to uncover mysteries, where nothing is quite as it seems.

25. Murder ? in Dunsborough.

Sanitee T'Chong

E-Pub ISBN: 9781005221706

smashwords.com/books/view/1141728

A Murder? A very cold case. A poltergeist. A pregnant betrayal? A diary. A missing Coroner's Report. A prize-winning novel. And a blossoming romance. What more could you want? In 1969 Mrs. Foster and her ward, Amanda, return to an English village 10 years after being coerced out. Amanda finds a news-clip of an "accidental" shooting in 1914. They set out to prove a very old murder indeed. Possibly.

26. WHO WILL CARE FOR THE CHILDREN?

Foreign Domestic Helpers and Female Labour Force Participation in Singapore, Hong Kong and Australia.

Dr. Paul W Mathews.

Non-Fiction.

In these papers I explore how FDHs have contributed, and continue to contribute, to the economic and social development of Singapore and HK, using primarily Filipina and Indonesian domestic helpers (maids, nannies, yaya) as a primary focus. I explore how government and economic policies and opportunities translate to the HH level by presenting several case studies that support the general thesis that FDHs contribute a hitherto unrecognized added value. I argue that it was (is) not merely the sheer numbers of FDHs that enabled local (skilled) women to enter the economy; rather, and more importantly, FDHs not only contributed to general productivity but to productivity at a higher added value (and continue to do so). Thus, while local women should be recognized for their LFP and at a higher level, so too should FDHs who provided that opportunity for the former to do so, and thereby (indirectly) added substantial value to the economy. Finally, I suggest that the Australian Productivity Commission (Report, 2014) was moralistic and myopic, and I put forward a case for and a draft model for employing FDHs in Australia.

FREE

smashwords.com/books/view/1178346

27. ROLL ON... a Changi PoW Remembers.

The Secret Diary Kept by Corporal Joseph Nutter R.A.M.C.

By Joseph Nutter.

smashwords.com/books/view/1074253

Corporal Joseph Nutter was only 21 when he enlisted in the British Royal Army Medical Corps (R.A.M.C) in 1936, to train as a Nursing Orderly. He left a note on the mantel for his mother, advising her, "Gone to join the Army !"

When the Japanese invaded Singapore in 1942 Joe was working at Alexandra Hospital. He was captured, and interred in Changi POW camp. He recorded in a secret diary of four small books the conditions and events between February 1942 and July 1943. Entries were recorded daily, meticulously written in his copperplate handwriting. They include the Selarang Barracks incident and a forced march of 170 miles to the Burma railway. He was frequently called upon to assist in surgical operations without proper medical equipment and facilities. These horrific episodes for which he was not trained were in addition to his normal duties and responsibilities in the field of first aid, health and hygiene. During his 3½ years as a POW Joe experienced several ailments himself, including diarrhea, beriberi, malnutrition, malaria, dysentery and skin diseases.

He never returned to England, having migrated to Australia in 1945 after liberation.

This book replicates Joe's diary verbatim, with added annotations, explanations and illustrations.

ISBN: 9781005304072

28. A Virus of Everything.

Dr. Paul W. Mathews.

A new virus was sweeping the globe. How far would it challenge or sweep aside the endless diseases of desire, of human yearnings—of love, lust, passion, greed, ambition, selfishness, and calamities of poverty, tempest and soullessness?

Mark was soul sick. Once again he was alone, and hence vulnerable. His psyche was howling for a new role in life he could call his own, his soul was screaming to be loved and nurtured. It was at this point that he excavated his own life from the dismal heap of circumstances that surrounded him. Free to spend hours every night chatting to Asian girls on-line in search of a loving companion, he finally met poor Annie, both cute and endearing. He flew to her arms, befriended her family, sent her to college, bought her land, paid expenses.... A year of bliss. Then she changed, for the worse, but he was infected by her poison. A litany of demands followed. He began his search again, and again...

Five years later a new virus swept the globe. Annie was in trouble: a pandemic, a typhoon, death, floods that were meant to wash away the virus, brought him back to her. Nonetheless, once again he was alone. All he could have were memories past. Love, it seemed, was a virus, and he was still not immune.

E-book ISBN: 9781005020989

smashwords.com/books/view/1137064

29. A Robbery of Sorts.

Sanitee T'Chong.

2024.

What happens when a bank makes a mistake? When a bank manager takes advantage of that mistake? Rhianna Ghamble, the Manager of a local bank branch in Shepparton, accidentally becomes enlightened as to how she can take advantage of loopholes in the banking system to bank-roll a luxurious lifestyle she has always desired, and thought she deserved. But will she come unstuck when she goes too far and is challenged by Mark Messenger over a deceased Estate? A mystery of pretentious greed, fraud, deceased Estates, inhumane institutions, and the foibles of the human condition, exposed by an amateur sleuth.

Don't miss out!

Visit the website below and you can sign up to receive emails whenever Paul W. Mathews publishes a new book. There's no charge and no obligation.

https://books2read.com/r/B-A-WLMTB-FKTQD

BOOKS2READ

Connecting independent readers to independent writers.